I0801619

FROM REFLECTION AND CHOICE

THE McDONALD
CENTER FOR
AMERICA'S FOUNDING
PRINCIPLES

MERCER
UNIVERSITY

THE A. V. ELLIOTT CONFERENCE SERIES

The Thomas C. and Ramona E. McDonald Center
for America's Founding Principles

Guided by James Madison's maxim that "a well-instructed people alone can be permanently a free people," the McDonald Center exists to promote the study of the great texts and ideas that have shaped our regime and fostered liberal learning.

Directors
Will R. Jordan and Charlotte C. S. Thomas

Published Volumes

Charlotte C. S. Thomas, ed., *No Greater Monster nor Miracle than Myself: The Political Philosophy of Michel de Montaigne* (2014)

Charlotte C. S. Thomas, ed., *Of Sympathy and Selfishness: The Moral and Political Philosophy of Adam Smith* (2015)

Will R. Jordan and Charlotte C. S. Thomas, ed., *The Most Sacred Freedom: Religious Liberty in the History of Philosophy and America's Founding* (2016)

Will R. Jordan, ed., *Promise and Peril: Republics and Republicanism in the History of Political Philosophy* (2017)

Will R. Jordan, ed., *When in the Course of Human Events: 1776 at Home, Abroad, and in American Memory* (2018)

Charlotte C. S. Thomas, ed. *Power and the People: Thucydides' History and the American Founding* (2019)

Forthcoming

Charlotte C. S. Thomas, ed., *Liberty and Tyranny in Plato* (2021)

Will R. Jordan, ed., On John Locke (2022)

From Reflection and Choice

The Political Philosophy of the *Federalist Papers* and the Ratification Debate

Edited by

Will R. Jordan

MERCER UNIVERSITY PRESS
Macon, Georgia
2020

MUP/ P604

Published by Mercer University Press
1501 Mercer University Drive
Macon, Georgia 31207

9 8 7 6 5 4 3 2 1

Books published by Mercer University Press are printed on acid-free paper that meets the requirements of the American National Standard for Information Sciences—Permanence of Paper for Printed Library Materials.

Printed and bound in the United States.

This book is set in Adobe Caslon Pro.

Cover/jacket design by Burt&Burt

ISBN 978-0-88146-744-4
Cataloging-in-Publication Data is available from the Library of Congress

CONTENTS

CONTRIBUTORS

Jeremy D. Bailey—Professor of Political Science, University of Houston, Houston, Texas

Roger Barrus—Elliott Professor of Government and Foreign Affairs, Hampden-Sydney College, Hampden-Sydney, Virginia

Murray Dry—Charles A. Dana Professor of Political Science, Middlebury College, Middlebury, Vermont

Elizabeth Kaufer Busch—Professor and Co-Director of the Center for American Studies, Christopher Newport University, Newport News, Virginia

Kimberly Hurd Hale—Assistant Professor of Politics, Coastal Carolina University, Conway, South Carolina

Will R. Jordan—Associate Professor of Political Science, Co-Director of the McDonald Center for America's Founding Principles, Mercer University, Macon, Georgia

Jon D. Schaff—Professor of Political Science, Northern State University, Aberdeen, South Dakota

Lynn Uzzell—Lecturer, Department of Politics, University of Virginia, Charlottesville, Virginia

Karl Walling—Professor of Strategy, U.S. Naval War College, Monterey, California

Michael Zuckert—Nancy R. Dreux Professor of Political Science, Emeritus, University of Notre Dame, Notre Dame, Indiana

Dedicated to the Memory of

A. V. Elliott

[1928–2019]

ACKNOWLEDGMENTS

A project of this sort comes together only with the hard work of a great many people. Most importantly, I would like to thank Jeremy Bailey, Roger Barrus, Elizabeth Kaufer Busch, Murray Dry, Kimberly Hurd Hale, Jon Schaff, Lynn Uzzell, Karl Walling, and Michael Zuckert for participating in the 2018 A.V. Elliott Conference on Great Books and Ideas at Mercer University and for contributing their essays to this volume. I thank them not only for their excellent scholarship, but for their collegiality during the conference along with the care and attention they showed to our students. Likewise, I commend the Mercer student participants at the conference—Jacob Harvey, David Stokes, and Mayah Waltower—for their excellent work. Carey Roberts and Greg Weiner also delivered papers and helped make the 11th Annual A.V. Elliott Conference a success.

There are also a number of people at Mercer deserving of special recognition here. First, the McDonald Center for America's Founding Principles, which sponsors the Elliott Conference, this volume, and a number of other important programs on campus, couldn't function without the tireless efforts of my co-director Charlotte Thomas. In turn, the Center has benefitted from strong institutional support provided by Mercer President William Underwood and College of Liberal Arts Dean Anita Gustafson. We also thank Thomas and Ramona McDonald for their generous and ongoing patronage of the Center and its mission. The Center's impact grows with every academic year, and all of these people have played a vital role.

In preparation for the 2018 Elliott Conference, a group of Mercer faculty and students participated in a reading group to study and discuss the debate between Federalists and Anti-Federalists. I would like to thank Garland Crawford, Sarah Gardner, Kevin Honeycutt, Gordon Johnston, Marc Jolley, Doug Thompson, Kyle Bligen, Jacob Harvey, Megan Hinkle, Hannah Keller, Macie Lee, Devyn Mode, Chase Peplin, Jordin Post, David Stokes, and Mayah Waltower for their excellent work and thoughtful conversation. I also thank the extraordinary teacher and scholar Ralph Lerner for his visit to campus in September of 2017, kicking off our year of thinking about this important subject.

I am also very grateful to Marc Jolley and his staff at Mercer University Press for their help in bringing this book to life. Their partnership on this entire series of books has been invaluable.

As ever, I am thankful for my wife Anissa and my sons Evan and Alex. Their love and support make everything possible.

Finally, this volume is dedicated to the memory of A.V. Elliott (1928–2019). Mr. Elliott was not only a generous benefactor and trustee of Mercer University, but his gift to our Center endowed the Conference and book series that now bear his name. Moreover, his strong and genuine commitment to the liberal arts continues to serve as a lodestar and inspiration in a time when so many seem to be so confused about the true purposes of higher education in a republic. We hope that this volume contributes in some small but fitting way to his immense legacy. He was a great Mercerian and a great American.

INTRODUCTION

Will R. Jordan

The essays in this volume were first prepared for the 2018 A.V. Elliott Conference on Great Books and Ideas at Mercer University. In planning the conference, we chose to focus on the debate between the Federalists and Anti-Federalists because we wanted our students to reflect deeply on the high quality of the political rhetoric and public philosophy produced in late eighteenth-century America. The ratification of the U.S. Constitution was a momentous event, fraught with danger for the young republic, yet friends and foes alike rose to the challenge by producing a veritable flood of thoughtful and reasonable commentary in the public press. When one compares this output to what passes for political analysis in the contemporary media landscape, it becomes rather difficult to avoid the suspicion that, as producers and consumers of political rhetoric, we have somehow lost our way.

Interestingly, the founding generation knew they were doing something unprecedented and extraordinary as they set out to debate the merits of the proposed constitution. In *Federalist* 1, Alexander Hamilton famously writes,

> it seems to have been reserved to the people of this country to decide, by their conduct and example, the important question, whether societies of men are really capable or not, of establishing good government from reflection and choice, or whether they are forever destined to depend, for their political constitutions, on accident and force.[1]

While we have taken the title of this volume from *Federalist* 1, it should be noted that the Anti-Federalists strongly agreed with Hamilton on this point. The Federal Farmer, for example, urged his readers to "remain cool and temperate," and promised to "attentively examine the system…with candor and fairness; and leave you to decide upon the propriety of my opinions, the weight of my reasons, and how far my conclusions are

---

[1] Alexander Hamilton, John Jay, James Madison, *Federalist* 1, in *The Federalist*, ed. George W. Carey and James McClellan (Indianapolis: Liberty Fund, 2001) 1.

well drawn."[2] Although both sides were capable of occasional intemperance and illogic,[3] the record reveals a remarkable level of success in accomplishing the ideal of establishing government from reflection and choice. If we twenty-first century Americans are to avoid backsliding to government by accident and force, we do well to reconsider the form and content of the ratification debate.

The book is divided into two major sections. In the first, we look at the ratification debate itself, to establish first principles, and to get a clearer sense of the founders' project. In the second, we turn to the ways in which the terms of the ratification debate echo down through American history and how they might be applied to inform contemporary political practice.

In the opening chapter, "The American Founders and the Fundamentals of Governance," Michael Zuckert takes James Madison as his guide in clarifying the characteristic ends and means of the American founding. For both ends and means, Zuckert distinguishes the distinctively modern and liberal republicanism of the founders from the prevailing, classical models. Zuckert focuses on the difficulties encountered in ensuring that this new republicanism would possess the requisite good will, or orientation toward securing the rights of all, as well as the basic competence required to govern effectively. The Madisonian solution, according to Zuckert, can be described as an "institutional republicanism," using carefully crafted institutions to generate the desired results even with imperfect human beings. This thoughtful study lays the groundwork for much of the rest of the book.

Murray Dry's "The Debate Over the Ratification of the Constitution: The Federalists vs. the Anti-Federalists" takes us from the realm of pure theory to the sometimes messy details of history and practice. Dry's chapter emphasizes the extent to which the debate between Federalists and Anti-Federalists, particularly on the core issues of federalism and republican government, is part of an ongoing political dialog that extends beyond the founding itself, making it exceeding difficult to determine clear

---

[2] *Federal Farmer* I, in *The Anti-Federalist Papers and the Constitutional Convention Debates*, ed. Ralph Ketcham (New York: Penguin, 2003) 268.

[3] In *Federalist* 85, Hamilton writes that it is possible that "circumstances may have occasionally betrayed me into intemperances of expression which I did not intend: it is certain that I have frequently felt a struggle between sensibility and moderation; and if the former has in some instances prevailed, it must be my excuse, that it has been neither often nor much," 453.

winners, losers, or even fixed answers at the founding. Dry takes us from the convention, through the ratification debates, and to the political drama of the 1790s to show that James Madison's apparent political shifts (away from Hamilton and his Federalist allies) can be accounted for by Madison's alternative understanding of how the politics of the ratification process should inform one's reading of the Constitution.

Madison's appropriation of Anti-Federalist arguments is also the subject of Lynn Uzzell's "Writing *Federalist* 10 for an Anti-Federalist Audience." Uzzell undertakes a close reading of *Federalist* 10 and Madison's several arguments in favor of the extended republic. Of particular interest is the relative ranking of two arguments: that the extended republic would produce representatives with superior wisdom and virtue; and that the extended republic would check majority factionalism through the multiplication of interests. Through a study of the convention notes and Madison's other defenses of the extended republic made in 1787, Uzzell finds that Madison supplemented his favored, more novel, case for the extended republic with an argument more familiar and preferred even by his Anti-Federalist foes. Uzzell's work encourages a reconsideration of both Federalist and Anti-Federalist writings in light of the rhetorical purposes they were written to serve.

Jeremy D. Bailey's "Federal Judges as a Source of Federal Authority in *Federalist* 39" revisits the subject broached in Dry's chapter about the potential inconsistency between Madison's writing in the *Federalist* and his later political views. In particular, Bailey explores Madison's possibly shifting views of federalism and the balance between state and federal authority. Bailey's chapter surveys Madison's record in the constitutional convention, his stance on the National Bank, his views on slavery, and his work on the Virginia Resolution in response to the Alien and Sedition Acts, making clear why scholars have long found Madison to be inconsistent or worse. Against this charge, Bailey argues that a consistent Madison can be found through a careful reading of *Federalist* 39. The role of the federal judiciary is key here, as No. 39 relies upon the courts to settle the inevitable controversies arising from the complexities of American federalism.

The focus shifts from Madison to Hamilton in Kimberly Hurd Hale's "'The Fate of an Empire': Alexander Hamilton's Baconian Project." In some ways, however, this chapter follows the trajectory suggested by Zuckert, as Hurd Hale emphasizes the distinctly modern roots of the

Federalist by describing the influence of Francis Bacon on Hamilton's thought. The major points of influence she discusses are their shared view of politics as a science, the support for commercial life and bourgeois virtues, and the need for military strength, especially naval power. Hurd Hale's treatment of Hamilton as a follower of Bacon carries with it important lessons about the size, scope, and ambition of the founders' new science of politics.

The book's second half, on the legacy and possible contemporary applications of the ratification debate, opens with Jon Schaff's "The American Constitution and Statesmanship: An Argument from Lincoln." Schaff suggests that Abraham Lincoln, perhaps surprisingly, integrates elements from both Federalist and Anti-Federalist thought. While Lincoln's view of the union clearly favors the Federalists, Schaff finds that Lincoln's suspicions of empire and of economic consolidation reflect some sympathy with Anti-Federalist concerns. Ultimately, however, Schaff suggests that Lincoln reveals the limits of both camps in that neither side sufficiently appreciates the need for statesmanship. Schaff both explores the chief characteristics of Lincoln's statesmanship, marked by prudence and moderation, and also offers some suggestions for why we seem to suffer from a dearth of statesmanship in contemporary America.

Roger Barrus' chapter, "Federalists and Anti-Federalists Then and Now: The Unfinished Ratification Debate," offers a helpful survey of the major points of divergence during the ratification struggle before carrying the debate forward to the present day. Of special interest in the first half is a careful discussion of how the Federalists and Anti-Federalists appealed to different arguments from Montesquieu to support their competing visions of republicanism. The chapter concludes that the relative weakness of the Anti-Federalist argument allowed the Federalists to win without ever fully delineating the fundamental goods of republican self-government. Barrus finds Zuckert's "institutional republicanism" insufficient, and suggests that a more rich, traditional understanding of republicanism, along with a more clear "dual federalism" would be needed to address the defects of contemporary American political life.

In her chapter "The Separation of Powers or the Normalization of Tyranny? Revisiting *Federalist Papers* 47–51," Elizabeth Kaufer Busch focuses on one of the defects introduced by Barrus: the growth of what Alexis de Tocqueville had referred to as administrative centralization. Kaufer Busch, however, sees this less as a problem of federalism than a problem of separation of powers. Her chapter describes the influence of Locke and Montesquieu on the American founders, clarifying the commitment to the rule of law and separation of powers that are necessary to avoid tyranny. She then examines how modern administrative agencies, by centralizing legislative, executive, and judicial functions, violate the Constitution's commitment to separation of powers. Her case study for this creeping Administrative tyranny involves the enforcement of Title IX of the Educational Amendments of 1972.

The book's final chapter is Karl Walling's "Old and New Testaments in American Grand Strategy, an Overview." Walling argues that the *Federalist Papers* should be read as a key component in the development of a novel American approach to republican security theory. Walling discusses how the *Federalist Papers*, along with the Declaration of Independence, the Articles of Confederation, the Constitution, Washington's Farewell Address, and the Monroe Doctrine, represent six key national security documents, together forming the Old Testament of American Grand Strategy. After defining this strategy—which includes liberty, independence, energetic and balanced republican institutions, non-intervention abroad, and counter-intervention in the Western Hemisphere—Walling questions whether or not this Old Testament is violated by the New Testament of mutual security (relying on international organizations such as NATO and the UN) that emerged in the twentieth century. Walling finds that the New Testament generally extends the benefits of republican security theory in a way not inconsistent with the Old Testament, and cautions against a rash rejection of this strategy.

Walling's piece reminds us, as do several of the chapters, that the founding generation—Federalists and Anti-Federalists alike—largely shared a view about the proper ends of government. They put liberty first. The great debates of the founding period were largely over the best means to secure that liberty. We see in this volume that the great debate did not end in 1788, and that many of the fundamental choices and challenges exposed during the ratification debate remain with us to this day, and indeed are endemic to republican self-government. This volume encourages scholars and citizens alike to continue the conversation, with the hope that we might strive to maintain and improve government from reflection and choice.

PART I

THE FOUNDERS' PROJECT

1

THE AMERICAN FOUNDERS AND THE FUNDAMENTALS OF GOVERNANCE

Michael Zuckert

The American Founders set out self-consciously to establish what we today would call a liberal republic or democracy. Such an order is marked by a variety of features, including both characteristic ends and characteristic means of governance. These ends and these means together constitute the "fundamentals of governance" as the Founders understood these. I propose to give a brief account of these fundamentals, but I must begin with some caveats at the outset.

Although there was a great amount of agreement among the founders, it is nonetheless a grave error to believe that there were no significant differences among them. I am thus going to construct a composite of their views on the fundamentals of governance, but my version is going to be tilted in a direction that emphasizes the political thought of James Madison. One could draw a picture centered more on Alexander Hamilton, John Adams, or James Wilson, and in all cases it would look somewhat different from the composite I will present.

There are a number of good reasons to take Madison as the central figure. He is rightly known as the "father of the Constitution," and since the governance we are most concerned with is governance under the Constitution, he seems a reasonable guide to it. Moreover, and this is perhaps a more contentious claim, Madison was, all in all, the greatest political thinker of the founding era, and it makes sense to look at the founders' views of the fundamentals of governance in the brightest light available.

I. The Ends of Governance in the Liberal Order

It is not in the least bit difficult to understand how the founders understood the ends of governance, for they expressed their thoughts on this topic at nearly every opportunity. The birth of the nation in a revolution against established authority was particularly conducive to their thinking about the ends of governance, for their grievances against British rule forced them to clarify for themselves the criteria of legitimate government. By the time they came to the decision for independence they had reached a remarkable consensus on the ends, a consensus they expressed most prominently in the Declaration of Independence, but they also enshrined the same view in many other documents produced during the conflict with Britain and in the constitutions they prepared for their newly independent states. Thomas Jefferson gave important testimony to that consensus when he explained his aim in the Declaration of Independence to have been merely to "express the American mind," to express the views of those who supported the dominant American position.[1] It must, of course, be noted that the American mind Jefferson expressed was the mind of the "Patriots," of the partisans of the revolution, the American Whigs. Many others, those who became Loyalists, did not always share the consensus Jefferson wrote into the Declaration.

That consensus was essentially Lockean in that the Declaration and related documents of the period expressed the fundamentals of governance in terms taken from the political philosophy of John Locke. Jefferson's Declaration is both beautifully concise and nobly explicit about the ends. Prior to and independently of government human beings possess "unalienable rights" to "life, liberty, and the pursuit of happiness." Without government, these rights would be insecure and that fact supplies the key to understanding the legitimate ends of governance: simply "to secure these rights." The rights are made secure through the existence of law and of police and courts to enforce the law.

When compared to other pronouncements on the ends of governance, the American founders appear to be very austere and limited. Aristotle and a long line of thinkers and political actors after him thought the end of governance was to promote or produce virtue in the citizen body. Even more common was the view that the end of governance was to promote the one true religion, to contribute to the salvation of the souls of the population, or to enforce the divine laws given to the people. There are regimes in the world today that understand themselves in just this way. The American founders were by no means indifferent to virtue in the

---

[1] Thomas Jefferson to Henry Lee, May 8, 1825, in *Writings*, ed. Merrill D. Peterson (New York: Literary Classics of the United States, 1984) 1501.

citizens, but they did not set it as the end of governance. Although they were not at all indifferent to religion or to the salvation of their souls, they set themselves yet more clearly against all notions that the ends of governance included any such religious purposes. For reasons partly secular and partly religious they turned away from the idea that civil society or the state exist to save souls or have any business establishing, maintaining, or enforcing the true religion or religious laws. The most "sacred" right they recognized was not the right to life, but rather the right to liberty of conscience.[2] Their understanding of the proper ends of governance was thus thoroughly secular even if the motives of many for accepting that view were religious in character.

Madison was among those who accepted the Declaration of Independence as an authoritative statement of the ends of governance, but at the same time he made another statement on ends that appears on its face to be quite different. In his single best known writing, *Federalist* 10, Madison made the following striking claim: "The diversity in the faculties of men, from which the rights of property arise, is...an insuperable obstacle to a uniformity of interests. The protection of these faculties is the first object of government."[3] Note what Madison is saying here: property rights arise from the "faculties of men." Protecting these faculties—and the rights to which they give rise—is "the first object of government." The diversity or difference in these faculties, however, leads to inequalities in property. Some acquire more; some acquire less. The inequality of property will provide constant occasion for a desire to interfere with property—to redistribute or even equalize it—but, says Madison, the protection of the faculties and the rights those faculties generate is "the first object of government."

Madison's formulation sounds less different from that in the Declaration when we recall that the more standard list of rights, endorsed elsewhere by Jefferson himself and incorporated in most of the other documents of the period, included life, liberty, and property.[4] But Madison's notion shares even more with the Declaration's statement of ends if we

---

[2] James Madison, "Property," *National Gazette*, March 29, 1792 in *Writings*, ed. Jack N. Rakove (New York: Literary Classics of the United States, 1999) 516.

[3] Alexander Hamilton, John Jay, and James Madison, *Federalist* 10, in *The Federalist*, ed. George W. Carey and James McClellan (Indianapolis: Liberty Fund, 2001) 43.

[4] For detail and speculation on why Jefferson omitted property in the Declaration of Independence, see Michael Zuckert, *Launching Liberalism: On Lockean Political Philosophy* (Lawrence: University Press of Kansas, 2002) 203–234.

note the common Lockean provenance of both versions. Madison is tracking Locke's discussion of property very closely. Property derives from human labor, i.e., the exercise of human faculties. Since property derives from labor, it is as dynamic as labor is; higher levels of labor lead to greater production of wealth. The protection of property not only protects rights that belong to individuals as personal rights, but also serves the common good, the good of society, by leading to the production of greater wealth through securing the fruits of the exercise of human faculties.

The connections between the Madisonian formulation and Jefferson's in the Declaration become clearer if we take into consideration Madison's broad reflections on property in an essay of that title that he wrote a few years after the *Federalist*. This essay follows the curious usage of Locke, who had spoken of all rights, or the objects of all rights, as property. Madison explains that property has two elements or dimensions—(1) "dominion which one man claims" (2) "in exclusion of every other individual."[5] The first dimension of property means that the right-holder has a kind of control or dominion over that to which he or she has a right; the second means that he or she has a kind of immunity from the intrusions of others on that to which he or she has a right, or what Madison calls "exclusion of others." Madison recognizes that the more usual meaning of the term "property" involves the "external things of the world," but, like Locke, Madison identifies a broader meaning. "In its larger and juster meaning, [property] embraces every thing to which a man may attach a value and have a right." He includes in property in this broad sense "safety and liberty of...person[s]...the free use of...faculties and free choice of the objects on which to employ them"—the rights the standard texts included in the catalog of rights as "life" and "liberty." In sum, Madison says, "As a man is said to have a right to his property, he may be equally said to have a property in his rights."[6] Government, Madison affirms in this context, is instituted to protect this very broad kind of property. The passage we have quoted from *Federalist* 10 ought to be read in the light of this other discussion. Madison is not obsessed, as he is sometime taken to be, with property in the narrow and external sense.

The discussion in his essay on property makes clear why he put the initial emphasis in *Federalist* 10 on the protection of the human faculties

---

[5] James Madison, "Property," 515.

[6] Ibid.

from which property derives. Human faculties and the right of their free use are the primary objects of governmental protection. Madison also helps bring out the nature of the political problem that lies at the bottom of the founder's treatment of the fundamentals of governance. The ambiguity in the notion of property contains the tension in the tasks of governance that a legitimate political system must grapple with. To equally protect the different and unequal faculties of citizens leads to the result that citizens are in part equal and in part unequal in their property, for they are equal in that part of their property that includes their lives, their bodies, their actions or liberty, but unequal in their property in external goods. The true ends of governance require that both sorts of property receive equal protection from law and government, but, as the always arising conflicts over the distribution of the burdens and benefits of social life show, no simple formula or political arrangement exists to produce this result. The problem can be put quite starkly if perhaps a bit too simply by saying that if political power is held by those who predominate in one sort of property, they tend to oppress the holders of the other sort of property. Thus if the propertied in the ordinary sense dominate they tend to "grind the poor." If the poor, i.e., the citizens who have property in their persons but much less property of the external sort, hold power, they tend to act to dispossess or take advantage of the others. This problem, universal in all government, becomes particularly acute in the kind of republic the founders established.

II. Fundamentals of Governance: Republicanism

Among the foundational ideas on which a great consensus existed at the time of the founding was the notion that "all men are created equal" because they are the bearers of natural rights, i.e., in the final analysis, of the right to give a shape to their own lives without needing the permission or direction of others. The founding generation meant something quite definite by the claim that all are created equal; they did not mean that all are equal in their faculties or abilities, as Madison made clear when he spoke of the unequal faculties of men producing unequal property holdings. They meant something more precise and realistic than this obviously false claim: they meant that all are equal in the sense that no one has a natural or divine right to rule another. No difference that exists between two men is sufficient to generate a claim that one of them has a right to rule the other. Thus Jefferson once said of Isaac Newton, the man whose intellect he seems to have most admired, that intelligent as Newton was he had no right to govern the most ignorant and dull-witted individual without that man's consent.[7] It followed, of course, that the institution of slavery was not legitimate, for that involved rule without consent and without recognition of rights. But that is another long story for another occasion.

Since there is by nature no authority, political power can only arise artificially, from some act by which men create it. Since men naturally have a right to govern themselves, others, including governments, can acquire that right only if the original right is delegated to them. Rational men will delegate only so much of their original right as is needed to protect the mass of remaining rights and they will delegate it only to a governing structure they have reason to believe will act to preserve their rights and not to oppress them.

Two large implications for the fundamentals of governance follow from this simple thought. First, as the Americans understood it, proper governments must be republics. By a republic they meant a government drawn from and ultimately responsible to the "great body of the people." A rational people will not delegate power to any body but themselves or to persons responsible to them, for that is the only way to begin to ensure that political power will be wielded in their interest and for the sake of securing their rights. "A will independent of the society,"[8] as Madison termed the other forms of government, is unreliable as a protector of the people and illegitimate in that it does not fully recognize the deep philosophic truth that "all men are created equal," or that nobody has a natural right to rule another.

They did not mean by this commitment to republicanism anything like direct democracy. They fully accepted representation and even the legitimacy of power indirectly derived and responsible only at a distance to the people. Thus an institution like the Supreme Court was considered legitimate even though it was to be selected by an indirectly chosen President and approved by an indirectly chosen Senate, and was to serve life tenure terms unless impeached for less than "good behavior." It was sufficient that there be a chain of connection back to the people both for how one comes to possess political power and how one could be removed from political office.

---

[7] Thomas Jefferson to Henri Gregoire, February 25, 1809 in *Writings*, 1202.

[8] *Federalist* 51, 271.

This may seem like a very lax notion of republicanism. This is how Thomas Jefferson saw it, but it did have real bite. It meant, first, that the great body of the people—at least the great body of the males—must have the right to vote. It meant, moreover, that no office-holder could be simply irremovable from office. It meant that no political body could be hereditary or self-selected. It would not be acceptable, for instance, to have a Senate organized in the way university Boards of Trustees are organized, with the existing board selecting its own replacements.

The other implications for the fundamentals of governance that followed from the ideas of natural rights and natural equality were the fundamental ideas I have already discussed a bit—that governments exist only to accomplish certain (limited) things. Thus it was common for constitutions at all levels in founding era America to have Bills of Rights denying to government the power to overstep its proper ends. Usually these Bills of Rights contained protections for freedom of conscience and for the basics of life, liberty, and property.

The commitment to republicanism responded to one of the problems the founders faced: given their understanding of the foundations of governance in rights and equality, what sort of government could achieve legitimacy? The republic and only the republic could be legitimate. However, the commitment to republicanism and thereby to majority rule by the great body of the citizenry brought with it its own set of problems. For the sake of simplicity let me reduce these problems to two: (1) would a republic have the will to do what it ought, i.e., to secure the rights of all? And (2) would a republic have the ability to do what it ought, i.e., to govern competently? Part of Madison's genius as a political scientist was that he saw these problems with greater clarity than any other member of his generation. Madison's analysis of the problem of the will to do right in a republic is well-known from his treatment of the problem of faction in *Federalist* 10. He defines a faction to be "a number of citizens…who are united and actuated by some common impulse of passion, or of interest, adverse to the rights of other citizens, or to the permanent and aggregate interests of the community."[9] He believed, alas, that human beings too often act in a factious manner, seeking their own interest at the expense of the rights and interests of others. Madison, like most of the other founders, was a very hard-headed analyst of human nature. "We well know" he tells us,

[9]*Federalist* 10, 43.

that "if the impulse and the opportunity...coincide...neither moral nor religious motives can be relied on as an adequate control."[10] More clearly than any others in the era, Madison saw that republicanism was only a partial solution to this universal problem. Operating on the principle of majority rule, the republic had the resources within itself to control factions that amounted only to a minority of the society. But what about a majority faction? On the basis of his analysis of the two types of property Madison was keenly conscious of the likelihood that majorities too could be factious. However, the republic was set up to empower majorities, even when factious, not to check and counter them. The republic, then, although demanded by the recognition of rights and equality, did not seem well suited to securing the equal rights of all.

Madison also supplied a profound analysis of the problem of republican competence. In republics political power rests in the hands of the representatives of the people, who tend to share the qualities of the people they represent. In monarchies and aristocracies one could count on a separate political class of men with special education, experience, and family tradition, which together fitted them with many of the skills needed for governing a complex society in a potentially dangerous world. In such regimes the monarch could supply the energy required for effective enforcement of the laws at home and for dealing with potential or actual enemies abroad. The nobility, in whose hands much of governance rested, could bring wisdom and stability to governmental deliberations. The American principled commitment to republicanism meant that no king or body of nobles would be part of American governments. Do republics have the wherewithal to make up for the lack of competencies the lack of a political class was likely to bring in its train?

III. Fundamentals of Governance: Institutional Republicanism

Prior to the American founding, there were two chief solutions to the problems I have just described. One was a solution characteristic of ancient republics like Sparta and Rome. That solution was virtue—the community had to be severely regulated so that the citizens learned to love the republic more than their private good, learned to submerge their interests in the common interest, learned to sacrifice their partial goods to the good of the

[10] *Federalist* 10, 45–46.

whole. The French philosopher Jean-Jacques Rousseau perhaps captured the spirit of the ancient republics best in the story he liked to retell of the Spartan mother who was told that her three sons had been killed in battle. Instead of showing any grief she asked the messenger, "But did we win?"[11] Her private interest was as nothing compared to that of the community. This kind of almost superhuman virtue was clearly a solution to the problem of will; it was also a kind of solution to the problem of competence, for it bred a community of men focused entirely on the common needs and the common good, a community where the only self-seeking was competition over who could serve the community best.

There were some Americans who were attracted to this model of the virtuous republic, but for the most part they did not take to it. They understood it to be contrary to the liberal or free character of the legitimate regime as articulated in the Declaration of Independence. The virtuous republic treated the individual as subordinate to the state; the Americans knew that this reversed the true relations between individual and society. The American founders thus had little faith in the virtuous republic model as the solution to their problem.

The other solution was characteristic of the monarchies of modern Europe. The government could draw into it men possessing the skills, the knowledge, the orientation required to perform competently the tasks of governance. This solution was equally out of the question, for it conflicted with the republican character of the regime to which the Americans were committed. No hereditary or self-appointed rulers could be relied on. All governors would be drawn from and by the governed.

In order for republicanism to work successfully—and the founders were agreed that the historical record for republics was pretty dismal[12]—new solutions to the problems of will and competence would have to be discovered. Much of the pride the founding generation took in their accomplishment derived from their belief that they had done just that. Their solution was an arrangement one can call "institutional republicanism," a system that would mimic the will to the public good promised by the ancient republics but in a fundamentally liberal environment, and would provide the competence promised by the modern monarchies but in a

[11] Jean-Jacques Rousseau, *Emile,* trans. Allan Bloom (New York: Basic Books, 1979) 40.

[12] *Federalist* 9 and 10, 37–49.

fundamentally republican context. The solution, in a word, was a set of institutions that would take in men as they are and produce the results that ought to be. The founders aimed at a sort of political alchemy—to produce an output better than the input would seem to warrant.

One of the central ideas of the founders' institutional republicanism was expressed in a passage by Madison we have already noted, but it is worth another look in this context. "If the impulse and the opportunity be suffered to coincide, we well know that neither moral nor religious motives can be relied on as an adequate control."[13] The classical republican or Christian reliance on individual virtue not only (in the former case) required a kind of oppressive regime the rights orientation of the founders turned them away from, but it was in fact ineffective and unreliable. In this respect the American founders were heirs of Machiavelli, who famously had said that we must take men as they are and not as they ought to be, for they do not reliably behave as they ought when they have the opportunity not to. One cannot count on political actors bringing into government the moral and religious restraints that will lead them to put the public good ahead of their own interests.

The general terms of the institutional solution were prefigured in Madison's dismissal of virtue as an adequate reliance: "if the impulse and the opportunity" to do the wrong thing are "suffered to coincide" then the wrong thing will often be done. The trick then is, first, not to allow "the impulse and the opportunity" to do wrong to "coincide." No power-holder can be simply free to do what he will; all power must be watched and held accountable. As Madison said in another place: "the policy of supplying, by opposite and rival interests, the defect of better motives" must be pursued.[14] One must "divide and arrange the several offices in such a manner as that each may be a check on the other; that the private interest of every individual may be a centinel over the public rights." In his famous trademark statement: "Ambition," a private and personal virtue often seen to be contrary to public virtue, "must be made to counteract ambition."[15]

Institutional republicanism assumes that men will be men, that they will not set aside their personal and private interests when they enter public life. The task is not to decry this fact, which is beyond our control in any

[13] *Federalist* 10, 45–46.
[14] *Federalist* 51, 269.
[15] *Federalist* 51, 268.

case, but to construct institutions cleverly to counteract and even take advantage of this all too human tendency. The center-piece of political science then becomes the design of constitutional structures that will allow and constrain action in the required ways. Chief among these devices is the central practice of republics—elections. Governors are to be periodically responsible to the governed, who can judge whether the governors are adequately attempting to serve the public good or not, and reward them with a continuance of a private good that they value, political office, or punish them by depriving them of that good.

Electoral control has many great virtues, but we must recall the problem Madison had discerned about majorities in a republic. They are not automatically sufficient to solve the problem of the need for a will to do the public good, for they too can be factious. At the end of the day, institutional republicanism must find a solution to the problem of majority faction. But can it?

Madison thought one of his greatest achievements was the discovery of a republican solution to this problem of republicanism. That solution lay in Madison's theory of the large or extended republic. Prior to Madison it was almost held to be a self-evident truth that republics must be small and could survive only if they were. The whole prior history of republics and the authority of the most respected political thinkers from Plato and Aristotle to Montesquieu seemed to agree on the proposition that republics must be small. Madison, however, went so far as to claim that largeness is so far from being the death of republics that it is their salvation.

Why should Madison expect the large republic to do a better job of favoring majorities aiming at justice and the common good than small republics? He has two answers—one simpler, and the other a bit more complex. The simpler answer is this: the larger the unit, the more different interests are likely to exist within it and thus to find representation in a republican legislature. Relative to the interests present in any given small republic, the number of interests present in the large republic is likely to be much greater. An interest that in itself makes up a majority in a small republic is much less likely to do so in the large republic. The interest that might dominate in a small republic will be outnumbered in the legislature of the large republic by interests more or less neutral relative to the political divisions of the small republic. Thus the raw materials exist in the large republic for the dominance of relatively neutral parties, able to make up non-factious majorities and produce more just decisions.

Madison also had in mind a more complex mechanism, which involves the replacement of natural majorities by artificial or constructed majorities. In a small, relatively undifferentiated society, there is a greater likelihood that there will exist a "natural majority"—that is, a set of interests that naturally amount to a majority of the politically empowered population and those of the republican legislature. In a larger, more heterogeneous society, it is much less likely that majorities will exist naturally; most interests will be distinct minorities. But governance requires majorities in the large as much as in the small republic; majorities will have to be constructed or put together from the smaller packets of interested minorities.

In *Federalist* 51, Madison makes one of his most important claims: "In the extended republic of the United States, and among the great variety of interests, parties and sects which it embraces, a coalition of the majority of the whole society could seldom take place upon any other principles than those of justice and the general good."[16] Madison is not looking to a stalemate system where no majorities can form, or to rule by minorities, as many of his interpreters believe, but rather to a process that almost by magic allows only good majorities to form. How can that be? Madison has in mind here the difference in character between natural and constructed majorities. Natural majorities have an immediate interest in common and are able to translate it, more or less unmodified, into law. Where there is no natural majority, however, the preexisting interests must undergo a process of transformation before they can become a majority. Common ground must be found on which the different interests can coalesce. That requires transformation and modification of the original interests in the direction of finding broader kinds of commonality. The process of majority construction leads to a search for common ground that approaches something like a common good and a more neutral or disinterested stance than any of the parties began with. There are, moreover, moderating effects imposed by the process of coalition formation in a system of fragmented interests. Coalition forming is not likely to be a once and for all matter; majorities are likely to be fluid and changing. Today's coalition partner is very possibly tomorrow's coalition opposition—and vice versa. Parties and interests come to view each other as long-run potential majority partners and recognize their mutual interest in treating each other moderately and fairly. Madison no doubt recognized that he overstated the case

[16] *Federalist* 51, 271.

when he said that the majorities would seek only justice and the general good, but he had a serious point beneath his hyperbole. The process pushes parties toward justice and the common good in a way that majority rule in small republics does not. One of the founders' fundamentals of governance is the taming of factious majorities not through reliance on human goodness, but through those "inventions of prudence"[17] that constitute "institutional republicanism."

However, it is not enough for the institutional republican solution that office holders be checked from doing the wrong thing. They must also be brought or at least encouraged to do the right thing. Governance is not merely a matter of preventing governors from doing harm (as many of the Anti-Federalist opponents of the Constitution and some of their latter day heirs, like the Tea Partiers, seem to believe). Government must accomplish things, and governors need institutions and structures to prompt them to actively search out and act on behalf of the public good. The general need is not only to prevent impulse and opportunity for ill from coinciding, but to engineer institutions in which the impulse for good will be generated and in which that impulse and opportunity then can be channeled to converge.

For this more positive task, Madison's idea of harnessing the ambition of the governors also comes into play. How can individuals be encouraged to think beyond their petty pre-existing interests and attach themselves to the public good? The founders expended much thought on this problem and were driven to make many changes in existing accepted practices in order to effectuate this engineering of will. It was, for example, nearly an axiom of political thinking that proper constitutional design should work to prevent office holders from identifying with their offices as separate "interests." Bad governance occurred, it was thought, when rulers thought of themselves as different from the ruled, as possessing different interests from the ruled, where they saw themselves as a self-conscious ruling clique. To counter the development of such a mentality, it was thought that short terms of office and rotation in office were required. Office-holders should not be allowed to develop psychic or physical distance from those they represented. They should come from the people and return to the people before they came to think of themselves as different from the people. Such was the dominant view in America between the

[17] *Federalist* 51, 269.

start of the Revolution and the making of the Constitution.

The founders rejected this reasoning in order to engineer the congruence between impulse, opportunity, and the public good. The more office holders valued their offices, the more they wished to remain in office, the more they would actively seek out those routes that would allow them to do so. The more they had the opportunity to remain in office, the more likely they would be to contract a desire to do so and thus to seek out the means of doing so. Thus the founders' institutional republicanism contained as one of its fundamentals of governance a commitment to relatively long terms of office with indefinite re-eligibility for reelection. This arrangement supplied the opportunity for men to form ambitions wholly different from what they may have started out with.

Alexander Hamilton gave one of the best defenses of the founders' ideas about engineering this convergence between ambition and the public good when he defended the provisions for indefinite re-eligibility for the Presidency. This provision ran counter to the political instincts of the nation, where suspicion and distrust of power was a very powerful force. "Nothing appears more plausible at first sight, nor more ill-founded upon close inspection," Hamilton tells us, "than a scheme...of continuing the chief magistrate in office for a certain time, and then excluding him from it."[18] The effects of this at first sight "plausible" scheme would be, he warns, "for the most part rather pernicious than salutary." The perniciousness of this arrangement lies in the "diminution of the inducements to good behavior" it would produce. The system requires, especially in the presidency, men who seek not only "the negative merit of not doing harm" but also "the positive merit of doing good." This latter more positive aim requires the same sort of intelligent constitutional design as does the achievement of the more negative aim, but it requires it on a grander and more daring scale. One must enlist or encourage "the love of fame, the ruling passion of the noblest minds." One needs not only men who wish to remain in office but men who wish for much more, men who wish to found a republic, or to save a republic, or to preserve the nation from economic crisis or war, or to establish a new system of health care. This love of fame "would prompt a man to plan and undertake extensive and arduous enterprises for the public benefit, requiring considerable time to mature and perfect them." But there is a necessary interaction between love of

[18] *Federalist* 72, 375.

fame and the great actions which that love would prompt, and the structure of offices. The lover of fame would be prompted to undertake these enterprises "if he could flatter himself with the prospect of being allowed to finish what he had begun." A short term of office with no possibility of extending his term "would, on the contrary, deter him from the undertaking, when he foresaw that he must quit the scene before he could accomplish the work, and must commit that, together with his own reputation, to hands which might be unequal or unfriendly to the task."[19] Although Hamilton does not bring out the point in this context, we must mention one other feature implicit in the argument. Long terms and re-eligibility not only provide incentives for the lovers of fame to act as Hamilton describes, but they also conduce to the transformation of the office-holder's psychological motives. A man who starts off with lesser aims, for example, to merely hold office, may come to higher motives, for example, the love of fame, by virtue of the opportunity the institutional structure provides. The kind of offices the founders designed not only gives scope for action to the lover of fame, but also conduces to the emergence of love of fame itself in their holders.

Institutional republicanism must not only solve the problem of creating the right kind of will in office-holders, but also provide the right kind of competencies in government so that government has the ability to do what governments need to do. Once again Madison provides the best formulation of the nature of the problem. In *Federalist* 37 he reminds his readers that governments require a number of different qualities in order to govern well. Recall the qualities we discussed earlier—energy, stability, wisdom. Can republics match the ability of aristocratic and monarchic regimes to supply these qualities?

In *Federalist* 37 Madison reveals just how complex the problem is, for he indicates that there are indeed institutional ways to encourage these qualities. For example, energy can be supplied by creating unitary offices armed with substantial powers, and organized in a way that we now call bureaucratic, i.e., where the head has the power to hire, fire, and direct subordinates. Likewise, stability can be supplied by institutions with multiple members, long terms of office and staggered membership. The majority of Americans in the 1780s were particularly concerned about the governmental quality they called republican liberty or safety.

[19] Ibid.

Governmental misconduct and oppression could best be prevented by having institutions composed of many individuals, where power is diffused, and short terms of office. A good republican system requires all of these qualities, but the institutional characteristics that produce one contradict the requirements for producing the others. It seems as though generally competent governance is beyond the reach of the founders and their republics.

Again the founders believed they had come up with a solution to the competence problem in their adaptation of the famous separation of powers scheme pioneered by the French philosopher Montesquieu. Earlier forms of republics had very undeveloped differentiation among governmental institutions, and had not come to a clear understanding of the functional division, now so familiar to us, among legislative, executive, and judicial powers. According to Montesquieu, the English constitutional order of the eighteenth century was the best yet devised for the sake of procuring liberty precisely because it divided governmental power into these three parts, and operated with mostly independent and differentiated political structures in the three domains of powers.[20] Montesquieu's theory of separation of powers copied the British prototype in that he maintained that the separation of powers scheme had to be embodied in a version of the older kind of constitutional order known as the mixed regime. The "mix" referred to was of the three classical types of regime—monarchy, aristocracy, and democracy. The British constitution, with its monarchic head, its aristocratic House of Lords, and its democratic House of Commons had long been considered an exemplary version of the mixed regime, but Montesquieu added that it should more fundamentally be seen as a separation of powers regime, with the mixed regime elements serving to give the institutions their necessary qualities of energy, stability, and so on.

The Americans were much impressed with Montesquieu's theory, but early on recognized that they could not match it because they were committed to wholly republican forms with no aristocratic or monarchic elements. However, they took a cue from Montesquieu and saw that they could use the separate institutions of the separation of powers scheme to produce the different governmental qualities that otherwise seemed so

[20] Montesquieu, *The Spirit of the Laws*, part I, book XI, chapter 6, trans. and ed. Anne M. Cohler, Basia Carolyn Miller, and Harold Samuel Stone (Cambridge University Press, 1989) 156–166.

difficult to combine. The Senate can provide stability and wisdom if constructed properly, the Presidency energy, and the House of Representatives republican liberty.

There are a number of lessons in the founders' way of thinking about the separation of powers that we ought to pause to notice. First, contrary to what we learn in the usual text book, the point of the separation of powers is not merely to supply checks and balances; it does far more than that. Second, we can notice the richness of the founders' political science. It is difficult not to contrast it with the approach typical of contemporary political science, which tends to view political institutions through the lens supplied by a simplistic democratic theory, which sees the point of political institutions as merely to collect and implement popular preferences. Although contemporary political scientists have many powerful tools for the study of politics that the founding generation lacked, their approach to it is quite impoverished at the more important conceptual level that sets out the agenda of what to study and why.

I have now sketched the chief "fundamentals of governance" as the founders saw them. It is admittedly nothing but a sketch, for I have omitted most of the detail on how to create the structures that will produce the needed qualities. I have omitted much of their most important thinking on the maintenance of separation of powers, and I have paid no attention whatsoever to federalism, an important part of their institutional republicanism. But I have attempted to highlight the general principles of their great insight into institutional republicanism.

2

THE DEBATE OVER THE RATIFICATION OF THE CONSTITUTION: THE FEDERALISTS VS. THE ANTI-FEDERALISTS

Murray Dry

Introduction

The debate over the ratification of the Constitution took place immediately after the Federal Convention completed its work on September 17, 1787 and transmitted the Constitution to Congress, with instructions to submit it to popularly elected state conventions. By the time New York voted for ratification, in July 1788, every state but North Carolina and Rhode Island had approved of the work of the Federal Convention. After federal elections took place, in 1789, the new government went to work establishing executive departments and considering promised amendments. The Constitution's ratification may be described as the final stage of the American constitutional founding, which began in 1776 with the Declaration of Independence from Great Britain and the establishment of new constitutions for eleven of the states, along with the country's first federal constitution, the Articles of Confederation.

Until the 1960s, the American founders were associated exclusively with the winning party, the Federalists, and the *Federalist Papers* were considered the only materials worth studying. While Cecelia Kenyon had written an important essay on the Anti-Federalists, entitled "Men of Little Faith,"[1] most of the work on the Anti-Federalists focused on the social background of the opponents of the Constitution.[2] Gordon Wood's

---

[1] Cecelia Kenyon, "Men of Little Faith: The Anti-Federalists on the Nature of Representative Government," *William and Mary Quarterly,* January 1955; also in Kenyon, "Introduction," *The Anti-Federalists* (Boston: Northeastern University Press, 1966).

[2] Charles A. Beard, *An Economic Interpretation of the Constitution* (New York: McMillan, 1913, 1935); Merrill Jensen, *The Articles of Confederation* (Madison: University

important work, *The Creation of the American Republic*, described the conflict between Federalists and Anti-Federalists in terms of social class: aristocracy versus democracy.[3] When political scientists Martin Diamond and Herbert Storing turned to the American founding, a name they gave to this period, they focused on the political thought of the parties involved in the debate over the Constitution. Diamond wrote several essays describing how the Federalists' conception of federalism departed from the traditional understanding, which came from Montesquieu's *Spirit of the Laws*. Storing wanted to discover how much the Anti-Federalists' understanding of good government differed from the Federalists'. His study of their major writings and convention speeches culminated in *The Complete Anti-Federalist*. In the first volume, Storing presented his account of Anti-Federalist thought, entitled "What the Anti-Federalists were For." This is how Storing began his essay:

> The Constitution of the United States was viewed by the founding generation as distinctive, even unique, in the extent to which it was the product of deliberation....[It] was framed by a numerous and diverse body of statesmen, sitting for over three months; it was widely, fully, and vigorously debated in the country at large; and it was adopted by (all things considered) a remarkably open and representative procedure. Viewed in this light, those who opposed the Constitution must be seen as playing an indispensable if subordinate part in the founding process. They contributed to the dialogue of the American founding.[4]

After noting the agreement that there would be amendments to provide for a bill of rights, as an illustration of that dialogue, Storing continues:

> The Constitution *did* settle many questions, and it established a lasting structure of rules and principles....But it did not settle *everything*; it did not finish the task of making the American polity. The political life of the

of Wisconsin Press, 1940); Jensen, *The New Nation* (New York: Knopf, 1950); Jackson Turner Main, *The Antifederalists: Critics of the Constitution* (Chapel Hill, N.C.: University of North Carolina Press, 1960).

[3] Gordon Wood, *The Creation of the American Republic, 1776–1787* (Chapel Hill, N.C.: University of North Carolina Press, 1969).

[4] *What the Anti-Federalists Were For* (Chicago: University of Chicago Press, 1981) 3. This book was also published as volume one of Herbert J. Storing's *Complete Anti-Federalist*, 7 volumes (Chicago: University of Chicago Press, 1981).

> community continues to be a dialogue, in which the Anti-Federalist concerns and principles still play an important role.[5]

A political dialogue, even at its best, is not the same as a Platonic dialogue. It is more like rhetoric than dialectic, to use a classical Greek distinction. It is good to keep this in mind when considering the American constitutional founding in general and the ratification debates in particular. I believe that Storing's point about dialogue refers to different views the founders had concerning federalism and republican government. While the Constitution settled some aspects of federalism and republicanism, it did not settle everything. I offer these two post-ratification observations about American government to illustrate this point. First, in his court opinion upholding Congress' authority to establish a national bank, Chief Justice Marshall described the main constitutional issue this way:

> This government has been acknowledged by all to be one of enumerated powers....That principle is now universally admitted. But the question respecting the extent of the powers actually granted, is perpetually arising, and will probably continue to arise, as long as our system shall exist.[6]

To illustrate the significance of such a formulation of federalism, Alexis de Tocqueville, who visited America in 1831–2, wrote that "the human mind invents things more easily than words," and then described America's "central power" as one that "acts without an intermediary on the governed, administers them and judges them by itself, as national governments do, but it acts this way only in a restricted sphere. Evidently, that is no longer a federal government; it is an incomplete national government."[7] These insightful observations about American government reveal the achievement of the American founding, as well as its open-endedness.

To understand both, I explain how and why the two major collaborators on the *Federalist Papers*, Alexander Hamilton and James Madison, could have come to disagree with one another as fundamentally as they did shortly after their successful efforts with the *Federalist Papers* and in their respective states' ratification conventions. Their disagreement over the proper course of American government in the 1790s is the source of our contemporary controversies over the meaning of federalism and executive

---

[5] Ibid.

[6] 17 US 316 (1819) 405.

[7] *Democracy in America*, trans. Harvey C. Mansfield and Delba Winthrop (Chicago: University of Chicago Press, 2000) 148–49.

power. These controversies reflect a fundamental disagreement over the nature of modern republican government: whether the major problem comes from too much or too little popular control over government. I begin my account of the debate over the Constitution with the Federal Convention (part one), and then I consider ratification by looking at the most important state ratification debates (part two) and considering the major differences between the political thought of the supporters and the opponents of the proposed Constitution (part three). During ratification especially, Hamilton and Madison subordinated their constitutional disagreements to their common goal of securing a more effective federal government. When President Washington acquiesced in Hamilton's economic plans, especially in the establishment of a national bank, and when he issued the country's Neutrality Declaration to avoid the war in Europe, the differences between the two major Publius authors became clear and very public. Because these contending views of the Constitution remain important today, I treat the major events of the first decade under the new Constitution (part four).

Part One:
The Federal Convention Proposes
a New Constitution

On February 21, 1787, the Confederation Congress authorized a federal convention to meet in Philadelphia in May "for the sole and express purpose of revising the Articles of Confederation" and reporting the proposed changes to Congress and the state legislatures. When Congress and the states agreed to these changes, they would "render the federal constitution adequate to the exigencies of government and the preservation of the union."[8] Despite that language, the Virginia Plan, which Madison wrote, departed fundamentally from the Articles of Confederation, in terms of the scope of power to be granted to Congress, a representation proportional to population and/or wealth, and ratification by popularly elected ratification conventions. Moreover, while the Constitution enumerated the legislative powers and reflected what was called the "Great Compromise" in proportioning the lower house by number and giving each state two

[8] "Report of Proceedings in Congress," Wednesday, Feb. 21, 1787, in *Documents Illustrative of the Formation of the Union of the American States*, Charles C. Tansill, ed. (Washington: Government Printing Office, 1927) 46.

senators, it retained ratification by popularly elected conventions and added the proviso that the ratification of nine states would bring the Constitution into being for those states. The framers' decision to depart from the amendment provision of the Articles, both by moving away from the approval of Congress and the state legislatures and by not requiring unanimity, greatly increased the chances of the Constitution's ratification. This was especially the case since Rhode Island never sent delegates to the Convention.

After the Convention spent two weeks considering the Virginia Plan, John Lansing and Robert Yates, framers from New York, joined David Brearly and William Paterson, framers from New Jersey, in arguing that the Convention was not authorized to consider or adopt the Virginia plan. And Luther Martin, in the Federal Convention and in Maryland's ratification convention, argued that the state legislatures needed to approve the change, since the people had divested themselves of the power to make such a decision. Patrick Henry made the same point in the Virginia ratification convention: "What right did they have to say 'We the People.' My political curiosity, exclusive of my anxious solicitude for the public welfare, leads me to ask who authorized them to speak the language of We, the People, instead of We the States? States are the characteristics and the soul of a confederation."[9]

This partly legal, partly conservative political argument did not gain much traction in the ratification debate. I think that was because a significant number of Anti-Federalist ratification convention delegates agreed with the most thoughtful Anti-Federalists, such as Federal Farmer and Brutus, that while amendments were necessary to make the proposed Constitution safe for republican liberty, it was better to work from that document than to work from the Articles of Confederation, with its reliance on state requisitions of men and money and each state's having a single vote and the power to control its federal delegation. Most of the Anti-Federalists also preferred to work from the proposed Constitution rather than the New Jersey plan. That plan adhered more strictly to the Congressional authorization; it added a limited tax on imports, a plural executive and a supreme court, with no change in state equality in voting and control

[9] Herbert J. Storing, ed. *The Anti-Federalist: Writings by the Opponents of the Constitution* (Chicago: University of Chicago Press) 297.

of their delegations.

The Great Compromise on representation also contained a sectional compromise; the framers drew on a Congressional proposal from 1783 to agree to count population for taxation and representation in the lower house on the basis of the whole number of free persons plus those bound to service for a limited term of years, excluding Indians not taxed, and "three-fifths of all other persons."[10] This is the first of three distinct places in the Constitution in which the institution of slavery is tacitly recognized, although the word is never used. The debate on this provision demonstrated that (1) there was no principled basis for recognizing this distinct form of property, i.e. in human beings, and (2) the provision was necessary because slaves were concentrated in the southern states, this sectional interest had to be accommodated, and the familiar provision effected a rough sectional parity in Congressional voting strength.

The Convention treated the two other sectional compromises involving slavery together. These involved proposed protections for slave importation and a special two-thirds requirement to pass a navigation act—a commercial regulation taking the form of a tariff on goods imported or exported. The dramatic and candid discussion concerning slavery and the principles of the American Revolution makes clear that the southern framers understood that "all men" in the Declaration of Independence meant all human beings, but, as John Rutledge asserted, "religion and humanity had nothing to do with this question. Interest alone is the governing principle with nations."[11] This meant it was impossible to eliminate slavery and retain the Union known as the United States. But, as it turned out, the southern states that most relied on slave importation—South Carolina, North Carolina, and Georgia—were satisfied by a proposal to allow such importation for twenty years, after which it was understood that Congress would prohibit it. In exchange for this "liberal" understanding, as General Pinckney described his eastern framers' position, enough framers from the southern states agreed to vote to delete the special majority for tariffs on goods shipped abroad in English rather than American ships. As Madison pointed out, the development of the American shipbuilding industry would enhance commerce throughout the union. And Gouverneur Morris

[10] *U.S. Constitution*, article I, section 2.

[11] James Madison, *Notes of Debates in the Federal Convention of 1787*, Adrienne Koch intro. (W.W. Norton & Co. New York and London 1987) 502.

pointed out that a strong navy was important for defense.[12]

Two other decisions by the Federal Convention facilitated subsequent ratification. First, the Convention rejected Madison's proposal that Congress have a national negative on all state laws, in order to redress what he described as the centrifugal force in all federal systems, whereby the power shifts from the center to the parts. Other supporters of a strengthened federal government doubted the practicality of such a measure, as it would take time for state legislation to get to the federal capital and then be considered. Such a proposal would surely have been a hard sell in ratification conventions. The Convention wisely adopted language from the New Jersey plan regarding federal supremacy, assuming that the matter would be handled in the courts.[13]

Finally, there was the matter of the executive. This was almost as difficult a subject as legislative apportionment. The Convention resolved early to have a single executive and to give that person a qualified veto. Then, after going back and forth on the mode of election and reeligibility issues, it finally decided on the indirectly popular "electoral college" mode of election. This decision reflected the Great Compromise by giving to each state the number of electors equal to its Congressional representation and then providing for state equality in the second stage of the election, should the electors' votes not produce a clear majority winner.

This mode of election, in contrast to election by the legislature, allowed for reeligibility. Both Edmund Randolph and George Mason opposed a single executive as "the foetus of monarchy," and Mason preferred legislative choice and a single term. It is noteworthy that while the proposal for a unitary executive produced "a considerable pause" in the Federal Convention, followed by these concerns about monarchy, in the ratification debate the Anti-Federalists rarely expressed any reservations about any part of the office of the president. I think that is because everyone knew that George Washington, who presided over the Federal Convention, would be selected as the first president. Their separation of powers

[12] See Madison *Notes*, August 29; the speeches of General Pinkney, Gouverneur Morris, and Madison are in Koch, 548–550.

[13] Compare the sixth resolution of the New Jersey Plan, in Madison's *Notes* (June 15) 120–121 in Koch with the Constitution's Supremacy Clause (article VI, section 2). The Federal Convention agreed to Luther Martin's motion to include a version of the sixth resolution of the New Jersey Plan when it defeated Madison's proposed national negative; see Koch, 305–306 (Madison's Notes, July 17).

concern was directed at the Senate.

Part Two: The Ratification Debate

First, I want to take note of the controversy surrounding the names of the contending parties. The supporters of the Constitution took the name Federalist and dubbed the opponents Anti-Federalists. The opponents claimed that they were the true federalists because they were the true republicans. When members of the Federal Convention distinguished federal from national, the former term referred to the voluntary principle of requisitions, characteristic of the Articles of Confederation, while the latter term referred to the coercion of law on individuals, characteristic of the proposed Constitution. In addition, however, as Storing pointed out, federal measures were then understood as measures aimed at supporting the authority of the Union. Federal authority referred to the government of the union; federal principle referred to requisitions.[14] Later on, both sides redefined federalism in a way that recognized the need for a true government of the union, one that acted directly on the people, and also one that recognized the importance of the states.

At its adjournment, on September 17, 1787, the Federal Convention resolved that the Constitution "be laid before the United States in Congress assembled" and then "be submitted to a Convention of Delegates, chosen in each state by the people thereof, under the Recommendation of its Legislature, for their Assent and Ratification."[15] Delaware was the first state to ratify the Constitution, and it did so unanimously on December 7, 1787. When Virginia became the ninth state to ratify the Constitution on June 26, 1788, that action affected the New York ratification convention, which, despite a substantial majority of Anti-Federalist delegates, ratified the Constitution 89 to 79 on July 26, 1788. North Carolina first voted against ratification on August 1, 1788, but then voted for ratification on November 21, 1789. Finally, Rhode Island voted for ratification on May 29, 1790. The total votes from the state conventions, counting North Carolina's two votes, were 1157 for ratification and 761 against. The outcome was much closer than that total would suggest. In three of the four major

---

[14] See Storing's discussion in *What the Anti-Federalists Were For,* 9–10.

[15] Max Farrand, *The Records of the Federal Convention of 1787*, 1937 edition in four volumes (New Haven: Yale University Press, 1937) vol. II, 665.

states, Massachusetts, Virginia, and New York, the votes for ratification were very close.[16]

The first serious ratification debate began in Pennsylvania in October, a month before that state's convention met. In the debate, James Wilson, who supported a strengthened federal government in the Federal Convention, strongly defended the Constitution. His State House Speech of October 6 and subsequent convention speeches made the Federalists' case for the Constitution. Centinel (thought to be Samuel Bryan),[17] along with John Smilie and Robert Whitehall, presented the Anti-Federalist position.

Viewed state by state, the ratification debates can be understood in terms of a contest over two different kinds of amendments: individual rights protections, which we associate with the first ten amendments, that is, the Bill of Rights; and amendments aimed at restricting the legislative powers of the government that the ratified Constitution would bring into being. After considering Pennsylvania, I take note of the Massachusetts convention's decision on recommendatory amendments, which led that state to ratify the Constitution by a close vote of 187 to 168 on February 6, 1788. With the Massachusetts decision as an impetus, Madison and the Virginia Federalists arrived at an unconditional ratification, and that greatly assisted Hamilton and the New York Federalists in their convention.

Published one day before Wilson's State House speech, Centinel's first letter began by lamenting the absence of any protections for freedom of the press and jury trials.[18] I assume Wilson was aware of it. In any case, some members of the Federal Convention had proposed such protections, but the Convention decided they were not necessary. In his defense of the Constitution without a bill of rights, Wilson distinguished between the completeness of a state's police power and the enumerated powers of the federal government: "in the former case, everything that is not reserved is given; but in the latter, everything which is not given is reserved."[19]

---

[16] For a chart that presents the dates and tallies of the state ratification votes, see Murray Dry, "The Debate over Ratification of the Constitution," in *A Companion to the American Revolution*, ed. Jack P. Greene and J. R. Pole, (Oxford: Blackwell 2000) 482.

[17] See Storing, *The Anti-Federalist,* 7.

[18] Ibid., 13.

[19] In John Bach McMaster and Frederick D. Stone, eds. *Pennsylvania and the Federal Constitution, 1787–1788* (Historical Society of Pennsylvania: 1888) 143.

Brutus directly responded to this point in his second essay, published in the New York Journal on November 1. He noted that the federal powers were substantial, and that the Constitution did contain some protections, which can be viewed as a partial bill of rights against Congress, in article one, section 9.[20] Jefferson made a similar argument to Madison in a letter dated March 15, 1789, which, among other things, persuaded Madison to lead the campaign for adding a bill of rights to the Constitution in the First Congress.

The other part of the amendments issue, however, would have amounted to a significant reduction in the powers of the federal government, and this was the major Anti-Federal objection to the current form of the proposed Constitution. While Centinel makes the point in his first Letter, the best statements came from Brutus and Federal Farmer. I quote two passages from Federal Farmer to show the link between the Anti-Federalist conception of federalism and their conception of representation and republican government: "The plan appears to be partly federal, but principally, however, [it is] calculated ultimately to make the states one consolidated government"[21] and "In examining the proposed constitution carefully, we must clearly perceive an unnatural separation of these powers from the substantial representation of the people."[22]

This view of representation and republican government would require more than an explicit protection of individual rights, such as freedom of the press and jury trials. It would require reducing the federal government's power to tax and to borrow money and to raise an army in time of peace. It would also suggest a limited federal judiciary: no lower courts. These are the kinds of amendments the Anti-Federalists proposed in several states, along with the individual rights or bill of rights provisions.

That is why the Massachusetts Convention's vote for unconditional ratification with recommendatory amendments was so important for the ratification of the Constitution. As Michael Gillespie, whom I follow here, has described it, Shays' Rebellion produced sharp divisions within the state, with a majority sympathetic to the protesting debtors. As a result, a

---

[20] See Storing, *The Anti-Federalist*, 119–121.

[21] Federal Farmer I, in Storing, *The Anti-Federalist*, 37.

[22] Federal Farmer II, in Storing, *The Anti-Federalist*, 41. See also Brutus I, 109, 114–115.

majority of the elected convention delegates opposed ratification.[23] Gillespie makes two related points about this state's convention, which remind me of the difference between carefully reasoned argument and rhetorically effective political speech. First, as the Federalist majority towns tended to be inhabited by the better educated citizens, the Anti-Federalists who were elected to the state convention, while roughly equal in number to the Federalists, were not equal in intellectual ability. Second, that disparity in intellect did not translate into an easy victory because the opponents of the Constitution were suspicious of "the clever rhetoric of the wealthy and well-born."[24] Gillespie points out that the Federalists had more success appealing to the different experiences of the several states, in the matter of frequency of elections, than when they made more principled arguments about government.

John Hancock and Samuel Adams were both moderates who were suspected of opposing the Constitution but who favored ratification with amendments. At the point where the two sides were in a stalemate, Hancock, who had not been present earlier, came forward with his proposal for unconditional ratification with recommended amendments. This was the decisive political action, because a conditional ratification would require another federal convention with no agreement on amendments, whereas unconditional ratification would have discussion of amendments take place under the new Constitution.

From the Massachusetts ratification on, the subsequent states all ratified the Constitution (except for North Carolina the first time) with recommended amendments. Interestingly, Massachusetts' own recommended amendments included both individual rights provisions and restrictions of the federal government's powers.[25]

The ratification contest in Virginia pitted Madison and Randolph against George Mason and Patrick Henry. (Randolph, who refused to sign the Constitution, came around to support it in ratification.) As Lance Banning pointed out in his essay on ratification in Virginia, everyone save Henry was committed to preserving the union and preferred to work from the proposed Constitution. They disagreed over two regional issues and

---

23 "Massachusetts: Creating Consensus," in *Ratifying the Constitution*, ed. Michael Allen Gillespie and Michael Lienesch (Lawrence, Kansas: University Press of Kansas, 1989) 145.

24 Ibid., 148.

25 See my chart in Dry, "The Debate over Ratification of the Constitution," 482.

their relation to the Constitution: the commerce power, which could affect exports, and the fear that a proposed treaty with Spain would include an agreement not to use the Mississippi River for twenty-five years, in exchange for commercial privileges.[26] Madison in particular responded on the first point, as he did in the Federal Convention, that the south would benefit as well as the country as a whole with a shipbuilding industry and the enhanced commercial activity that would result. In other words, the short-term cost of higher freight for shipping its agricultural goods to Europe would lead to enhanced benefits for Virginia and the south with increased trade. As for navigation of the Mississippi River, Madison argued that a stronger federal government would be less likely to consider such temporary concessions.[27]

After New Hampshire voted to ratify the Constitution on June 21, Virginia's vote to ratify on June 26 made it the tenth state. Madison's success in Virginia enabled New York's Federalists, outnumbered by 46 to 19, to eventually succeed in gaining unconditional ratification. Even Melancton Smith, a thoughtful and outspoken Anti-Federalist, voted for the Constitution.

The final stage of the subject of amendments took place in the First Congress and then in the states which ratified the proposed amendments. Madison took the lead in the House, insisting to his fellow Federalists that many people well-disposed toward the Constitution expected protections for individual rights. After putting Madison's proposed amendments at the end of the Constitution, rather than within the document, the House passed them. The Senate agreed, and the necessary three quarters of the states ratified ten of the twelve amendments, which came to be known as the Bill of Rights. The Federalists had such a commanding majority in the House that Thomas Tucker's attempt to put "expressly" into what became the tenth amendment failed by a substantial margin.[28]

---

[26] Lance Banning, "Virginia: Sectionalism and the General Good," in Gillespie and Lienesch, *Ratifying the Constitution*, 263–4.

[27] Ibid., 282.

[28] See *Creating the Bill of Rights: The Documentary Record from the First Federal Congress*, ed. Helen E. Veit, Kenneth R. Bowling, and Charlene Bangs Bickford (Baltimore and London: John's Hopkins University Press, 1991) 197, 199, and 51 for the vote; (the Congressional Register of August 18 and 21 records votes of 16–34 and 17–32 respectively).

Given the closeness of the votes for ratification in Massachusetts, Virginia, and New York, and the significance of the recommended amendments approach that came out of Massachusetts, it is surprising that the Anti-Federalists had so little success with amendments aimed at reducing the federal power. Somehow, the unconditional ratification of the Constitution, by eleven states by July 1788, took the wind out of the sails of the Anti-Federalists.

Part Three: The Political and Constitutional Thought of the Federalists and Anti-Federalists

I shift now from considering how the ratification process unfolded to judging the fullest thought in support of and in opposition to ratification of the Constitution. Earlier, I referred to Federal Farmer's argument that a substantial representation is possible in the state legislatures but not in the federal legislature. In a later letter, he identifies a natural aristocracy and a natural democracy and he argues that in the nature of popular elections, the former is going to dominate in the federal legislature by virtue of their talents as well as their wealth, while the latter, the middling sort, are more likely to be present if not dominate in more popular and less competitive state legislatures (see Letter VII). This is actually the obverse of Madison's famous argument in *Federalist* 10 that large heterogeneous constituencies will prevent majority faction more effectively than small, relatively homogeneous ones. The increased competition for places will result in more able representatives and no single faction is likely to command a majority in the larger more diverse constituency. It comes down to which concern is primary: the need to check majority tyranny or the need to check the tendency of government to become too exclusive—call it minority tyranny.

In the New York ratification convention, a similar exchange took place between Melancton Smith and Alexander Hamilton. Smith, denying that he would exclude the few and the great from power, makes the case for the predominance of the yeomanry, the middling farming class:

> A representative body, composed principally of respectable yeomanry, is the best possible security to liberty. When the interest of this part of the community is pursued, the public good is pursued, because the body of every

> nation consists of this class. And because the interest of the rich and the poor are involved in that of the middling class.[29]

Smith continues by pointing out that the number of representatives in Congress is too small and will be so even after the representation reaches one for every 30,000 people. He points out, as does Federal Farmer, that the middling class, or the natural democracy, will be more substantially represented in the state legislatures, and therefore the powers of government need to be recalibrated lest the federal government eventually overrun the state governments and effect a complete consolidation.[30]

Responding, Hamilton took issue with Smith's claim that the yeomanry is the virtuous class and therefore deserves preference.

> It is a harsh doctrine that men grow wicked in proportion as they improve and enlighten their minds. Experience has by no means justified us in the supposition, that there is more virtue in one class of men than in another. Look through the rich and the poor of the community; the learned and the ignorant. —Where does virtue predominate? The difference indeed consists, not in the quantity but kind of vices, which are incident to the various classes; and here the advantage of character belongs to the wealthy. Their vices are probably more favorable to the prosperity of the state, than those of the indigent; and partake less of moral depravity.[31]

Hamilton expressed himself more diplomatically in *Federalist* 35, where he argued that the kind of representation the Anti-Federalists were calling for, a reflection of the entire community, was inconsistent with elections. He went on to identify three main classes in the country: the farming class, the commercial class, and the learned professions, particularly lawyers. He contended that the large land owners were the natural representatives of all land owners, the merchants were the natural

---

[29] June 21, 1788, in *The Debates in the Several State Conventions as Recommended by the General Convention at Philadelphia in 1787*, ed. Jonathan Elliot (hereinafter Elliot) in 5 volumes (Philadelphia: Lippincott Company, 1891) II, 248; also, in *The Debate on the Constitution*, ed. Bernard Bailyn, (New York, NY: Literary Classics of the United States) vol. II, 762.

[30] Robert H. Webking has argued that Smith authored the Letters of the Federal Farmer. See "Melancton Smith and the Letters from the Federal Farmer," *The William and Mary Quarterly*, vol. 44, No 3, 510–528.

[31] June 21, 1788, in vol. II, Elliot, 257; and in *The Debate on the Constitution*, vol. II, 771–772.

representatives of mechanics and manufacturers, and the learned class acted as arbitrators.

Brutus makes the same argument Smith and Federal Farmer did with respect to the need to coordinate representation with the powers of government. His treatment of the powers is more detailed than Federal Farmer's and it constitutes a direct reply to Alexander Hamilton's argument in *Federalist* 23 about the necessity of granting full powers to raise money and armies to achieve the objects of government, especially when those objects include the common defense and general welfare of the country. Hamilton argued that because a polity cannot know the extent of the danger from without, it must be prepared to defend itself with all available means; hence the need for a full taxing power and the power to raise an army in peacetime. Brutus responds that preserving the states was equally important in a federal system and that required that the state powers be secured against federal encroachment. Therefore, Brutus recommended amendments to the Constitution that would limit the taxing power to import duties and allow Congress to raise standing armies in peacetime only with the vote of two-thirds of each House.[32]

The most thoughtful Anti-Federalists, as I said, preferred to seek amendments to the proposed Constitution. Given the significant compromises that took place in the Federal Convention, between the north and the south and large and small states, the major issue in ratification turned on whether some revision of the powers and/or structure of the proposed government would both be an improvement and gain consent. Since it was known that George Washington would be the first president, that took the possible disagreement over the executive out of consideration. The major issue thus became the scope of Congress's powers to tax, to raise armies, and, to a lesser extent, the scope of the necessary and proper clause. As I have mentioned, Hamilton addressed this issue in *Federalist* 23 by insisting that the federal government have the full powers to provide for the common defense:

> The powers are not too extensive for the objects of federal administration, or, in other words, for the management of our national interests.... If it be true... that the difficulty arises from the nature of the thing, and that the extent of the country will not permit us to form a government in which such ample powers can safely be reposed, it would prove that we ought to contract

[32] See Essays of Brutus, V–X, in Storing, *The Anti-Federalist*, 133–162.

> our views and resort to the expedient of separate confederacies….For the absurdity must continually stare us in the face of confiding to a government the direction of the most essential national concerns, without daring to trust it to the authorities which are indispensable to their proper and efficient management. Let us not attempt to reconcile contradictions, but firmly embrace a rational alternative.[33]

This is what Storing was referring to when he wrote:

> The Anti-Federalists lost the debate over the Constitution not merely because they were less clever arguers or less skillful politicians but because they had the weaker argument….The Federalists…reminded Americans that the true principle of the American Revolution was not hostility to government but hostility to tyrannical government. They sought to recover the balance that Americans had lost in the zeal for revolution.[34]

For all the regional differences that affected the ratification debates, as well as the different views about the rich and the poor, or the natural aristocracy and the natural democracy, the Americans' commitment to the Union and their realization that the traditional federal system had failed led them to ratify a Constitution that, as Tocqueville noted, involved the creation of a new form of government in terms of the relationship between the whole and its parts.

Part Four: After Ratification: the Contest Between the Federalists and the Republicans

So, what happened almost immediately after James Madison engineered a complete victory with amendments that the Anti-Federalists had insisted upon and yet which did nothing to weaken the structure or the powers of the government under the Constitution? My answer draws on Lance Banning's study of Madison and Ron Chernow's biography of Hamilton.[35] Hamilton proposed an economic development program that Madison did not foresee and did not believe was consistent with republican government.

---

[33] *The Federalist: A Commentary on the Constitution of the United States,* ed. Robert Scigliano (New York: Modern Library) Number 23, 144.

[34] Storing, *What the Anti-Federalists Were For*, 71.

[35] Lance Banning, *The Sacred Fire of Liberty: James Madisn and the Founding of the American Republic* (Ithaca, NY and London: Cornell University Press, 1995); Ron Chernow, *Alexander Hamilton* (New York, NY: Penguin Books, 2004).

Hamilton's plans included paying off the federal debt at par, assuming the state debts, establishing a national bank, and enacting tariffs to give incentives to manufacturing. He achieved all but the last objective. Madison disagreed with him on paying all federal bond holders, including speculators, at par (he wanted to make discriminations, presumably based on when the bonds were bought); he reluctantly agreed to the assumption of state debts when credit was given to Virginia, which had paid down its debt, and the capital was moved to the Potomac. He openly broke with Hamilton over the desirability and constitutionality of a national bank. Did this opposition to a national bank, on "strict construction" grounds, coming from the father of the Constitution, who kept "expressly" out of the tenth amendment, amount to a shift away from Madison's extended republic argument? Hamilton certainly thought so and conveyed that view in a letter to Edward Carrington.[36] Here is Madison's reported position.

> Mr. M., 'As to the other branch of the subject, I deserted Colonel Hamilton, or rather Colonel H deserted me; in a word, a divergence between us took place—for his wishing to administration, or rather to administer the government (these were Mr. M's very words), into what he thought it ought to be; while on my part, I endeavored to make it conform to the Constitution as understood by the Convention that produced and recommended it, and particularly by the state conventions that *adopted* it.'[37]

Was Madison consistent in the way he interpreted the Constitution, as Banning argues, or was Hamilton right to note a significant shift in Madison's constitutionalism? Banning does acknowledge that the Madison who wrote about the threat of majority faction in *Federalist* 10 had come to discern, after Hamilton proposed his financial plans, an apparently greater threat: "The danger posed by a minority with sinister designs—a faction fully capable of masking its intentions under cover of the Constitution—could be harder to defeat than number ten suggested."[38] This threat became all the more apparent to Madison when Hamilton persuaded President Washington to declare neutrality at the outbreak of war, with Revolutionary France facing off against Europe and England. From

[36] Letter of Alexander Hamilton to Edward Carrington, May 26, 1792, in *The Papers of Alexander Hamilton,* Harold C. Syrett, editor, Jacob Cooke, associate editor (New York: Columbia University Press, 1961-1977) volume XI, p. 438.

[37] This comes from Memoranda of N. P. Trist, 27 September 1834; see vol. III, Farrand. 534.

[38] Banning, *The Sacred Fire of Liberty*, 374.

that point on, until the election of 1800, Madison and Jefferson were convinced that Hamilton and the Federalist party leaders, including President John Adams (1797–1801), supported England against France because they favored monarchy over republicanism. Consequently, Madison and Jefferson considered the Federalist party leaders a threat to the American Revolution.[39] Other events in the 1790s further divided Madison and the incipient Republican Party from the Federalists: the Jay Treaty of Peace with England in 1795, the Alien and Sedition Acts of 1798 and the Kentucky and Virginia Resolutions of 1799–1800 in response, the undeclared war with France, and, finally, the election of 1800, called by the Republican victors "the second American Revolution."[40] Banning, whose work on Madison is thorough and fair, argues that Madison was consistent in his views on federalism. He refers to Madison's position in the Virginia Ratification convention to support his position. In response to Anti-Federalist concerns about consolidation, or an excess of power in Congress under the proposed Constitution, Madison argued that the state governments would retain the affections of the people, and hence their authority, because "[t]hey have the care of all of local interests..., for which men have the strongest predilections."[41] And to minimize the significance of the change from the Articles of Confederation to the proposed Constitution, Madison contends not only that "[t]he powers of the general government relate to external objects, and are but few," but "that the powers vested in the proposed government are not so much an augmentation of powers in the general government, as a change rendered necessary for the purpose of giving efficacy to those which were vested in it before."[42] He is referring, as he notes in the sequel, to the replacement of reliance on state requisitions,

---

[39] To explain such a result, Banning wrote that Madison could be described, as much as Thomas Paine or Jefferson, as "first to last the theorist—and not infrequently the ideologist—of the party of the Revolution." Ibid., 373.

[40] That phrase derives from a letter Jefferson wrote to Spencer Roane, dated September 6, 1819. Praising Roane for his Hampden essays, which opposed extensive federal power and the Supreme Court's authority to interpret the Constitution, Jefferson wrote: "They contain the true principles of the revolution of 1800, for that was the real revolution in the principles of our government as that of 1776 was in its form; not effected indeed by the sword, as that, but by the rational and peaceable instrument of reform, the suffrage of the people." In *The Portable Thomas Jefferson*, ed. by Merrill D. Peterson (New York, NY: Viking Penguin, 1975) 562.

[41] In Elliot, vol. III, 257.

[42] Ibid., 259.

of both men and money, with a complete tax power and the power to raise armies. So, not only does Madison offer a moderate view of the powers of Congress under the proposed Constitution, but he also places special weight on the views of the state conventions that adopted the Constitution.[43] Let it be noted, however, that as the Constitution's critics' strongest point concerned an excess of power in the general government, the Federalists had a rhetorical interest in playing down the enhancement of the federal government's powers, especially concerning the enumeration of legislative powers and the concluding "necessary and proper" clause.[44] Moreover, Madison's expressed preference for the understanding of the ratifiers over the framers of the Constitution draws on the requirement of ratification to bring the Constitution into being as law. But that valid point does not preclude the framers providing a fuller understanding of the meaning of the Constitution.

Conclusion

The ratification of the Constitution brought a new form of federalism into being and that, in turn, brought a new form of republican government into being, as well. Tocqueville, who described the first achievement as the creation of a new thing for which an old word, federalism, was given a new meaning, still described republicanism in America in terms of Montesquieu's emphasis on the smallness and homogeneity of the people in the separate states. But the Constitution lends itself to a more robust form of republican government, one in which the enumerated powers with respect to taxation, commerce, and foreign policy, all acting directly on individuals, lead to what we call "big government" today. From the 1790s on, Madison envisioned the farming class as the core of republicanism, as did the Anti-Federalists. Southern agrarianism depended on slavery. However, a capitalist economy, if Adam Smith was right, would eventually become more commercial and industrial, because the more extensive division of

[43] In addition to the passage from Trist's Notes, Jack Rakove quotes and discusses Madison's speech in the House of Representatives in April 1796, when he was contending for a constitutional role for that Body in connection with the controversial Jay Treaty. See Madison's speech of April 6, 1796, in J. C. A. Stagg, ed. 16, *The Papers of James Madison*, 290, 295–96; as quoted in Jack N. Rakove, "The Original Intention of Original Understanding," 13 *Constitutional Commentary* 159, Summer, 1996: 160–161.

[44] Rakove reminds his readers of the political context within which Madison's House speech was given; see Ibid., 161.

labor in those parts of the economy would produce more wealth. The Constitution, with a new federalism and a new republicanism, is closer to Montesquieu's account of England than it is to Montesquieu's account of republican government. Montesquieu said England's constitution had liberty as its end, not love of equality and love of country, which is how he defined political virtue.[45] Likewise, the Declaration of Independence has government securing the rights to life, liberty, and the pursuit of happiness, without referring to virtue. Moreover, Montesquieu mentions representation only in connection with England, not republics, and yet even the several states are large enough to require representation. England's constitutionalism differs from America's because it relies on hereditary institutions and America, lacking such, relied entirely on elections. Here is how James Wilson described the American system of government in the Pennsylvania Convention: "In its principles, Sir, it is purely democratical; varying, indeed, in its form, in order to admit all the advantages and to exclude all the disadvantages which are incidental to the known and established constitutions of government."[46] This is characteristic of the Federalist argument concerning representation and republican government. It is their reply to the Anti-Federalist demand for a more numerous representation, which in their view is necessary to maintain republicanism.

In *The Creation of the American Republic*, Gordon Wood described ratification as a social conflict between aristocracy and democracy. He then maintained that the Federalists, in making the kind of argument they did with election and representation,

> appropriated and exploited the language that more rightfully belonged to their opponents....By using the most popular and democratic rhetoric available to explain and justify their aristocratic system, the Federalists helped to foreclose the development of an American intellectual tradition in which differing ideas of politics would be intimately and genuinely related to different social interests.[47]

I think Wood stretches the term "aristocracy" here because the framers left the determination of voting rights in the hands of state

[45] See Montesquieu, *The Spirit of the Laws* (Cambridge: Cambridge University Press, 1989) part I, book XI, chapter 6.

[46] McMaster and Stone, 231, Speech of November 24; cf. 217.

[47] Wood, *The Creation of the American Republic*, 562.

government, and they understood that the trend was toward democratization. They also rejected any property qualifications for office holding. Better to say, especially with Madison's shift from a concern about majority tyranny to a concern about government tyranny, that the Constitution allowed for a continuation of the dialogue over the distribution of power between the nation and the states. In place of a debate about the power to tax and raise armies in time of peace, the future debates would be over the scope of the commerce clause and the tax and spend clause. Eventually the Reconstruction Amendments further enhanced the federal government's authority.

Where Wood charged the Federalists with a dubious appropriation, Jeffrey Tulis and Nicole Mellow have offered a more nuanced, and hence more persuasive, interpretation of the Federalists' successful ratification strategy. They maintain that by emphasizing the limitation of the enumeration of powers and playing down the significant structural shift away from the reliance of the Articles of Confederation on the state governments, the Federalists allowed the Anti-Federalists, thanks to Jefferson and Madison, to snatch victory from the jaws of defeat with the election of 1800 and the apparent triumph of strict construction federalism.[48] After all, "strict construction" is an adaptation of the Anti-Federalist advocacy, during ratification, of restrictions on the powers of government. Tulis and Mellow maintain that the Federalists, by softening their position, allowed their opponents to redefine federalism and republican government. As a result, a current majority of the Supreme Court embraces the view that the founders' Constitution comprehends federalism understood as the structural preservation of the authority of state government, when, in fact, that very Constitution provided a structure of government reflective of a national government.[49] Much of this careful argument sounds compelling, particularly the discussion, which draws on Storing, of the difference between the Federalist's and the Anti-Federalist's conceptions of federalism. My reservation concerns the extent to which the resulting weight given to "strict construction" by present day Conservatives can be identified

---

[48] Jeffrey K. Tulis and Nicole Mellow, *Legacies of Losing in American Politics* (Chicago and London: The University of Chicago Press, 2018) 45–54.

[49] Tulis and Mellow begin their chapter on the Founding, also called "The Anti-Federalist Appropriation," with a discussion of the Supreme Court's decision in the Affordable Care Act case (*National Federation of Independent Business v Sebelius* 567 U.S. 19 2012); see Ibid., 29–30.

primarily with the Anti-Federalists. After all, Madison took this position as early as 1790, with the proposal for a national bank, and he professed a limited view of federal power in the Virginia ratification convention in 1788.[50] The difference between the Tulis and Mellow interpretation, which merits careful consideration, and mine may turn on the significance of the structure of the Constitution on the one hand and the enumeration of powers in Article I, Section Eight, on the other. Tulis and Mellow seem to regard "strict construction" as a repudiation of the clear implications of the founders' Constitution. I think the closeness of the ratification votes, the importance of the promise of amendments, and the range of amendments proposed, to say nothing of the text of the Constitution itself, including what became the Tenth Amendment, made it possible for Madison to reconsider what threatened republicanism and to join Jefferson in making the case for a more traditional conception of republicanism.

Today, given the increased size and racial and ethnic diversity of the country and the increased importance of national security, the American people must find a way to reconcile "big government" with meaningful popular consent. But, as Chief Justice Marshall predicted in *McCulloch*, "the extent of the powers actually granted, is perpetually arising, and will probably continue to arise as long as our system shall exist."[51] That means we Americans need to think for ourselves about how to apply the lessons of our constitutional founding to today's conditions and problems.

---

[50] See above text at note 39.

[51] *United States Supreme Court Reports* 4 Wheaton 316, 405.

3

WRITING *FEDERALIST* 10 FOR AN ANTI-FEDERALIST AUDIENCE

Lynn Uzzell

Too often, the *Federalist* essays are examined as though they were a philosophical treatise rather than rhetorical discourse. This is a mistake, first, because it is not true. The authors of *The Federalist* were seeking to persuade a particular audience at a particular moment in time, and they sometimes defended positions with which they personally disagreed, or at least exaggerated the strengths or weaknesses of certain arguments for the larger goal of ratifying the Constitution.[1] Second, it is a mistake because it may cause readers to miss unexpected twists or eccentricities in the argument in pursuit of the abstract purity of its logic. This has been the case even with the most famous of all the arguments contained within these essays: Madison's defense of an extended republic in *Federalist* 10.[2]

Anyone with an elementary education in American constitutional government is already familiar with the basic argument of *Federalist* 10. Majority factions are the mortal disease of popular governments. Factions

---

[1] Others have made the same point, such as Paul Peterson, "The Rhetorical Design and Theoretical Teaching of *Federalist* No. 10," *Political Science Reviewer*, no. 17 (Fall 1987): 192–218; Quentin P. Taylor, "Publius and Persuasion: Rhetorical Readings of *The Federalist Papers*," *Political Science Reviewer*, no. 31 (2002): 236–82; Murray Dry, "Anti-Federalism in *The Federalist*: A Founding Dialogue on the Constitution, Republican Government, and Federalism," in *Saving the Revolution: The Federalist Papers and the American Founding*, ed. Charles R. Kesler (New York: Free Press, 1987) 40–60; and the most sophisticated rhetorical analysis to date probably belongs to Larry Arnhart, "The Deliberate Rhetoric of *The Federalist*," *Political Science Reviewer*, no. 19 (Spring 1990): 49–86.

[2] Alan Gibson has written: "With the exception of the Declaration of Independence and the Constitution itself, none of the documents of the founding era has generated such intense interest, nor been the object of such close textual exegesis or the subject of such profound and persistent scholarly disputation" as *Federalist* 10. Alan Gibson, "Inventing the Extended Republic: The Debate over the Role of Madison's Theory in the Creation of the Constitution," in *James Madison: Philosopher, Founder, and Statesman*, ed. John R. Vile, William D. Pederson, and Frank J. Williams (Athens: Ohio University Press, 2008) 65.

cannot be prevented; the best that can be done is to mitigate their pernicious effects. Extending the sphere of republican governments offers the best remedy for this (potentially fatal) disease of factions. Then Publius proceeds to list three advantages to be gained by extending the sphere of republican government. Thus far, no one disputes the general outlines of the argument. However, it is when ranking the relative importance of Madison's three advantages that we discover some disagreement among the scholars who have addressed this question. Since I will be examining the ranking of these three advantages throughout this chapter, for ease of reference I will assign each one a number. This number does not accord with the order in which they are listed in the *Federalist*; rather, the number accords with the strength of their adherents: from the greatest number of enthusiasts to the least.

Three Advantages of Extended Republics, and Three Curiosities about their Rankings

Advantage Number One is that extending the sphere of republican government—extending it both in geographic size and in the number of inhabitants—will encompass a greater number and variety of interests and parties; this multiplicity of interests will make it far less likely that any one faction will achieve a majority. This feature of the extended republic is the overwhelming favorite among scholars who have taken any position on the relative importance of Madison's three advantages. Some expositors of *Federalist* 10 treat this benefit of the extended republic as if it were the only one that Madison offered; others acknowledge the other advantages while explicitly or implicitly relegating them to a position of lesser importance.[3]

[3] David F. Epstein, *The Political Theory of* The Federalist (Chicago: University of Chicago Press, 1984) 99 and 109; Richard K. Matthews, *If Men Were Angels: James Madison and the Heartless Empire of Reason* (Lawrence, KA: University Press of Kansas, 1995) 71–79, esp. 77; Lance Banning, *The Sacred Fire of Liberty: James Madison and the Founding of the Federal Republic* (Ithaca, N.Y.: Cornell University Press, 1995) 203, 208; Lance Banning, "The Hamiltonian Madison: A Reconsideration," *Virginia Magazine of History and Biography* 92, no. 1 (January 1984): 13–14; Alan Gibson, "Impartial Representation and the Extended Republic: Towards a Comprehensive and Balanced Reading of the Tenth Federalist Paper," *History of Political Thought* 12, no. 2 (Summer 1991): 282–83; Martin Diamond, "Democracy and The Federalist," in *As Far as Republican Principles Will Admit: Essays by Martin Diamond*, ed. William A. Schambra (Washington, D.C.: AEI Press, 1992) 33; Martin Diamond, "Ethics and Politics: The American Way," in *The Moral*

Advantage Number Two is that extending the sphere of republican government will result in the election of representatives with superior wisdom, virtue, and patriotism. Madison argues that, since the ratio of meritorious leaders to the rest of the population should remain constant whether in a small or large republic, there will be a higher number of "fit characters" to choose from in the large republic. Furthermore, when the body of electors for each candidate is likewise enlarged, it is more difficult to practice with success the "vicious arts" of demagoguery; therefore, the people's choice "will be more likely to center on men who possess the most attractive merit and the most diffusive and established characters."[4] Although the advantage of securing a more virtuous representative body is a distant second among those who write on *Federalist* 10, it has some notable adherents. Gordon Wood, Garry Wills, Woody Holton, Joseph Kobylka, and Bradley Kent Carter all contend that the goal of securing superior representatives was paramount in *Federalist* 10; this priority supposedly

---

Foundations of the American Republic, ed. Robert H. Horwitz (Charlottesville: University Press of Va., 1990) 84–85 and 93; David Freeman, "Reflections on Human Nature: The Federalists and the Republican Tradition," in *The Federalists, the Antifederalists, and the American Political Tradition*, ed. Wilson Carey McWilliams and Michael T. Gibbons (New York: Greenwood Press, 1992) 33–35; Issac Kramnick, "The Discourse of Politics in 1787: The Constitution and Its Critics on Individualism, Community, and the State," in *To Form a More Perfect Union: The Critical Ideas of the Constitution*, ed. Herman Belz, Ronald Hoffman, and Peter J. Albert (Charlottesville: Published for the United States Capitol Historical Society by the University Press of Virginia, 1992) 170–71, 183–84, and 214; Thomas L. Pangle, "The Philosophical Understanding of Human Nature Informing the Constitution," in *Confronting the Constitution: The Challenge to Locke, Montesquieu, Jefferson, and the Federalists from Utilitarianism, Historicism, Marxism, Freudianism, Pragmatism, Existentialism...*, ed. Allan Bloom (Washington, DC: AEI Press, 1990) 20–21; Thomas L. Pangle, *The Spirit of Modern Republicanism: The Moral Vision of the American Founders and the Philosophy of Locke* (Chicago: University of Chicago Press, 1988) 110; Douglass Adair, *Fame and the Founding Fathers: Essays by Douglass Adair* (New York, Published for the Institute of Early American History and Culture at Williamsburg, Va., by Norton, 1974) 103; Harvey C. Mansfield, *America's Constitutional Soul* (Baltimore, Md.: Johns Hopkins University Press, 1991) 179; George F. Will, *Statecraft as Soulcraft: What Government Does* (New York: Simon and Schuster, 1983) 39–40; Charles R. Kesler, "Federalist 10 and the American Republicanism," in *Saving the Revolution: The Federalist Papers and the American Founding* (New York: Free Press, 1987) 36–37 and 39. Kesler is unique in arguing that, although No. 10 emphasizes the multiplicity of factions as the principal advantage, No. 63 gives a contradictory account, recognizing that the extended sphere is perhaps even more important for procuring "the right kind of representation."

[4] Alexander Hamilton, James Madison, and John Jay, *The Federalist Papers*, ed. Clinton Rossiter (New York: New American Library, 1961) 77.

burnishes Madison's credentials as a classical republican, or perhaps even a closet aristocrat.[5]

The final advantage can sometimes be the forgotten stepchild of the three. Madison also claims that the extended sphere of republican government will make it logistically more difficult for majority factions to form. The greater the number of people necessary to carry out some unjust combination, and the greater the expanse of territory over which it is necessary to communicate such a scheme, the less likely that it will be successful. It would be difficult to contend that this argument was the most important to Madison. Indeed, within Madison's various formulations of the same argument, the third advantage is sometimes portrayed as if it were simply an adjunct to Advantage One. Nevertheless, at least one author, Sanderson Schaub, has ventured to pull this advantage out of the shadows and into the limelight, so all three advantages have been given a shot at the top spot within the scholarly literature on *Federalist* 10.[6]

There are three curious facts that render the previous rankings rather

---

[5] Garry Wills, *Explaining America:* The Federalist, 1st ed (Garden City, N.Y.: Doubleday, 1981) 217–19, 223–30, 236–37, 259, 264–65, and 269; Joseph F. Kobylka and Bradley Kent Carter, "Madison, The Federalist, and Constitutional Order: Human Nature and Institutional Structure," *Polity* 20, no. 2 (Winter 1987): 202, 205, and 208; Woody Holton, "'Divide et Impera': *Federalist* 10 in a Wider Sphere," *The William and Mary Quarterly* 62, no. 2 (April 2005): esp. 193; Gordon S. Wood, *The Creation of the American Republic, 1776-1787* (New York: Norton & Co, Inc, 1969) 500, 612, and 615; Gordon S. Wood, "Democracy and the Constitution," in *How Democratic Is the Constitution?*, ed. Robert A. Goldwin and William A. Schambra (Washington, D.C.: AEI Press, 1980) 11, 13, and 15–16; Gordon S. Wood, "Interest and Disinterestedness in the Making of the Constitution," in *Beyond Confederation: Origins of the Constitution and American National Identity*, ed. Richard Beeman, Stephen Botein, and Edward C. Carter II (Chapel Hill: University of North Carolina Press, 1987) 82–83, 91–92, and 109. Interestingly, Wood argues that the intentions of the Federalists were to institute aristocratic leaders, but their deceptively democratic rhetoric (and he cites No. 10 in particular) misled people into believing that the means of combating the vices of democracy were entirely democratic. Contrary to Wood, I find that Madison's rhetoric became *more* focused on the need for virtuous leaders when he was addressing the larger audience; his private ruminations on the same subject were manifestly more engrossed with discovering democratic remedies for democratic diseases.

[6] Sanderson Schaub, "Justice and Honor, The Surest Foundation of Liberty: The Natural Law Doctrine in *The Federalist* No. 10," in *Constitutionalism in Perspective: The United States Constitution in Twentieth Century Politics*, ed. Sarah Baumgartner Thurow, vol. 3, Constitutionalism in America (Lanham, MD: University Press of America, 1988) 2–30, esp. 24–26 and 28.

peculiar. Curiosity Number One is that Madison provides his own ranking within *Federalist* 10 (and it is not oblique; it is explicit). Curiosity Number Two is that, in spite of the gallons of ink that have been devoted to publishing expositions of No. 10, apparently no one has ever highlighted *Madison's* ranking of the three advantages. And Curiosity Number Three is that Madison's hierarchy contradicts the two most popular alternatives heretofore given (yet still casts doubt on the third).

Since Madison's ranking is discreetly lodged within the summation sentences at the close of the essay—a deceptively simple repetition of his main points—it requires close attention. Madison sums up his main argument by explaining why the new federal Congress can be expected to be superior to the existing state legislatures. In framing his case, he begins (as he begins the essay as a whole) with Advantage Number Two:

> Does the advantage consist in the substitution of representatives whose enlightened views and virtuous sentiments render them superior to local prejudices and schemes of injustice? It will not be denied that the representation of the Union will be most likely to possess these requisite endowments.

He then proceeds to explain that we may also expect the federal Congress to be characterized by what scholars have considered to be Advantage Number One:

> Does it consist in the greater security afforded by a greater variety of parties, against the event of any one party being able to outnumber and oppress the rest? *In an equal degree* does the increased variety of parties comprised within the Union, increase this security.[7]

In other words, when Madison gives his own ranking of the three advantages, he states that if we are seeking security against unjust legislation (and if we are paying attention to his argument, that is the whole point of *Federalist* 10) then Advantage One increases this security to "an equal degree" as Advantage Two. He then concludes by saying that Advantage Number Three will give a "palpable advantage" to the Union over the state governments.

Given Madison's explicit statement on the equality of the two main advantages in *Federalist* 10, what could account for the widespread belief, and sometimes mere assumption, that Advantage One is more significant than Advantage Two? There are three possible reasons, each one of which

[7] *Federalist* 10, p.78 (emphasis added).

probably contributes to this misperception; however, these reasons may be ranked in ascending order of logical cogency (from least to most compelling).

Three Reasons for Reordering Madison's Ranking

The first reason for preferring Advantage One doubtless arises from our retrospective knowledge of the way the U.S. Constitution has worked in practice. When observing our political process today, we find it easier to believe in Advantage One than Advantage Two. Political pluralism, interest-group politicking, K-Street lobbyists, and even gridlock are ordinary features of our legislative process. But do we find in an equal degree (in the words of *Federalist* 10) representatives "whose wisdom may best discern the true interest of their country" and who are distinguished for their "patriotism and love of justice"? Representatives possessing such exalted intellectual and moral fiber are less evident.[8] For years now, approval ratings for Congress have rarely managed to top 20 percent, and they occasionally dip below 10 percent. And this low opinion of our nation's representatives is no new phenomenon. When Tocqueville surveyed the ranks in the House of Representatives in the 1830s, he was immediately "struck by the vulgar aspect of this great assembly." The moral caliber of the people's representatives was no better than the general population, he thought, and their intellectual acuity was perhaps worse.[9] Such grim reflections on our actual political experience under the Constitution probably accounts for the most immediate and visceral reason why people today believe that the pluralistic advantages of an extended republic take precedence in *Federalist* 10. Yet logically it makes no sense to import subsequent empirical knowledge—knowledge that would have been inaccessible to Madison—into his understanding when he composed the essay.

The second reason for believing that Madison had given priority to Advantage One appears logical on its face, but it disintegrates upon closer scrutiny. Among those who contend for its superiority, there are some who

[8] Gordon Wood has said that Madison's expectations that an extended republic would lead to "the filtration of talent" have "turned out to be as unrelated to reality as his idea of a congressional power to veto all state laws had been," in, "Is There a 'James Madison Problem?'," in *Liberty and American Experience in The Eighteenth Century*, ed. David Womersley (Indianapolis: Liberty Fund, 2006) 439.

[9] Alexis de Tocqueville, *Democracy in America*, ed. and trans. Harvey C. Mansfield and Delba Winthrop (Chicago: University of Chicago Press, 2000) 191–92.

claim that Madison explicitly asserts that the multiplicity-of-interests is the most important feature of the extended republic within *Federalist* 10. Indeed, they supposedly find that ranking in the paragraph immediately preceding the one quoted above, the one that contends for the equality of the two leading advantages. If this reading of the foregoing paragraph were correct, it would mean that there was an internal contradiction within *Federalist* 10: with Madison first giving a priority to Advantage One over the other two, then immediately claiming that One and Two were equal in the paragraph that follows.

In point of fact, this has been a misreading of Madison's argument. The source of the misunderstanding comes from the widespread but mistaken belief that when Madison speaks of "extending the sphere" of republican government, the phrase is the equivalent to Advantage One (ensuring "a multiplicity of interests," to borrow the phrase used in *Federalist* 51).[10] However, enlarging the geographical extent and population of republican government is the means of achieving all three of the advantages on offer; it is a mistake to identify that phrase with just one of them. Nevertheless, as a result of that error, several scholars have failed to understand the flow of Madison's argument in Number Ten and his statement regarding which circumstance is "principally" responsible for keeping us safe from majority faction.

After Madison has finished delineating the lethal and intractable problem of factions in republican governments, and before he launches into the advantages to be had from enlarging their sphere, he segues into an explanation of the "two great points of difference between a democracy and a republic." Within this passage, Madison numbers these two differences, but in order to better distinguish them from the three advantages, I will here assign each one with a letter: "The two great points of difference between a democracy and a republic are: [Difference A], the delegation of the government, in the latter, to a small number of citizens elected by the rest; [Difference B], the greater number of citizens, and greater sphere of country, over which the latter may be extended." *Federalist* 10 proceeds to argue that the first difference may yield the advantage of superior representation; then again, it may not, for "the effect may be inverted" in small republics. Madison then provides the "two obvious considerations" which make it plain that the advantage of superior representation, Advantage

[10] *Federalist* 51, p. 321.

Two, can only be expected within large republics with a correspondingly large population and electoral districts.[11]

Madison concludes his discussion of the second advantage by admitting that the number of electors may sometimes be too large for a truly representative government, but that the number anticipated by the federal Constitution supplies a happy medium. It is at this point, at the transition sentence between the conclusion of Advantage Two and the introduction of Advantage One, that scholars have so frequently misinterpreted Madison as giving a priority to the latter. "The other point of difference" between democracies and republics, according to Madison, "is, the greater number of citizens and extent of territory which may be brought within the compass of republican than of democratic government; and it is this circumstance principally that renders factious combinations less to be dreaded in the former than in the latter."[12] Within the context of Madison's argument, his meaning should be clear enough. When comparing the two points that distinguish republics from democracies, Difference A (a scheme of representation) is no advantage at all, unless coupled with Difference B (enlarging the size). Therefore, "the greater number of citizens and extent of territory" is the circumstance that "principally" makes factious combinations less to be dreaded. After all, Difference B (extending the sphere) is responsible for procuring all three of the advantages that he names.

Several scholars have erred because they treat Difference A (any scheme of representation) as if it were the equivalent of Advantage Two (superior representation), and they regard Difference B ("the greater number of citizens, and greater sphere of country") as the equivalent of Advantage One (breaking up majority factions through a multiplicity of interests).[13] Thus David Epstein, in an otherwise penetrating explication of

---

[11] *Federalist* 10, p. 76, 77.

[12] *Federalist* 10, p. 78.

[13] Epstein, *The Political Theory of* The Federalist, 99–101; Banning, *The Sacred Fire of Liberty*, 203, 208; Gibson, "Impartial Representation," 282–83; Kesler, "Federalist 10 and the American Republicanism," 36–37; John Patrick Coby, "The Long Road toward a More Perfect Union: Majority Rule and Minority Rights at the Constitutional Convention," *American Political Thought* 5, no. 1 (January 2016): 28–31 and 37. To be fair, Coby is analyzing Madison's argument on June 6 from the Constitutional Convention, not *Federalist* 10; in the former case, treating "extending the sphere" as synonymous with "multiplying interests" is far more justifiable, especially if one were examining Madison's *Notes of the Convention* in isolation from the other records for the same date.

The Federalist, draws on this passage to claim that "Madison calls the extended sphere the principal solution to the dangers of faction," and he elsewhere claims that "The diversity of parties is in Madison's view the more important solution," and his analysis in between seems to suggest that the two claims are interchangeable.[14] In fact, only the first claim is faithful to a plain reading of *Federalist* 10. The proper relationship between these concepts can almost be expressed in mathematical formulations: A scheme of representation added to an enlarged republic equals superior representation (Difference A + B = Advantage 2). On the other hand, an enlarged republic equals (or at least makes possible) all three advantages (Difference B = Advantages 1, 2, and 3). Therefore, a faithful reading of *Federalist* 10 must distinguish between "the two great points of difference between a democracy and a republic" and the three advantages to be expected from the second point of difference, the extension of territory and population that can take place only in a republic and is impossible in a democracy.

To sum up this almost algebraic analysis: Madison does not state in *Federalist* 10 that Advantage One is the "circumstance principally" responsible for making factions less fearsome; therefore, there is no internal contradiction when he subsequently claims that Advantages One and Two provide equally efficacious securities against oppressive majorities. Nevertheless, it may have been only too natural for scholars to misinterpret that passage; that is, there is a compelling reason for anticipating that Madison should be giving priority to the multiplicity-of-interests argument.

Among the three reasons for supposing that Advantage One ought to be considered the most important in *Federalist* 10, the last is logically the most formidable. *Federalist* 10 *seems* to contradict all of Madison's previous statements on the same subject. In the year 1787, Madison gave no fewer than four separate formulations of his extended-sphere argument. It was a dominant feature in the essay, "Vices of the Political System of the United States" (probably written around April of 1787), in a speech at the Constitutional Convention (delivered on June 6), within the letter he wrote to Jefferson several months later (October 24), and fourth and last, in *Federalist* 10 (published on November 23). In the first three of his formulations of the same argument, Madison gives an unambiguous preference to Advantage One. The clearest statement of his ranking comes in

---

[14] Epstein, *The Political Theory of* The Federalist, 101, 109.

his first articulation, the "Vices," in which he calls the combined effects of Advantages One and Three "the great desideratum in Government," but he names any process of elections that would "extract from the mass of the Society the purest and noblest characters" merely "an auxiliary desideratum."[15] The rankings in Madison's next two formulations are not stated as clearly as they are in the "Vices," but that is because Madison's account of the June speech and the October letter both omit any explication of Advantage Two altogether; in these instances he names only Advantages One and Three as the benefits derived from extending the sphere. Therefore, while there is no internal contradiction within *Federalist* 10, there is a contradiction, or at least an apparent inconsistency, between that essay and all previous iterations of the same argument. Our task, therefore, is to seek an explanation that would account for the apparent inconsistency.

Three Possible Explanations for the Anomaly in *Federalist* 10

There are three possible explanations, any one of which would account for the anomaly, but I propose to rank them in ascending order of plausibility—that is, from the least to the most likely explanation. The first possibility is the simplest: perhaps Madison changed his mind. It is possible that, from April through October of 1787, he believed that the multiplicity of interests was more important than securing virtuous representatives, but by November of that same year he believed otherwise. There is nothing impossible about this scenario, but it does not seem very likely. The contrast is too striking, and the change too sudden, to be believable without an intervening cause.

Possibility Number Two is considerably more plausible, though far less simple to explain. It is possible that *Federalist* 10 provides a different ranking of the three advantages than previous articulations because it is in fact answering a different kind of question and addressing a different problem. After all, any time we alter the parameters of a political problem, we may find that we reach a different solution. This explanation has real merit, and it should be given its due defense. Ultimately, however, it will

---

[15] "Vices of the Political System of the United States," in *The Papers of James Madison Digital Edition*, ed. J. C. A. Stagg, (Charlottesville: University of Virginia Press, Rodunda, 2010) (Henceforth abbreviated as *PJMDE*.). http://rotunda.upress.virginia.edu/founders/JSMN-01-09-02-0187.

not be found as convincing as the third explanation: that Madison's anomalous claim in *Federalist* 10—that the two leading advantages are of equal importance—expresses what he did not personally believe, and that he ranked them in this somewhat disingenuous way for rhetorical reasons. But before defending the third possibility, due weight should be given to the second.

In all of Madison's previous iterations of the extended-sphere argument, he was seeking a remedy for the injustices and instability he found in the *state legislatures*, and he defended a popularly elected continental legislature as the solution to that problem. In these formulations, he sought "some disinterested & dispassionate umpire in disputes between different passions & interests in the State."[16] At this stage, Madison viewed *Congress* as that "dispassionate umpire," and his idea of the "federal veto" (whereby Congress would have the power to void state laws) was the proposed instrument whereby it could exercise its impartiality when remedying injustices in the states. From April through October of 1787, all three previous iterations of the argument explicitly addressed the problem of injustices in the states, and all of them either implicitly or explicitly appealed to Madison's preferred plan for the federal veto as the structural solution to that problem.

When Madison wrote *Federalist* 10, however, his idea for the federal veto had been decisively rejected, and Congress could no longer be seen as the arbiter of justice when reviewing state laws. For the first time, therefore, Madison was applying his earlier reflections on extended republics to an entirely different question.[17] Instead of asking, "why trust Congress to act as an 'impartial umpire' when judging state laws?" the question was now, "why trust Congress to act as an 'impartial umpire' when passing federal legislation?" It seems perfectly plausible that these two questions might have two distinctly different answers.

If Congress were judging *state legislation* by means of the federal veto, then Advantage One, the multiplicity of interests to be expected from diverse representatives (most of whom were *not* drawn from the state which passed the offending law), would be the most important feature

[16] Letter from Madison to George Washington, April 16, 1787, in Stagg, *PJMDE*. http://rotunda.upress.virginia.edu/founders/JSMN-01-09-02-0208.

[17] Michael Zuckert, "James Madison in *The Federalist*: Elucidating 'The Particular Structure of This Government,'" in *A Companion to James Madison and James Monroe*, ed. Stuart Leibiger (Malden, MA: Wiley-Blackwell, 2013) 92.

guaranteeing impartiality. When Madison first proposed the idea of the federal veto to George Washington, he asked: "Might not the national prerogative here suggested be found sufficiently disinterested for the decision of local questions of policy...?"[18] On questions of "local policy," indeed, the disinterestedness of Congressmen living outside that locality would generally be above reproach. However, when considering the deliberative process leading to *federal legislation*, the impartiality derived from a diversity of interests is lessened, because it would often be less disinterested. When presenting this new circumstance in *Federalist* 10, Madison asked an entirely new question: "what are the different classes of legislators but advocates and parties to the causes which they determine?"[19] Therefore, when applying the operations of the extended sphere to the new question of federal legislation, we can expect that the influence of the multiplicity of interests in breaking up factions would be weakened, whereas the force of virtuous representatives elected from larger districts would remain the same. Consequently, it may be inferred that the comparative efficacy of Advantages One and Two for controlling factions has been equalized when applying Madison's already established benefits from extending the sphere to this new question of passing federal legislation.

This explanation is certainly possible; it even sounds plausible when focusing exclusively on the distinctions between *Federalist* 10 and the previous iterations of the same argument. But its plausibility begins to break down when we consider other aspects of Madison's earlier versions of the extended-sphere argument. While it is true that all previous formulations were addressing the immediate problem of unjust state legislation, it is also true that Madison was making some grandiose claims about the importance of his new theory—claims that went far beyond its immediate application to the federal veto.

Most telling of all is Madison's October letter to Thomas Jefferson, which is probably the most thorough explication of Madison's theory as he originally formulated it: as a defense of the federal veto. In a previous letter he sent to Jefferson in September, Madison expressed his doubts that the new Constitution could succeed, and he promised to explain his reasons for these doubts (the Convention's rejection of the federal veto) in a

[18] Letter from Madison to George Washington, April 16, 1787, in Stagg, *PJMDE*. http://rotunda.upress.virginia.edu/founders/JSMN-01-09-02-0208.

[19] *Federalist* 10, p. 74.

future letter. By defending the extended-sphere argument in his October letter, a month before composing *Federalist* 10, Madison was practicing his rhetorical chops on Jefferson. Moreover, he knew that he was addressing an unsympathetic audience (although a close friend), because Jefferson had preemptively expressed skepticism over the necessity and wisdom of Madison's proposed federal veto in a letter he penned from Paris in June.

Although Madison's October letter was ostensibly written to give Jefferson a post mortem on the outcome of the Convention, Madison indulged in an "immoderate digression" in which he defended his rebuffed proposal for a federal veto (filling approximately 40 percent of a letter that ran to 17 manuscript pages). Madison rested his argument on the sweeping claim that "private rights will be more secure under the Guardianship of the General Government than under the State Governments." He promised that the analysis establishing that premise "would, if I mistake not, unfold the true principles of Republican Government, and prove in contradiction to the concurrent opinions of theoretical writers, that this form of Government, in order to effect its purposes, must operate not within a small but an extensive sphere." Then, as we proceed through the letter, we find that these "true principles" that apply to *all* republican Governments (not merely to those, like the U.S., that are subdivided into smaller republics)—the principles that are going to upend all the prevailing "opinions of theoretical writers"—have nothing to do with the superior virtue of the representatives. As noted above, Advantage Two is not even mentioned in this letter. The revolutionary theory that Madison predicts will overturn all previous theories on republicanism is Advantage One, the multiplicity of interests, with a brief nod to Advantage Three.[20]

Madison would compose the tenth *Federalist* before he had a chance to receive Jefferson's response to his October letter, which must have come as a disappointment when it arrived. Although his friend responded to various points in the letter, he had nothing whatsoever to say on the subject of the "immoderate digression" that had so preoccupied his correspondent. Jefferson's indifference was to be the denouement in a string of cold receptions Madison would encounter when trying to persuade his contemporaries about the significance of his new theory. However, in stark

[20] Madison to Jefferson, October 24, 1787, in Stagg, *PJMDE*. http://rotunda.upress.virginia.edu/founders/JSMN-01-10-02-0151; see also, Madison to Jefferson, September 6, 1787, and Jefferson to Madison, June 20, 1787.

contrast to the lackluster notice given by Jefferson and others, Madison's enthusiasm for the theoretical importance of Advantage One in October of 1787 was undeniable. So why was it that, after the interim of only one month following unfolding the revolutionary theory described in this letter, he would claim that Advantage One was the equal to Advantage Two (an advantage about which he had not, apparently, given much thought since the previous spring)? The shift in focus that takes place in *Federalist* 10 (from the federal veto over state legislation to the quality of federal legislation) does not in itself seem sufficient to explain such a drastic realignment in his thinking. It seems more probable that Madison scaled back his claims for the multiplicity of interests, and exaggerated the importance of improving the caliber of representatives, for the very reason that he knew the former theory was revolutionary and the latter would be more readily acceptable. Since the multiplicity-of-interests theory was novel, untested, and contrary to prevailing opinions, he knew it would be a difficult hurdle to persuade his readers of its validity. When we consider the rhetorical headwinds Madison was facing, we at last gain insight into the most plausible reason why he framed the argument in *Federalist* 10 as he did.

Madison's Logic Bows to Rhetorical Necessity

We can better appreciate the rhetorical challenges faced by Madison if we look closely at his first attempt to persuade a contemporary audience of the superiority of the extended republic: his June 6 speech in the Constitutional Convention. Piecing together this speech is difficult because there are multiple, somewhat conflicting accounts of it. Taken together, they tend to show that there was some discrepancy between what Madison remembered saying and what the other delegates recorded hearing. Madison's account of his own speech, which he must have recreated from memory at least some hours after its delivery, lists only Advantages One and Three as being the explicit benefits derived from the extended sphere. He does record himself as saying that popular elections "under proper regulations had the additional advantage of securing better representatives."[21] But that curt and vague formulation is a far cry from the lengthy exposition that Advantage Two receives in *Federalist* 10—which dawdles over four

[21] Max Farrand, ed., *The Records of the Federal Convention of 1787*, Rev. ed, vol. 1 (New Haven: Yale University Press, 1937) 134.

paragraphs—an exposition that is there accorded at least twice the length that is devoted to defending Advantage One.

Some of the other delegates at the Convention, however, heard Madison present a somewhat more prominent case for Advantage Two on June 6 than his records relate. According to Hamilton's notes of the Convention, "Maddisons Theory" included all three advantages of the extended republic (which Hamilton conflated into "Two principles:" the first principle being a composite of Advantages One and Three, the second being Advantage Two). Robert Yates wrote a few lines indicating that Madison had argued for extending the sphere of government, but he listed no reasons that would explain why an enlarged republic would be superior. Rufus King also wrote a very cursory account of the June 6 speech, and he listed *only* Advantage Two. According to him, Madison was defending the enlarged republic merely as a means to prevent "bad elections."[22] However, King frustrates our attempts to piece together Madison's June 6 speech even further, because he apparently tried to reformulate Advantage One and apply it to a different subject altogether; worse still, he appears to have appended that reformulation to the end of his notes for June 4. By misunderstanding the argument, misapplying it to a different context, and recording it on the wrong date, King has bewildered scholars of the Constitutional Convention ever since.[23]

Examining the various and conflicting accounts of Madison's June 6 speech shows, first of all, that piecing together any historical event is difficult when the surviving records are imperfect. Second, it appears from the other records that Madison's public, more rhetorical presentation of his argument gave greater prominence to refining elections than his private recollections would suggest. As he was reconstructing the speech later that evening, alone in his room at Mrs. House's boarding house, the prominence of Advantage Two receded almost to nonexistence in his own mind. But it was remembered as being of at least equal significance to those who

---

[22] Farrand, 1:146-47 (Hamilton) 141 (Yates) 143-44 (King); James H. Hutson, "The Creation of the Constitution: The Integrity of the Documentary Record," *Texas Law Review* 65 (November 1986): 35.

[23] Lynn Uzzell, "A New Investigation into Madison's Notes of the Convention: Solving the Mystery of His June 6 Speech," *American Political Thought* 6, no. 4 (Fall 2017): 517–49; cf. Mary Sarah Bilder, *Madison's Hand: Revising the Constitutional Convention* (Cambridge, Mass.: Harvard University Press, 2015) 72–74, 117 (arguing that King's notes were accurate, and that Madison's version of the June 6 speech was a later fabrication).

heard it. Finally, the surviving records indicate that Madison's maiden attempt to persuade others of the importance of his revolutionary new theory—to convince his peers to trust the efficacy of Advantage One, that factions may be neutralized by multiplying interests and parties—was a rhetorical failure.

Although it appears that Madison did present all three advantages of the extended republic to the Convention on June 6, the three were not appreciated equally by those who heard it. Hamilton may have been the only one to treat Advantages One and Two equally, but only insofar as he devoted equal space to refuting and criticizing them: "There is truth in both" of Madison's principles, he says, "but they do not conclude so strongly as he supposes." King did not appear even to understand the argument for Advantage One, much less was he persuaded by it. Nor did anyone else at the Convention appear to appreciate the significance of the multiplicity-of-interests argument at the time, because no one either responded to it or repeated it all summer. All indications suggest that Madison's first audience was wholly unmoved by this groundbreaking theory. It is even possible that Madison defended his theory on more occasions than the surviving records indicate, because on August 14 he declared: "The enlargement of the sphere of the Government was indeed a circumstance which he thought would be favorable as he had on several occasions undertaken to show." The records do not indicate that there were "several occasions" when Madison defended this argument; instead, Advantage One seems to have been sadly forgotten, misunderstood, rejected, or disregarded by almost everyone except Madison.[24]

But if the other delegates seemed singularly unpersuaded by Advantage One, how did the second advantage go over at the Convention? If we return to the June 6 debates, we find that Madison is not the only Framer (or even the first one) to formulate the argument about larger

---

[24] Farrand, *The Records of the Federal Convention of 1787*, 1:146 (Hamilton's notes for June 6) 2:291 (Madison on August 14); Larry D. Kramer, "Madison's Audience," *Harvard Law Review* 112, no. 3 (January 1999): 611–79 (also arguing that Madison's theory failed to persuade because it was new and difficult to understand). Madison perhaps won only one convert in Philadelphia, Charles Pinckney, who delivered a fair rendition of Madison's theory in the South Carolina Ratifying Convention on May 14, 1788, as recorded in John P. Kaminski et al., eds., *The Documentary History of the Ratification of the Constitution Digital Edition* (Charlottesville: University of Virginia Press, 2009). http://rotunda.upress.virginia.edu/founders/RNCN-02-27-02-0005-0005-0004.

districts yielding more virtuous representatives. Indeed, the argument that large electoral districts improved the odds of electing qualified candidates was repeated numerous times over the course of the summer. Moreover, the same argument was made by delegates coming from a variety of different perspectives. It was defended by the populist Federalist James Wilson, the high-toned, aristocratic Federalist Gouverneur Morris, and the more classically republican Anti-Federalist George Mason. In other words, the argument on behalf of Advantage Two was a crowd-pleaser; it had the potential to appeal to almost everyone.[25]

When comparing the potential rhetorical appeal of Advantages One and Two, as these arguments were actually received by Madison's original audience, we have probably discovered the key to understanding why Madison composed *Federalist* 10 as he did. He began (as any good rhetorician does) with the arguments that unite the presuppositions of both speaker and audience. Madison lists what we've been calling Advantage Two—the virtue of the representatives—first. Only after developing the more acceptable thesis does he proceed to the revolutionary theory: that there is a way to secure justice and stability within a republic even when virtue fails. Here, Madison is asking his audience to be willing to accept strategically arranged human vices, and not merely hope and contrive for the best from human virtue. Finally, in his conclusion, Madison argues that his revolutionary new theory is "equal" to (or, to put it another way, "just as good as") the argument that would be more familiar and acceptable to his audience. He does this even though all other indications suggest that Madison privately believed the multiplicity of interests was by far the more important advantage.

It may be countered that Madison's decision to lead with Advantage Two was perhaps necessitated by his explication of the "two great points

---

[25] Farrand, *The Records of the Federal Convention of 1787*, 1:56 (Madison was the first to make the argument about large electoral districts on May 31, according to King's notes alone) 133–34, 135 (Wilson, Mason, and Madison on June 6) 154 (Wilson on June 7); vol. 2:54 (Morris on July 19). To say that this argument was a crowd-pleaser is not to say that the sentiment was universally embraced. Elbridge Gerry on June 2 and Roger Sherman on June 20 both expressed some skepticism about elections in large districts (1:80, 342). However, even with these outliers, the overarching rhetorical framework remains constant. All the delegates were seeking that form of election that would secure the most virtuous representatives, even when they disagreed about the means. When Madison took a stand on popular elections in large districts, he was adopting the presupposition that was shared by everyone in the room and defending the mechanism that was shared by most.

of difference between a democracy and a republic." But in point of fact, there is something oddly superfluous about interjecting the topic of direct democracy into this discussion at all, just as there is something logically incongruous in the subsequent ordering of the three advantages. Both the interjection and the ordering are unique to *Federalist* 10 and are not found in any of his other presentations of the enlarged sphere. Paul Peterson has argued that Madison's decision to introduce the topic of pure democracy into this essay should itself be considered "a masterful rhetorical ploy" and "a kind of rhetorical smoke screen." After all, none of Publius' readers were contending for direct democracy as a viable option, even at the state level, so its invocation would seem to be irrelevant or unnecessary, and hardly the most efficient route to the conclusion of his argument. Nevertheless, introducing the subject serves a rhetorical purpose. Madison begins with a proposition with which his audience will agree (that democracies are impracticable for America and have "ever been spectacles of turbulence and contention"). He does this in order to move them gently toward an argument which overturns all their previous presuppositions (that small republics are subject to the same tumults as small democracies, and may at times be worse). In other words, Madison is attempting, by starting from a common ground and taking small steps away from it, to move his audience in the direction of his radical thesis.[26]

But there is another reason why the digression into pure democracies and the primacy of Advantage Two (primacy at least in the order of presentation) should strike the reader as odd. When Madison first delineated the problem of factions, he established that there was no feasible way to remove the causes of faction; they must therefore seek to control its effects. However, when he arrives at the point in the argument where he finally reveals how these dangerous forces within republics will be contained, he leads with Advantage Two, which is plainly a means of eliminating the cause of factions rather than controlling its effects. It is true that electing virtuous representatives will do nothing to remove the causes of faction in the electorate. But to the extent that elections in large republics really could work as advertised—securing "representatives whose enlightened views and virtuous sentiments render them superior to local prejudices and schemes of injustice"—to that extent the process of election has

[26] Peterson, "Rhetorical Design," 205, 206–207ff; see also, Dry, "Anti-Federalism in *The Federalist*," 41.

eliminated the causes of faction within the legislative body.

It is almost as if, when Madison was formulating his argument about the intractability of factions, he was still mentally leading with Advantage One, similar to the line of reasoning as it had originally been presented in the "Vices." The logical flow of the argument leads us to expect that benefit to come first, and that Advantage Two will again be appended to the end of the main discussion as an "auxiliary desideratum." Yet, instead of following his argument down its logical path, instead of leading with the two advantages (One and Three) that actually do control the effects of faction, he somewhat unnaturally and awkwardly inserts a digression about pure democracy and elevates Advantage Two by giving it pride of place within the structure of the argument. Both of these hiccups in the construction of the argument are difficult to defend logically, but both may be seen as attempts to disarm his readers by introducing familiar propositions before clobbering them with the more radical theory. In a similar fashion, his surprising assertion within the summation paragraph that the multiplicity-of-interests argument was of "equal" efficacy as virtuous representatives was likely an attempt to win over his readers to the more controversial argument.

Consequently, those scholars who believe that *Federalist* 10 gives priority to Advantage One have been mistaken. But those who believe that Advantage One is the most important consideration *to Madison* are probably correct, even though he offered an altogether different and even surprising reversal within his most celebrated essay. Why does the distinction between Madison's private opinions and his public expressions matter? When we read *Federalist* 10 (or any of the *Federalist* essays) as if it were a philosophical treatise divorced from its historical and rhetorical context, we are liable to read into the argument what we logically expect to find there rather than appreciating the odd quirks and unexpected maneuvers that its author actually assembled. Madison is justly recognized as a preeminent political theorist, and he will never be remembered as a preeminent rhetorician. Nevertheless, he was not entirely tone-deaf to the constraints placed upon him by his historical milieu.

Finally, although the "crowd-pleasing" argument in Advantage Two was suitable for most audiences, it was aimed especially at the Anti-Federalists. During the Convention, both Gouverneur Morris and George Mason had endorsed the proposition that larger districts could improve the odds of securing more virtuous representatives. But like many

Federalists, Morris tended to take the darker view of human nature.[27] Morris might use an argument from virtue when it suited his purposes, but his views of republicanism didn't require elevating the moral tenor of the people or their rulers. Mason, by contrast, like so many Anti-Federalists, believed that virtue was the vital principle of republican governments. That is why we find him in the Convention "descanting on the extravagance" of American manners; he even attempted to counter these troubling tendencies by twice moving (unsuccessfully) to empower Congress "to enact sumptuary laws."[28] Madison's Anti-Federalist audience generally took for granted that the success or failure of republican governments hinged upon the virtue of its people, and they believed that virtue was dependable only in a small republic. Madison was attempting to replace those presuppositions with radical new theories: that human virtue was never dependable within popular assemblies, that republican government could only be secure if virtue was not the only guarantee of its success, and that the best security arose from larger republics. The novel and groundbreaking potential of the multiplicity-of-interests theory made it exhilarating for Madison to formulate dialectically, but those same qualities posed a challenge when seeking a formulation that could succeed rhetorically.

---

[27] On July 11 in the Convention, Madison described Morris as "a member who on all occasions, had inculcated So strongly, the political depravity of men, and the necessity of checking one vice and interest by opposing to them another vice & interest." In Farrand, *The Records of the Federal Convention of 1787*, 1937, 1:584.

[28] Mason on August 20 and September 13, in Ibid., 2:344 and 606.

4

FEDERAL JUDGES AS A SOURCE OF FEDERAL AUTHORITY IN *FEDERALIST* 39

Jeremy D. Bailey

Scholars have long written of a "James Madison problem." The problem is that there seems to have been two Madisons: one in the 1780s who joined with Hamilton to defend the Constitution against local-minded critics and another in the 1790s who seemed to join those very critics to create an opposition party based on states' rights.[1] But the James Madison problem is not a new construction framed by scholars looking to publish new books and articles. Rather, it was known to Madison's contemporaries. Hamilton, for example, believed that it was Madison who changed in the 1790s, not Hamilton. But more than that, Madison's Republican allies also charged Madison with inconsistency as a Republican. For them, Madison was for the Bank of the United States after he was against it, and, given the centrality of the Bank to the Republican understanding of the Constitution, this turnaround was inexplicable. For these Republicans, there were not two Madisons, but three.

Madison was well aware of these charges, and, late in life, he went to great effort to answer them as controversies over the meaning of federalism became intertwined with a growing sectionalism and eventually with the crisis over nullification. The running thread in these explanations is that Madison frequently pointed to his *Federalist* 39 as a way to both demonstrate his own consistency and to illustrate the true meaning of the Constitution. In an 1823 letter to Jefferson, for example, Madison wrote that he had "never yielded my original opinion indicated in the *Federalist* No. 39 to the ingenious reasonings of Col. Taylor against this construction of the Constitution."[2] Throughout his retirement, Madison responded to

---

[1] For a review of this scholarship, see Jeremy D. Bailey, *James Madison and Constitutional Imperfection* (New York: Cambridge University Press, 2015) 1–14.

[2] James Madison to Thomas Jefferson, June 27, 1823, in *James Madison: Writings*, ed. Jack Rakove (New York: Library of America, 1999) 801–2.

charges of inconsistency by pointing to his argument in *Federalist* 39 as the foundational logic of what he believed to be his basic consistency regarding the line between state and national authority. That is, he offered *Federalist* 39 with a reading in mind that would be able to accommodate both his efforts to make a nation *and* his efforts to defend the rights of Virginia.

In this essay, I ask whether such a reading is possible. Before I turn to *Federalist* 39, I will summarize a few of Madison's positions during controversies over the division of state and national authority.

The Bank of the United States

During the controversy in the 1790s over Hamilton's proposal to create the Bank of the United States, Madison sided firmly with Jefferson in arguing that the Constitution did not grant the Congress the power to incorporate a bank. His argument rested on the history of the Convention and the text of the Constitution. As to the history, Madison pointed out that the Convention had explicitly voted down a proposal to give Congress the power to grant "charters of incorporation." As to text, Madison proposed a theory of interpretation to counter Hamilton's argument that the power was implied because it "is inherent in the very definition of Government." Madison instead argued that the Bank fell short in terms of proximity and importance to explicitly enumerated powers. He connected the two arguments with another claim, that the "meaning of the parties" to the Constitution would shed light on the particular characteristics of the constitution in question. Because an interpretation cannot be allowed to change the nature of a constitution, a constitution's particularity is of utmost importance. Because the Constitution of 1787 rejected the Bank as an enumerated power, and because the people who ratified the Constitution did not believe that the power to incorporate a bank was part of the deal, it would be inappropriate to add the power by way of construction.[3]

Later, however, Madison supported renewing the charter of the Bank and then, in 1816, signed a bill chartering the Second Bank of the United States. Madison defended himself against inconsistency on the Bank question on many occasions throughout his retirement. In 1817, Madison explained to the new President, James Monroe, that the question of the Bank was different from the ongoing controversy over the national road and

[3] Madison, "Speech in Congress Opposing the National Bank," February 2, 1791, in *Madison: Writings*, ed. Rakove, 480–490

internal improvements. What made the Bank different was that it had been the subject of extensive public discussion and had been approved by all three departments.[4] In the aftermath of John Marshall's decision for the constitutionality of the Bank in *McCulloch v. Maryland*, Madison wrote Spencer Roane to reflect on the controversy. In a passage that has been quoted often, Madison writes:

> It could not but happen, and was foreseen at the birth of the Constitution, that difficulties and differences of opinion might occasionally arise in expounding terms & phrases necessarily used in such a charter; more especially those which divide legislation between the General & local Governments; and that it might require a regular course of practice to liquidate & settle the meaning of some of them.[5]

In other words, Madison argues that some questions about the constitutional line between state and national authority were unresolved or unclear but could be resolved as the meaning of the Constitution became settled—or liquidated—over time. In 1830, to C. E. Haynes, Madison used similar reasoning to claim that his position was actually consistent: "in the case of a Constitution as of a law, a course of authoritative expositions sufficiently deliberate, uniform and settled, was an evidence of the public will necessarily overruling individual opinions."[6] For Madison, it seems the Bank could be made constitutional by public deliberation even though it was not constitutional in the first place. Importantly, this deliberation could happen at the national level—among Congress, the president, and the Supreme Court—even though the controversy in question was about whether the national government had this power.

---

[4] Madison to James Monroe, December 27, 1817, in *The Papers of James Madison, Retirement Series*, vol. 2, ed. David B. Mattern et. al. (Charlottesville: University of Virginia Press, 2013) 190–91. It is worth noting that Madison believed that the power over internal improvements, especially canals, was also explicitly considered and rejected by the Convention. See Madison to Edward Livingston, April 17, 1824, in *The Writings of James Madison*, vol. 9, ed. Gaillard Hunt (New York: G. P. Putnam's, 1910) 188.

[5] Madison to Spencer Roane, September 2, 1819, in *Madison: Writings*, ed. Rakove 735.

[6] Madison to C. E. Haynes, February 25, 1831, in *Writings of James Madison*, vol. 9, ed. Hunt, 433.

Madison in the Convention

Another difficulty in assessing Madison's argument in *Federalist* 39 has to do with the textual record of the Convention of 1787. Madison left the most extensive records of the Convention, but a handful of other delegates left fragmentary accounts of the deliberations. One of those delegates was the New Yorker Robert Yates, whose account was necessarily incomplete because he left the Convention on July 10. Yates's records of Madison's speeches are different than Madison's records of Madison's speeches. For example, on June 12 and June 26, Yates records Madison defending the Senate as an institution that would represent wealth, as a protector of the rights of the "opulent" man "who lolls on his sofa or rolls in his carriage."[7] Madison, however, records himself defending the Senate as a protector of stability and justice, not the opulent per se. Many years later, in a letter to Jared Sparks, Madison wrote that Gouverneur Morris wanted to balance the weight of wealth against the weight of numbers, but he did not ascribe to himself the idea that the Senate would represent wealth.[8]

The difference between Yates's and Madison's accounts are also suggestive with respect to Madison's desired version of federalism under the Constitution. Yates records Madison on June 21 to say that it was impossible to mark the boundary between state and national authority: "To draw a line between thc two, is a difficult task. I believe it cannot be done."[9] Madison does record this statement, but he does not record himself as saying it. Rather, he ascribed it to Hamilton on June 19, with Hamilton asserting that "no boundary could be drawn between the National & State Legislatures." To be fair, these textual differences may not by themselves add up to a new revelation. After all, Madison had come very close in *Federalist* 37 to arguing that no line could be drawn, or, at a minimum, that is a conclusion that is held out to the reader in that essay. But the difference is that Madison's *Notes* have Hamilton making this point to conclude that the national legislature must have "indefinite power."[10] Yates's version records Madison moving in that direction, too, saying that because no line

---

[7] Robert Yates and John Lansing, *Secret Proceedings and Debates of the Constitutional Convention* (Honolulu, HI: University Press of the Pacific, 2002 [1986]) 124.

[8] Madison to Jared Sparks, April 8, 1831, in *Writings*, vol. 9, ed. Hunt, 447–51.

[9] Yates and Lansing, 159.

[10] James Madison, *Notes of Debates in the Federal Convention of 1787 as Reported by James Madison*, ed. Adrienne Koch (Athens: Ohio University Press, 1966) 152.

could be drawn, he was "inclined for a general government."[11] Madison's version, however, has Madison saying that even if the general government were given indefinite powers, the states would still retain their powers because of the preference of the people in the states.[12]

Likewise, Yates records Madison differently on the question of the sovereignty of the states. The question arose during the heat of the debate between large states and small states. According to Yates, William Samuel Johnson said that the controversy boiled down to two competing views of the states. On one side, the large states viewed the states "as districts of people composing one society," and the small states viewed the states as distinct "political societies." Yates records Madison as rejecting the premise: the states "never possessed the rights of sovereignty" because these "were always vested in Congress."[13] Madison's version is more qualified: "too much stress" was placed on the states as "political societies," and under the Articles of Confederation there were in fact some "limitations on the sovereignty of the states."[14]

If Yates is to be trusted, and that is a big if, one possibility would be to stop here and conclude that Madison simply did not believe in the prior sovereignty of the states either under the Articles of Confederation or before the adoption of the Articles of Confederation. In this view, *Federalist* 39 reveals that the division between state and nation in Madison's mind was really more one of process than of line-drawing. What matters is that some institutions are federal, others national, and others partly federal and partly national, *not the limits on the national government's powers over the states.* This would make a certain sense when read as a continuation of *Federalist* 37 and 38. In No. 37, we learn that it is impossible to draw such lines because of the limits of human understanding and human language, and sometimes meaning has to be settled over time. In No. 38, we learn that regimes governed by deliberation and consent are often founded without deliberation and without consent. Thus, in *Federalist* 39, the argument is meant to show that the new Constitution is both sufficiently republican

---

[11] Yates and Lansing, 159.

[12] Madison, *Notes*, 165. His example is the townships in Connecticut, which are incorporated. If the states were "reduced to corporations" under the General Government, it would not follow that the General Government would find it inconvenient to take away their powers. The threat actually comes from the states, not from the nation.

[13] Yates and Lansing, *Secret Proceedings*, 199–200.

[14] Madison, *Notes*, 213.

and sufficiently federal, *but this first requires that readers lower their expectations for both republicanism and federalism.* Deliberation does not seem to be necessary for republicanism, and federalism is more a matter of process and negotiation than a compact.

This would seem to mean that Madison was impatient with, or skeptical of, arguments that began from the premise of sovereign states which existed prior to the Constitution and Union. The problem with this reading is that Madison goes further toward a stronger notion of state sovereignty in later explications of the Constitution. One example is his response to the Alien and Sedition Acts. Another is his treatment of slavery.

Slavery

Madison's later opinions on slavery are enough to frustrate anyone trying to save the Founders by giving them a Lincolnian reading of the Constitution and slavery. While Madison did prefer a gradual colonization policy that would be consented to by all parties and therefore require compensation to slaveholders (with money raised from sale of western lands), he seemed to believe this required a constitutional amendment.[15] Meanwhile, like Jefferson, he favored the spread of slavery on diffusionist grounds, that is, Madison believed that diluting it would weaken it as well as improve the conditions for the enslaved.[16] Likewise, Madison objected to the Missouri Compromise on the grounds that it was beyond the constitutional authority of Congress.[17] One problem was that reformers were trying to change the meaning of the Constitution by giving old words new meanings. In particular, they were reading Congress' power over the *importation*

---

[15] Madison to Robert Evans, June 15, 1819, in *Madison: Writings*, ed. Rakove, 728–33

[16] Madison to James Monroe, February 10, 1820, in *Madison: Writings*, ed. Rakove, 771–72. He believed that the conditions for the enslaved had improved since the Revolution of 1776 because there was more attention to human rights and because reforms regarding entail and primogeniture had resulted in a decreasing proportion of enslaved persons to masters. Madison to Robert Walsh, March 2, 1819, in *Madison: Writings*, ed. Rakove, 723. See Thomas W. Merrill, "The Later Jefferson and the Problem of Natural Rights," in *The Political Thought of the Civil War*, eds. Alan Levine, Thomas W. Merrill and James R. Stoner, Jr., (Lawrence, KS: University Press of Kansas, 2018) 1–47.

[17] Madison to Spencer Roane, May 6 and June 29, 1821, in *Madison: Writings*, ed. Rakove, 772–79.

of slaves to include the *migration* of slaves from one state to another.[18] In particular he wrote President Monroe to inform him of the meaning of the Constitution based on his memory of the Convention Debates, noting that he was "astonished" that the novel interpretations used by members of Congress had not used the true meaning of the words, that is, the meaning used by the men who ratified the Constitution.[19] But more than having the wrong interpretation of words, the deeper problem was that it admitted new states to the Union on different terms than old states. It would thus upset the "political equality of the states."[20] More than a rationalization made on behalf of Southern states, this was actually an application of a principle Madison had used during ratification, when he argued that states such as New York could not conditionally ratify the Constitution because that would create unequal levels of ratification.[21] A special ratification was necessary to make the Constitution an actual constitution, but this presumed that that every state ratified exactly the same document.

The Alien and Sedition Acts

Madison veered most toward the authority of the states in his response to the Sedition Act of 1798, passed by a Federalist Congress, and signed by John Adams. Under that law, any person who published "scandalous and malicious" writings with intent to defame or stir up opposition against the President or either house of Congress would be subject to a fine of up to two thousand dollars and two years in prison. There were fourteen indictments under the Sedition Act, plus three more done before the law under the common law. Twelve of the seventeen were printers, and the majority occurred during the spring of 1800, right in the middle of the election.

It is important to note that Federalists were operating under conventional readings of freedom of the press, readings made popular by William Blackstone. Under that understanding, freedom of the press was only freedom from prior restraint, not from prosecution after the fact. It is also important to note that the Sedition Act took a major step toward a more

[18] Robert Walsh to Madison, November 11, 1819, *Madison Papers Retirement*, 1: 548–9; Madison to Walsh, November 27, 1819 and January 11, 1820, in *Madison Papers Retirement*, 1: 553–59, 584–85.

[19] Madison to James Monroe, February 10, 1820, *Madison Papers Retirement*, 2: 6–7.

[20] Madison to James Monroe, November 19, 1820, in *Writings of James Madison*, ed. Hunt, 9: 31.

[21] See Bailey, *James Madison and Constitutional Imperfection*, 70–88.

libertarian understanding by allowing truth to be a defense, whereas Blackstone's did not. It is also important to note that Federalists were not unanimous.[22]

In response, Madison and Jefferson secretly authored resolutions to be acted upon by the legislatures of Virginia and Kentucky. In his draft of the Kentucky Resolutions, Jefferson began from the premise that the fundamental principle of the Constitution is the Tenth Amendment, that is, that all powers not delegated to the national government are reserved. Importantly, Jefferson labeled the Union a compact, with each "party" having "equal right to judge for itself" the "infractions" upon the compact. The federal government cannot be the judge because it was not a party to the compact; rather, it was created by the compact. Because the states are the parties, the states were the ultimate judges of the compact and had the power to nullify laws that violate the Constitution.

Madison made the same general argument in his draft of the Virginia Resolutions, but he was more moderate in key places. Unlike Jefferson, Madison began by proclaiming Virginia's "warm attachment to the Union of the States," and he did not mention nullification. Like Jefferson, however, Madison characterized that Union as a "compact to which the states are parties." Further, he argued that as the parties to the compact, the states have a duty to "interpose" when powers not delegated are exercised.[23] Later, in his longer Report on the Virginia Resolutions, Madison repeated

[22] Recent scholarship has shown that not every Federalist supported the Blackstonian notion that a free press required only freedom from prior restraint: it appears that the justices on the original Supreme Court were evenly divided on this question, with men like John Jay, James Wilson, and John Rutledge going beyond the Blackstone standard. Later, with respect to the Act itself, a "sizeable minority of the Federalist Party opposed the Sedition Act, generally on grounds of unconstitutionality." But that minority did not include Alexander Hamilton and John Marshall. Both held practical misgivings about the political effects of the law but none about its constitutionality. After the response by Kentucky and Virginia, their positions hardened. See Wendell Bird, *Press and Speech Under Assault: The Early Supreme Court Justices, the Sedition Acts of 1798, and the Campaign Against Dissent* (New York: Oxford University Press, 2016) 454.

[23] Madison, "Virginia Resolutions Against the Alien and Sedition Acts," December 21, 1798, in *Madison: Writings*, Rakove, 589. As to the liberty of the press, Madison calls it the "only effectual guardian of every other right." Like Jefferson, and unlike Marshall, he argues that press and religion have similar protection. He quotes from the VA ratifying convention: "the liberty of conscience and of the press cannot be cancelled, abridged, restrained or modified by any authority of the United States." See *Madison*: *Writings*, ed. Rakove, 590.

his insistence that the Union is a "compact" among the states. This means that the states preceded the national government as the "parties" to the compact that created the national government. It also means that the national government has only those powers that were given to it and any remaining governmental powers were necessarily "withheld" by the states. In Madison's view, this reading was supported by "all the contemporary discussions and comments" surrounding the formation and ratification of the Constitution, as it was "constantly justified and recommended" on that "ground."[24]

A lot depends on the meaning of the word interpose, so it should be pointed out that Madison persuaded Jefferson against nullification. In particular, he pointed out that the parties to the Constitutions were state ratifying conventions, not state legislatures, so it made little sense to say that a state legislature had the power to nullify law. Jefferson agreed. Moreover, while Jefferson was president, either Jefferson or Madison wrote a memorandum deciding that in cases when a state believed a law was unconstitutional, the president was obligated to enforce federal law until the Constitution was formally amended by three fourths of the states.[25] Later, after Jefferson's death, Madison went to great effort to save Jefferson from attempts by nullifiers to claim Jefferson as their model. In a series of letters to Nicholas Trist, Madison expressed dismay that they had invoked Jefferson as the "pedestal for their colossal heresy."[26] Specifically, he directly countered the claim that Jefferson believed that one state could put a federal law on hold until the convention could sort it out: "No man's creed was more opposed to such an inversion of the Repub[lican] order of things."[27] It is likely that Madison was right, at least in the sense that Madison had persuaded Jefferson on several occasions to walk back from his more extreme position on nullification.[28]

---

[24] Report on VA Resolutions, 1799, in *Madison: Writings*, ed. Rakove, 610.

[25] See Bailey, *Thomas Jefferson and Executive Power* (New York: Cambridge University Press, 2007) 98.

[26] Madison to Nicholas Trist, 23 December 1832, in *Writings*, ed. Hunt, 489–92.

[27] Madison to Nicholas Trist, Dec. 1831, in *Writings*, ed. Hunt, 472–3. Madison did concede that Jefferson's letter to Giles suggests otherwise, but he concluded that it was a letter written in old age and did not outweigh the many opinions on the other side.

[28] For example, Jefferson wrote to Wilson Carey Nicholas that Madison persuaded him in 1799 that the states should not "reserve" the right to use the Sedition Act's violation of liberty as grounds "of doing in the future whatever we might now rightfully do." Jefferson

Coordinate Review and the Supreme Court

More than moderating Jefferson's theory of nullification, Madison moderated his own compact theory with a doctrine of judicial finality. While it is true that Madison, like Jefferson, supported a doctrine of coordinate review with respect to separation of powers, he did not with respect to questions of federalism. In his 1817 message explaining his veto of an internal improvements bill, Madison explained that one of the reasons for his veto was that the bill had the result of "excluding the judicial authority of the United States from its participation in guarding the boundary between the legislative powers of the General and the State Governments."[29]

In an 1821 letter to Spencer Roane, Madison went further, this time in the aftermath of *Cohens v. Virginia*. He clarified his position to be that on the "abstract question whether the federal, or the State decisions ought to prevail, the sounder policy would yield to the claims of the former." The reason why the national judiciary had to prevail—and it is worth noting that Madison calls the national judiciary the federal judiciary—is because the alternative is unacceptable. "Were this trust to be vested in the States in their individual characters, the Constitution of the U.S. might become different in every state, and would be pretty sure to do so in some; the State Govts. would not stand all in the same relation to the General Govt., some retaining more, others less of sovereignty; and the vital principle of equality, which cements their Union thus gradually be deprived of its virtue."[30] Later, in an exchange of letters with Joseph C. Cabell, Madison entered the controversy over whether the Constitution gives Congress the power to pass a tariff, a controversy that would be settled eventually by Andrew Jackson's Nullification Proclamation. Madison believed that Congress did have the power, but he also believed that the question had been obfuscated by both "judicial and anti-union heresies."[31] In his view, the states could not reserve to themselves the final say over constitutional interpretation.

---

to Wilson Carey Nicholas, September 5, 1799, in Barbara O'Berg, ed., *The Papers of Thomas* Jefferson, vol. 31 (Princeton, NJ: Princeton University Press, 2004) 178.

[29] Madison, "Veto Message to Congress," March 3, 1817, in *Madison: Writings*, ed. Rakove, 719.

[30] Madison to Spencer Roane, June 29, 1821, in *Madison: Writings*, ed. Rakove, 778.

[31] For his explanation of the power, see Madison to Joseph C. Cabell, 18 September 1828, in *Madison: Writings*, ed. Rakove, 813–823. The statement about heresies comes from Madison to Cabell, September 7, 1829, *Founders Online*, National Archives, last modified February 1, 2018, http://founders.archives.gov/documents/Madison/99-02-02-1877.

"Were this a mere league, each of the parties would have a right to expound it." But such a league, without a provision for a "peaceable and effectual decision of all controversies arising among the parties," would be a "mere Treaty between Independent Nations," and "not a Government." While a state may "shake off the yoke" by appealing to the right of revolution in "extreme cases," the states do not reserve the power to be the final say on the Constitution. Madison added a postscript with the following comments:

> note that there can of course be no regular Arbiter or Umpire, under any Governmental System, applicable to those extreme cases, or questions of passive obedience & non-resistance, which justify & require a resort to the original rights of the parties to the System or compact, but that in all cases not of that extreme character, there is & must be an Arbiter or Umpire in the Constitutional authority provided for deciding questions concerning the boundaries of right & power. The particular provision, in the Constitution of the U.S. is in the authority of the Supreme Court, as stated in the "Federalist" No. 39.

The passage from *Federalist* 39 he has in mind occurs in his discussion of the extent of the powers the general government would have under the new Constitution. There, he writes that the extent cannot be national, because that would imply "an indefinite supremacy over all persons and things."[32] This is not the case. Instead, the government's "jurisdiction extends to certain enumerated objects only." Just as important, the Constitution "leaves to the several states a residuary and inviolable sovereignty over all other subjects." But this does not mean that the state sovereignty includes the right to decide "controversies relating to the boundary between the two jurisdictions." Rather, "to prevent an appeal to the sword and a dissolution of the compact," there must be some "tribunal" to make impartial rules "according to the rules of the Constitution." And this tribunal "ought to be established under the general rather than under the local governments."[33] The fact that the national judiciary would be determining the meaning of the boundaries is less important than the fact that there are boundaries. These boundaries were agreed to by way of a ratification process that was federal and not national in character. It would

[32] Madison, *Federalist* 39, in *The Federalist*, ed. Robert Scigliano (Modern Library, 2000) 245.

[33] Ibid.

seem, then, that Madison's complicated position—treating the Union as a compact among states *and* as a Union wherein controversies would have to be settled by a judiciary created by those parties to that compact—goes all the way back to *Federalist* 39 and therefore suggests a basic consistency.

It is worth noting, however, that Madison does not discuss the national judiciary in the next paragraph when he discusses the other two departments of government. In examining "the sources from which the ordinary powers of government are to be derived," Madison explains that the House is national, the Senate is federal, and the presidency is partly national and partly federal.[34] Curiously, he does not say whether the judiciary is national or federal. Indeed, by the logic used for the executive and legislative branches, the judiciary would seem to be more federal than national, because the president is at least partly federal and the Senate is wholly federal. Owing its selection to a compound body (the president) and its confirmation to a federal body (the Senate), the judiciary would have to be federal.

But this is clearly ridiculous. As Brutus saw, the members of the federal judiciary are nothing if not national officials. Supported by a lifetime tenure that would protect them from any electoral constituency, the judges would find that their own power was intimately connected to the power of the national government.[35] Indeed, the reason Madison left judges out of the discussion is likely because he perceived how ridiculous it would be to call federal judges mostly federal. More than that, by calling attention to the strangeness of the logic behind this category, the question of judges would implicate the other two branches as well. Is it true, for example, that the House is national when members are necessarily tied to local constituencies? Why is the formula for representation a more important variable than the constituency being represented?

An 1825 letter to Henry Lee demonstrates this point. In response to the election of 1824, Henry Lee sent Madison his newspaper editorial condemning the House's choice of John Quincy Adams, a candidate who received fewer Electoral Votes than Jackson. Madison responded by reflecting on representation and on the merits of a plurality system. As to representation, Madison acknowledged two views on representation, noting that there is no way to legally bind representatives to their constituents'

---

[34] Ibid.

[35] See Brutus, Nos. 10–15.

wishes, so this must be left to the conscience of the legislator and the prudence of the constituent. Although this has not been appreciated by the scholarship on Madison, this was Madison's standard way of threading the needle on the meaning of representation.[36] As to the merits of a plurality requirement, Madison noted that a lot depended on how many candidates were under consideration. But Madison did not stop there. Rather, he argued that the Constitution complicated the question as to the meaning of the will of the "majority of voters": "In our complex system of polity, the public will, as a source of Authority, may be the will of the people as composing one nation; or the Will of the States in their distinct & independent capacities; or the federal will as viewed, for example, thro' the Presidential Electors, representing, in a certain proportion both the nation & the States." These divisions should be "regarded as the result of a compromise, between the larger & smaller States." And thus the large states were given the advantage in choosing the president from the people, and the small states were given the advantage in choosing the president from among the candidates.[37] Elsewhere, Madison frequently criticized this part of the compromise and tried to change it.[38] To Robert Garnett, Madison observed in 1824 that the Constitution is "sui generis" because nothing like it had existed in prior history, and, as a result the usual vocabulary with words like "national" and "federal" were not applicable.[39]

Madison's explanation that the Constitution creates various and competing wills goes hand in hand with his going out of the way to remind readers in *Federalist* 37 that the Constitution could not settle the question of line drawing between state and nation. In addition to there being no line, there is no single finite will. Rather there are competing wills that speak on behalf of different constituencies. These competing wills will inevitably claim, sometimes rightly so, that they represent the final authority. But judges would represent another will, and this will would try to act as if it had no constituency at all. The missing constituency of judges in *Federalist* 39 reveals not only that the meaning of the Constitution would have to be settled but also that the national and federal constituencies under the Constitution are not and cannot be straightforward.

---

36 Bailey, *James Madison and Constitutional Imperfection*, Chapter 3.

37 Madison to Henry Lee, January 14, 1825, in *Writings*, ed. Hunt, 215–8.

38 Bailey, *James Madison and Constitutional Imperfection*, Chapter 6.

39 Madison to Robert S. Garnett, February 11, 1824, in *Writings*, ed. Hunt, 176–77.

5.

"THE FATE OF AN EMPIRE:" ALEXANDER HAMILTON'S BACONIAN PROJECT

Kimberly Hurd Hale

The intellectual and philosophical inspirations of the American Founders are well-traversed topics. Whether it be Thomas Jefferson's homage to John Locke's *Second Treatise of Government* in the Declaration of Independence, or the Framers' constitutional adaptation of the Baron de Montesquieu's argument in the *Spirit of the Laws* about the virtues of dividing power into three branches of government, the Founders clearly learned much from their Enlightenment predecessors. In this chapter, I argue that the influence of one key early Enlightenment thinker on the American project has thus far been largely overlooked, namely that of Francis Bacon (1561–1626). I argue that Alexander Hamilton, in particular, can be viewed as an adherent to Bacon's vision for the possibility of a deliberately planned, scientifically grounded political society. Bacon's Great Instauration, as his planned re-structuring of British society is known, lays the groundwork for much of the Enlightenment thought that follows in the seventeenth and eighteenth centuries. Using Hamilton's contributions to the *Federalist Papers* and selections from Bacon's *Essays*, I examine the extent to which Hamilton's vision for the American republic can be understood as a manifestation of Bacon's intended Instauration.

Bacon's role as a forerunner, and perhaps architect, of Enlightenment thought is well established. Thomas Hobbes, who in his youth worked as Bacon's secretary,[1] is a clear proponent of Bacon's vision for a politics and a philosophy grounded in the principles of science. Both Bacon and Hobbes recognize that modern science will irreversibly change the way

---

[1] Howard White, *Peace Among the Willows* (The Hague: Martinus Nijhoff, 1968) 254; Paul A. Rahe, *Republics Ancient and Modern,* Vol. 2 (Chapel Hill: University of North Carolina Press, 1994) 137.

man exists in society; their arguments differ, however, on how this knowledge should be applied to political philosophy. Howard White argues that "Bacon would have considered Hobbes' effort premature. Few, if any, experiments in natural science which developed between Bacon and Hobbes were of sufficient magnitude to justify, in Baconian terms, the assurance that Hobbes could arrive at the 'two maxims of human nature' [that form the basis of Hobbes' natural rights argument]."[2] White also makes clear, however, that, "While Hobbes claimed to know more than Bacon believed he (or any person) could know, the foundations of Hobbes' claim are assuredly Baconian."[3] The founders of the Royal Society also freely acknowledged their debt to Lord Verulam.[4] In the century after Bacon used his position in James I's court to initiate his Instauration, the idea of a science of politics, aimed at progression towards a perfect (or near-perfect) future captured the imaginations of many prominent thinkers, including those most commonly cited as the American Founders' greatest inspirations.[5] Yet, very little attention has been paid to the sympathies between Bacon's "project of progress"[6] and that of the American Founders. I argue that by investigating these sympathies, we can better understand the origins of Hamilton's vision for the development of American political thought and better evaluate how that vision compares to the reality of American political life.

Hamilton's essays in *The Federalist* are rich, detailed works of political theory and rhetoric. As the chief architect of the project, Hamilton wrote

---

[2] White, *Peace*, 255. White quotes: Thomas Hobbes, *De Cive*, ed. Sterling Power Lamprecht, (New York: Appleton-Century-Crofts, 1949) "Epistle Dedicatory," 5.

[3] White, *Peace*, 255.

[4] Baron Verulam is Bacon's official title in James I's court. Benjamin Farrington, *Francis Bacon: Philosopher of Industrial Science* (London: Lawrence and Wishart, Ltd, 1951) 17; Graham Rees, "Reflections on the Reputation of Francis Bacon's Philosophy," *Huntington Library Quarterly*, 65, 3/4 (2002): 379-394, 380.

[5] Paolo Rossi, "Bacon's Idea of Science", in *The Cambridge Companion to Bacon*, edited by Markku Peltonen, (Cambridge: Cambridge University Press, 1996) 39. See Kimberly Hurd Hale, *Francis Bacon's New Atlantis in the Foundation of Modern Political Thought* (Lanham: Lexington Books, 2013) Chapter 6 for a discussion of Bacon's influence on later Enlightenment thinkers, in particular the Marquis de Condorcet.

[6] This term is taken from the title of Robert K. Faulkner's excellent book, *Francis Bacon and the Project of Progress* (Lanham: Rowan & Littlefield Publishers, Inc. 1993).

approximately two-thirds of the *Federalist Papers*, about fifty essays.[7] He discusses the role of each branch of the proposed government at length, giving special attention to the powers and scope of the executive branch. Despite his sometime reputation as a thinker enamored with executive power, Hamilton, unlike Bacon, is not an overt monarchist.[8] And though evidence exists that calls into question Bacon's sincerity in his defense of monarchy, the purpose of this chapter is not to interrogate either the esoteric possibilities of Bacon's thought or Hamilton's arguments about the superiority of republican government. Instead, I focus on three areas of thought where Hamilton's arguments explicitly echo those of Bacon: 1) the view of politics as a science, 2) the encouragement of commerce, and 3) the advocacy in favor of developing naval strength. These three arguments demonstrate that Hamilton's vision for America's future is decidedly Baconian in scope, and in character.

The Science of Politics

My examination of Bacon's influence on Hamilton's thought begins at the very beginning of the *Federalist Papers*. Hamilton begins *Federalist* 1 with a remarkable declaration of the scope of the founders' endeavor:

> The subject speaks to its own importance; comprehending in its consequences nothing less than the existence of the UNION, the safety and welfare of the parts of which it is composed, the fate of an empire in many respects the most interesting in the world...it seems to have been reserved to the people of this country...to decide...whether societies of men are really capable or not of establishing good government from reflection and choice, or whether they are forever destined to depend for their political constitutions on accident and force.[9]

The decision of the American Founders to pursue a constitutional, republican, federal form of government must be appreciated for its

---

[7] Officially, John Jay is the acknowledged author of five essays, James Madison of twenty-nine essays, and Hamilton of fifty-one essays. Madison disputed this count however, claiming that he was the author of several more.

[8] Several scholars, including Robert K. Faulkner in *Project of Progress* and Hale in *Francis Bacon's New Atlantis*, argue that evidence can be found that Bacon is somewhat open to the nascent republicanism emerging in England at this time. However, Bacon never openly acknowledges this affinity in his writings.

[9] Alexander Hamilton, *Federalist* 1, in *The Federalist Papers*, by Alexander Hamilton, James Madison, and John Jay, ed. Clinton Rossiter (New York: Signet Classics, 2003) 27.

intentionality. At the time, received wisdom held that a republic as large as that of the United States would be undesirable, if not dangerously unstable. Yet, the Founders found a way to turn these perceived liabilities into the strengths of the new Constitution. Hamilton's passage, quoted above, is notable for two reasons: 1) he likens the new Union to an empire; and 2) he emphasizes that the Constitution is the result of reflection. First, Hamilton is known to harbor grand ambitions for the newly formed United States; in this essay, he makes those ambitions clear. The thirteen states already cover a geographical territory of impressive size, with great potential for expansion. Though the obstacles to empire are numerous at this stage of American development, Hamilton clearly views them as surmountable. He believes that the United States can continue to grow, and become a preeminent political, economic, and military force in the world.

Second, Hamilton emphasizes that the design of the American Constitution is one made from reflection and choice, rather than haphazard development made necessary by the accidents of history and force. Unlike other political organizations throughout history, there is intentionality in the American structure. Moreover, the process of designing this Constitution is framed by Hamilton as scientific. He claims the Framers aimed for a "judicious estimate of our true interests, unperplexed and unbiased."[10] This striving for unbiased evaluation of political principles evidences the extent to which Hamilton views the project as grounded in scientific methods. Hamilton draws upon both reason and history in forming his defense. He compares the American experiment to past republics, noting that though these governments generally failed to live up to their promise, "the science of politics, like most other sciences, has received great improvement [in the modern age]."[11] He argues that "the efficacy of various principles" is much better understood by modern thinkers than by ancient ones.[12] Though the Founders are undoubtedly indebted to Greek thinkers such as Plato and Aristotle in their embrace of the possibility of public life and public virtue, the Founders also view themselves as incorporating ancient wisdom into the modern scientific practice of politics. Hamilton can thus argue in favor of the "vigor of government"[13] as a means to preserve

[10] Hamilton, *Federalist* 1, p. 27.
[11] Hamilton, *Federalist* 9, p. 67.
[12] Hamilton, *Federalist* 9, p. 67.
[13] Hamilton, *Federalist* 1, p. 29.

liberty. Contrary to much Enlightenment thought, most notably that of Locke, Hamilton proposes that a free government need not be a minimal government, but rather it must be an efficient one, free of corruption and waste. This view of state power as a tool to be wielded by wise statesmen accords with both Bacon's Instauration, and contemporary understandings of "progressivism." Though there are important differences between the thought of Bacon and Hamilton on one hand and twentieth-century progressivism on the other, they are differences in scale, not in kind. Bacon and Hamilton both acknowledge the practical limitations of current human understanding. Unlike many contemporary progressive thinkers, they are humble before nature's secrets, aware that our comprehension of both human nature and natural law are not yet sufficient for certainty in applying scientific knowledge to political rule.

The phrase "science of politics" is anachronistic to Bacon's time. Science is instead understood as "natural philosophy," which Bacon views as intrinsically linked to both political philosophy and moral philosophy.[14] For Bacon, the greatest danger of the modern project is the creation of a permanent divide between the study of nature and the study of man, which includes the study of how men live together. That said, Bacon's understanding of how natural law works is certainly scientific. After all, "nature can only be commanded by being obeyed."[15] It is humanity's task to uncover the laws of nature, so that they may be manipulated for our improvement. This task applies to all branches of science, including physics, biology, and politics.

A key feature of Bacon's inductive science is experiment. Observation of historical trends and contemporary events is necessary to discern patterns and general principles, but scientific knowledge can only truly be gained by testing these theories. Political science, unlike the natural sciences, does not lend itself well to controlled laboratory conditions; any experiment in the realm of political science will, of necessity, fail to rise to the standards of measurement and control required by natural scientists.

[14] Francis Bacon, *Great Instauration* in *The Works of Francis Bacon, Volume 4*, 5–33, eds. James Spedding, Robert Leslie Ellis, and Douglas Denon Heath (Cambridge: Cambridge University Press, 2011[1858]) 18–21; for an extended discussion, see Hale, *Francis Bacon's New Atlantis*.

[15] Bacon, *Great Instauration*, 22. See Alan Wade Davenport, "Thomas Reid and His Contemporaries," *The Monist* 70, no. 4, (October 1987): 496–507, 496 for a discussion of Bacon's influence on subsequent British scientists, including Isaac Newton.

But does this mean that no experimentation is possible? After all, are not the American states termed the "laboratories of democracy?"[16] Ours is a compromised science, without doubt, but Bacon was hopeful that true political science would one day be a reality. After all, "[H]e that will not apply new remedies must expect new evils; for time is the greatest innovator."[17]

There is little doubt that Bacon, a skilled courtier,[18] viewed governance as a distinct skill to be acquired, one that required study and practice. In "Of the True Greatness of Kingdoms and Estates", in reference to Nero's skill as a musician, he writes:

> For if a true survey be taken of counsellors and statesmen, there may be found (though rarely) those which can make a small state great, and yet cannot fiddle: as on the other side, there will be found a great many that can fiddle very cunningly, but yet are so far from being able to make a small state great, as their gift lieth the other way; to bring a great and flourishing estate to ruin and decay.[19]

Political wisdom is separate from other types of wisdom, and the ability to govern effectively is still further separate. Bacon argues that skill in one area, such as war, business, or art, does not necessarily translate to skill in politics. Though it may borrow from history, economics, philosophy, and natural science, statesmanship is an area of learning unto itself. Bacon hopes, through his accounting of past and present knowledge, to bring forth the principles of good governance, so that future statesmen may be

---

[16] Louis Brandeis, *New State Ice Co. v. Liebmann*, (March 21, 1932) retrieved from https://www.law.cornell.edu/supremecourt/text/285/262.

[17] Francis Bacon, "Of Innovations" in *Essays or Counsels Civil and Moral* in *The Works of Francis Bacon, Volume 6*, 433–434, eds. James Spedding, Robert Leslie Ellis, and Douglas Denon Heath (Cambridge: Cambridge University Press, 2011 [1858]) 433.

[18] Bacon rose to prominence in the court of James I, at one point serving as Lord Chancellor of England, until he fell from grace through the machinations of his political enemies, who arranged for Bacon to be convicted of bribery and removed from office. As Erin A. Dolgoy succinctly puts it, "Bacon is an adept, albeit controversial, political performer until he suddenly is not." Erin A. Dolgoy, "Francis Bacon, Self-Knowledge, and the Art of Lies," in *Leadership and the Unmasking of Authenticity*, 113–137, eds. Brent Edwin Cusher and Mark A. Menaldo (Northampton: Edward Elger Publishing, 2018) 116.

[19] Francis Bacon, "Of the True Greatness of Kingdoms and Estates", in *Essays or Counsels Civil and Moral* in *The Works of Francis Bacon, Volume 6*, 444–452, eds. James Spedding, Robert Leslie Ellis, and Douglas Denon Heath (Cambridge: Cambridge University Press, 2011 [1858]) 444. Bacon, "Of the True Greatness of Kingdoms and Estates," in *Essays*, eds. Spedding, et. al., 433.

able to truly design a science of politics that will avoid the pitfalls of the past.

Hamilton shares this hope, though he appears to be operating on an accelerated timeline, compared to that of Bacon's more ardent followers, such as Condorcet and even Jefferson.[20] Hamilton rejects the type of "Utopian speculations" that lead critics of the Constitution to romanticize decentralized, agricultural, yeoman republics.[21] While the Anti-Federalists' vision of self-reliant, independent citizens exercising absolute democratic control over vigorous local governments is certainly appealing, Hamilton understood that pursuing that type of political development would leave the states vulnerable to international influence and domestic strife. Unless the states are united into a functioning whole, the weaknesses of the Articles of Confederation will only continue to be exacerbated, eventually leading the states to suffer the same discord as the European powers. And, given that the European colonial powers appear all too eager to reassert their domination of the New World, the American states do not have the luxury of developing their own spheres of power in peace. Hamilton thus intends to use the science of politics to establish a political empire that will be safe from foreign invasion, domestic strife, and the vicissitudes of time. In order to accomplish these goals, he again turns to decidedly Baconian policies.

The Commercial Republic

Hamilton is perhaps best known to modern readers as a friend of commerce. In addition to advocating for a standing army and vigorous executive as safeguards against encroaching foreign powers, Hamilton argues strenuously for forming a national bank, which could be used to "jumpstart" domestic manufacturing and industrialization. Unlike many of the Founders, most notably Jefferson, Hamilton neither idealized rural life nor longed for a society of self-reliant yeoman farmers. He viewed the security and liberty of the country as inexorably tied to its economic prosperity. For example, in reference to Shays' Rebellion (1786–1787), Hamilton argues in *Federalist* 6 that, "If Shays had not been a *desperate debtor*,

[20] I argue that Hamilton's rejection of utopianism actually indicates a truer understanding of and affinity with Bacon's vision. See Hale, *Francis Bacon's New Atlantis*, Ch. 6–7 for an extended discussion of the various ways later thinkers interpret Bacon's legacy.

[21] Hamilton, *Federalist* 6, p. 48.

it is much to be doubted whether Massachusetts would have been plunged into a civil war."[22] Furthermore, Hamilton argues that the rivalry between agriculture and industry is false. He notes, "It has been found in various countries that in proportion as commerce has flourished land has risen in value."[23] Unless American farmers truly wish to resign themselves to sustenance farming, they are well served by an alliance with champions of commerce.

Commerce, like any other form of power, must be guided in its development in such a way that it will unite the states, not divide them. In *Federalist* 7, Hamilton again identifies "competitions of commerce" between the states as a potentially serious source of civil discord.[24] He argues that the "unbridled spirit [of enterprise]," which forms one of Americans' primary characteristics, will not abide by any public policy that seeks to give preferential treatment to citizens of one state over another.[25] Americans, in Hamilton's view, have always depended on their economic freedom to improve their circumstances. The hard work and ingenuity required to succeed in the colonies have rendered American citizens unfit for anything other than open and free competition with one another. The republican spirit of American politics must extend to a liberal economic policy.

Though Bacon never openly breaks with monarchy as his preferred regime, his understanding of a "good" monarchy is decidedly in line with classical liberalism. Though Bacon certainly believes that scientific investigation can move human understanding closer to the truth of things, he acknowledges that the ability of human beings to interpret scientific findings will always be flawed.[26] The uncertainty of all knowledge, including newly discovered scientific knowledge, helps explain the necessity of liberalism (and perhaps nascent republicanism) for Bacon's project.

---

[22] Hamilton, *Federalist* 6, p. 50. Hamilton refers to Shays' Rebellion, in which economically depressed farmers throughout several states took up arms against local and state tax collectors. Though it never seriously threatened the stability of the country, the event served as a prominent impetus to call a Constitutional Convention for the purpose of revising the Articles of Confederation.

[23] Hamilton, *Federalist* 12, p. 86.

[24] Hamilton, *Federalist* 7, p. 57.

[25] Hamilton, *Federalist* 7, p. 57.

[26] See Dolgoy, "Art of Lies," 118–122 for an excellent explanation of Bacon's "Idols of the Mind." Bacon identifies four main types of bias, or "idols," that prevent human beings from grasping the objective truth of the world.

Statesmen must be cautious when pronouncing political truths and forming laws; the wisest path may be the most cautious. By insisting on the primacy of individual rights and the need to limit government intrusion into citizens' private lives, liberalism helps prevent tyrannical policies enacted based on flawed or biased conclusions arrived at through faulty reasoning. It hinders governments that would act on incomplete information without acknowledging their limitations. By preserving the greatest possible amount of individual liberty, statesmen will also free scientists to pursue new avenues of inquiry. A liberal society will foster innovation and technological advancement, while protecting the public from the tyrannical possibilities of a modern science manipulated for unjust ends.[27]

In "Of Seditions and Troubles," Bacon warns against the dangers of "want and poverty," citing them as the material root cause of sedition.[28] For Bacon, scarcity is the primary cause of injustice and vice. As he notes in "Of Goodness and Goodness of Nature," "the inclination to goodness is imprinted deeply in the nature of man."[29] The vast majority of individuals seek to dominate others only as a result of insecurity; they only engage in destabilizing activities, such as crime or sedition, out of a desire for economic and material security. As a remedy, Bacon recommends "the opening and well-balancing of trade; the cherishing of manufactures; the banishing of idleness; the repressing of waste and excess by sumptuary laws...and the like."[30] In this context, one finds a strong support of free trade and the emerging middle class. If the power of nature can be harnessed into technological advancement, many of the natural plagues of humanity, such as famine, drought, and disease, can be eradicated. Freed from these material worries, the public will be capable of pursuing higher things.

Bacon recognizes the value of active nobles, committed to a

---

[27] See Robin Neill, "Francis Bacon, John Rae, and the Economics of Competitiveness: Capital Theory and Trade Policy," *The American Journal of Economics and Sociology*, 58, 3 (July, 1999): 385–398, 385–386 for a discussion of the influence of Baconian science on British economists, most notably John Rae, "whose work on the nature of economic growth, development and trade was founded on Baconian science."

[28] Francis Bacon, "Of Seditions and Troubles," in *Essays*, eds. James Spedding, et al., 408.

[29] Francis Bacon, "Of Goodness and Goodness of Nature," in *Essays*, eds. James Spedding, et al., 403.

[30] Bacon, "Of Seditions and Troubles," 410.

commercially powerful empire, but he especially targets idle nobility as a hindrance to the Instauration. Bacon well understands that even if a society were to solve the problem of material scarcity, certain objects of men's desire, such as power and honor, will always, necessarily, be available only in limited quantities. But by expanding the avenues to honor and reputation to include the type of commercial success traditionally disdained by the nobility, who favor military prowess, Bacon succeeds in increasing the total amount of these intangible goods available in the society. Bacon was no advocate for democracy, but he needed an active, industrious nobility who would value learning and understand technological advances. The common man may be the primary consumer of technology, but because they wield political and economic power, the nobles would be largely responsible for securing the scientists' freedom to experiment and create new technologies. Given that Bacon believes stability to be a prerequisite for scientific advancement,[31] it is understandable that he would encourage the stability that comes from the nobility adopting middle class virtues, and the channeling of nobility into commercial, rather than military, pursuits.

Commerce opens up a wide variety of avenues to material prosperity; Bacon is unwilling to discount any of them. Unlike some of his successors, Bacon does not even wholly condemn usury, for "[I]t is a vanity to conceive that there would be ordinary borrowing without profit; and it is impossible to conceive the number of inconveniences that will ensue, if borrowing be cramped."[32] Therefore, talk of abolishing usury completely is "idle," for it is impractical. However, Bacon does not refrain from criticizing the "lazy trade" on several fronts. Usury has the effect of "making fewer merchants" by causing money to "lie still," instead of being used in commercial activity. It also causes merchants to be poorer, and consolidates the "wealth of the realm" into a few hands.[33] One can see in this critique an early acknowledgement of the virtues of economic competition and entrepreneurship. Bacon grounds the possibility of empire in a robust commercial life of the people.

Bacon argues that "money is like muck, not good except it be spread."[34] Merchants are the backbone of a vital economy, and a vital

[31] White, *Peace*, 1.
[32] Francis Bacon, "Of Usury," in *Essays* eds. James Spedding, et al., 475.
[33] Bacon, "Of Usury," 474.
[34] Bacon, "Of Seditions and Troubles," 410.

economy is the backbone of the Instauration. Bacon, following Plato's example in the *Laws*, elevates merchants to a place of honor.[35] Bacon recognizes that the fruits of modern science will quickly become commodities; he also recognizes the emerging power of international trade. International trading will lead to the dissemination of information. A vigorous populace (both noble and common) will be necessary if a state is to remain strong in the face of constant interaction with foreign influences. Liberated merchants will ensure the health of the state's economic life; Bacon and his intellectual heirs must ensure the health of its political life.

The importance of merchants is again pressed in "Of Empire," which describes the many woes of monarchs. In fact, "Of Empire" could lead the reader to entirely mistrust the judgment of monarchs, who have more power to fulfill their desires than do other people. Bacon notes that, "It is a miserable state of mind, to have few things to desire, and many things to fear."[36] Because their normal human desires (comfort, wealth, power, sex) are readily fulfilled, kings will seek out things to desire; these desires can range from the virtuous to the depraved. Those counselors who wish to keep their kings from turning into depraved tyrants must give the king something to desire that will also benefit the society as a whole. To that end, Bacon notes that empire is "a thing rare and hard to keep,"[37] because lasting empires require skill in governing, not just desire for more power. Kings cannot simply "command the end," they must also "endure the means."[38] Kings who would gain empires must know how to tune their governments as skillfully as Nero tunes his fiddle, discerning when to tighten their rule and when to relax it. Skillful governance benefits both the ruled and the ruler.

Bacon is particularly concerned with the monarch's regulation of merchants. He notes, "For their [the society's] merchants; they are *vena porta*; and if they flourish not, a kingdom may have good limbs, but will have empty veins, and nourish little."[39] Bacon warns monarchs against the temptation to overtax merchants in order to support military campaigns. The increase in revenue is useful in the short term, but damaging in the long term, as it depresses commercial activity and economic growth.

---

[35] See Hale, *Francis Bacon's New Atlantis*, Chapter 4 for further discussion.
[36] Francis Bacon, "Of Empire," in *Essays*, eds. James Spedding, et al., 419.
[37] Bacon, "Of Empire," 419.
[38] Bacon, "Of Empire," 420.
[39] Bacon, "Of Empire," 422.

Moreover, "neither will it be, that a people overlaid with taxes should ever become valiant and martial."[40] Bacon argues that the robustness of the common people depends on their belief in the possibility of social or economic advancement. If the common people are economically depressed, overtaxed for the benefit of the honor of king and nobility, they become "a peasant and base swain, driven out of heart, and in effect but the gentleman's labourer."[41] Such a people will not have the necessary spiritedness for successful expansion, either military or commercial.

Hamilton is likewise wary of over-taxation as a means of raising revenue. He argues that "Revenue must be had at all events." If it cannot be drawn from commerce, as he hopes and recommends, then "it must fall with oppressive weight upon land," in the form of property taxes.[42] A country facing hostile foreign powers, or domestic unrest, must have the means available to keep the peace. Hamilton argues that a commercial nation will produce enough revenue through "taxes on consumption" to fund the necessary defense expenditures, without turning to oppressive taxes on property.[43] He maintains that taxes upon consumption, or sales taxes, "contain in their own nature a security against excess."[44] Taxes on consumption of goods cannot be raised beyond what consumers are willing to pay, otherwise the tax is self-defeating. Of course, Hamilton's argument on this point does not account for taxes on necessary goods, such as food, though one can safely assume that a just government would not tax its citizens to the point of starvation. His argument emphasizes the difficulty of obtaining an accurate assessment of the value of land in a country "imperfectly settled and progressive in improvement."[45] By its very nature, Hamilton implies, taxation of property discourages development.

At first glance, Bacon's arguments in favor of free trade and minimal taxation seem at odds with Hamilton's best known work on economic policy, his "Report on Manufactures," which argues in favor of using the power of the federal government to encourage domestic industrialization. Douglas A. Irwin, in fact, notes that the report is "the quintessential American document against *laissez faire* and free trade to promote

[40] Bacon, "Of the True Greatness of Kingdoms and Estates," 446.

[41] Ibid.

[42] Hamilton, *Federalist* 12, p. 91.

[43] Ibid.

[44] Hamilton, *Federalist* 21, p. 138.

[45] Hamilton, *Federalist* 21, p. 139.

industrialization."[46] Irwin goes on, however, to argue that the "Report on Manufactures," along with *Federalist* 35, actually promotes a policy of *encouraging* manufacturers, not *protecting* them in a mercantile system.[47] The report argues in favor of tariffs, but not for the purpose of protecting domestic manufactures. Rather, Hamilton's purpose is to generate revenue for the funding of public debt, in case of national emergency.[48] As he argues in *Federalist* 30:

> Money is, with propriety, considered as the vital principle of the body politic; as that which sustains its life and motions...A complete power, therefore, to procure a regular and adequate supply of revenue...may be regarded as an indispensible ingredient in every constitution. From a deficiency in this particular, one of two evils must ensue: either the people be subjected to continual plunder, as a substitute for a more eligible mode of supplying the public wants, or the government must sink into a fatal atrophy and...perish.[49]

A government "half-supplied and always necessitous"[50] cannot hope to actually promote the security or prosperity of the people. Those who do not support an active national government will no doubt respond that *no government at all* can effectively take on such a responsibility, that the security and prosperity of the people is dependent on the individual liberty of the people. While that is a fair objection worthy of serious debate, both Bacon's and Hamilton's projects are so vast in scope that they require not only the consent of government, but the active employment of governmental authority to secure their ends.

The Occupation of Arms

As a thinker acutely concerned with the future of his enterprise, Bacon spends a considerable amount of time discussing what he believes must be the "principle point of greatness" in any society aspiring to greatness: military prowess.[51] Though he does recommend grounding imperial aspirations in commercial power, Bacon, like Hamilton, also recognizes the

---

46 Douglas A. Irwin, "The Aftermath of Hamilton's 'Report on Manufactures,'" *The Journal of Economic History* 64, 3 (2004): 800–821, 800.

47 Irwin, "Aftermath," 814.

48 Irwin, "Aftermath," 801.

49 Hamilton, *Federalist* 30, p. 184.

50 Hamilton, *Federalist* 30, p. 187.

51 Bacon, "Of the True Greatness of Kingdoms and Estates," 446.

connection between economic might and military security. His project requires stability, and the best way to ensure stability is to tie the interests of rival states to one another as closely as possible. For example, in "Of the True Greatness of Kingdoms and Estates," Bacon argues in favor of liberal naturalization policies, as a means of stabilizing one's empire. He advocates the easy acceptance of conquered peoples into military, economic, and political society, as exemplified by the Romans at the height of their power.[52] This increases the human resources of the conquering empire, while also extending the ties of patriotism beyond the immediate seat of power, as the newly enfranchised citizens will hopefully recognize and appreciate the justness of the policy. As discussed earlier, Bacon fervently believes, as does Niccolò Machiavelli, that the true measure of an army's power is in the disposition of the people, not the material stores of the crown.[53]

Bacon argues that the conditions for both economic and scientific advancement are dependent on military security. Though he longs for the stability of peacetime, the stability he aims at is of a decidedly *Pax Romana* flavor. He warns strongly against civil strife, comparing it to "the heat of a fever," while noting that foreign military campaigns more closely resemble "the heat of exercise," which keeps a body politic healthy.[54] Bacon does not desire a nation of soft merchants, unable to defend their power against armed invaders or pirates; he rather aims at an empire that channels the ambitions of common men and nobles alike, rendering them "rather busy than dangerous."[55]

Both Bacon and Hamilton endorse naval power as the key to past and future greatness. Bacon argues that the ruler "that commands the sea, is at great liberty, and may take as much and as little of the war as he will," while those confined to land armies often find themselves in "great straits."[56] Hamilton, in the same vein as Bacon, argues that, "If we mean

[52] Bacon, "Of the True Greatness of Kingdoms and Estates," 447–448.

[53] Bacon, in "Of the True Greatness of Kingdoms and Estates," 445, writes, "Walled towns, stored arsenals and armories, goodly races of horse, chariots of war, elephants, ordnance, artillery, and the like; all this is but a sheep in a lion's skin, except the breed and disposition of the people be stout and warlike." See also Niccolo Machiavelli, *Discourses on Livy*, trans. Harvey C. Mansfield and Nathan Tarcov, (Chicago: University of Chicago Press, 1998) 148–149.

[54] Bacon, "Of the True Greatness of Kingdoms and Estates," 450.

[55] Francis Bacon, "Of Ambition," in *Essays*, eds. James Spedding, et al., 465.

[56] Bacon, "Of the True Greatness of Kingdoms and Estates," 451.

to be a commercial people, or even to be secure on our Atlantic side, we must endeavor, as soon as possible, to have a navy."[57] The "powerful marine" will safeguard American merchants, allowing us to counteract our enemies' goal of "preventing our interference in their navigation, of monopolizing the profits of our trade, and of clipping the wings by which we might soar to a dangerous greatness."[58]

Though it is possible to guide a kingdom to greatness, Bacon laments that these things are usually left to chance.[59] This discussion reveals Bacon's greatest enemy: the vicissitude of things. Bacon's Instauration is not just a project of progress. It is also a defense against the type of regression witnessed in Europe after the fall of the Roman Empire. It is an effort to overcome the vicissitudes of time, and nature. He warns, "Upon the breaking and shivering of a great state and empire, you may be sure to have wars."[60] These wars come about because the empire, during its time of power, depresses the native power of the subdued territories. Once the central power collapses, civil war breaks out and all parts of the empire are open to invasion. Furthermore, "When a war-like state grows soft and effeminate, they may be sure of a war. For commonly such states are grown rich in the time of their degenerating; and so the prey inviteth, and their decay in valour encourageth a war."[61] It is therefore in the best interest of political rulers to maintain the valor and energy of subdued people. Rather than attacking new religions or sects, a wise ruler will incorporate their leaders into the existing regime, keeping the people united.[62] The people must all be given the chance to order their lives, and seek advancement, as they can.

Hamilton seemingly absorbs this lesson of Bacon's wholesale. He repeatedly emphasizes the precarious situation of the new republic with regard to foreign militaries, arguing that "*Divide et impera* [Divide and command] must be the motto of every nation that either hates or fears us."[63] Unless the states present a united front to the world, foreign powers will

[57] Hamilton, *Federalist* 24, p. 158.

[58] Hamilton, *Federalist* 11, p. 80.

[59] Bacon, "Of the True Greatness of Kingdoms and Estates," 452.

[60] Francis Bacon, "Of the Vicissitude of Things," in *Essays*, eds., James Spedding, et al., 515.

[61] Bacon, "Of the Vicissitude of Things," 516.

[62] Bacon, "Of the Vicissitude of Things," 514.

[63] Hamilton, *Federalist* 7, 60.

seek to entangle the various states in their power struggles. Hamilton fears the states' opposition to a standing national army, and the Articles of Confederation's prohibition against nationally funded troops, believing that the lack of a cohesive, regular army leaves the new republic vulnerable to invasion and the temptation of civil war.[64] He argues fervently that the states' liberty will only be secure if the nation's sovereignty is secure from threats both foreign and domestic.

Though economic might is championed throughout Hamilton's writings, it can never truly be divorced from arms. Hamilton rejects the position of military neutrality, arguing that the United States will not be permitted to engage freely in international trade, without opening itself to the dangers of warring nations, unless it is itself a feared power. He writes that, "The rights of neutrality will only be respected when they are defended by an adequate power."[65] He cautions his fellow citizens against over reliance on the states' geographic isolation and natural resources. Those congenital advantages are important, but they are of limited value unless they are developed and put to productive use by an active, purposeful government. Most of all, he fears that constitutional prohibitions against standing armies, such as those found in the Articles of Confederation, will render the United States, "a nation incapacitated by its Constitution to prepare for defense before it was actually invaded."[66] If American citizens continue to fear their own government more than they fear hostile foreign armies, the republic will die in infancy.

Bacon lays forth his vision of the life of an empire: "In the youth of a state arms do flourish; in the middle age of a state, learning, and then both of them together for a time; in the declining age of a state, mechanical arts and merchandise."[67] If Bacon's Instauration is successful, then humanity can perhaps transcend this cycle, preserving the best parts of each stage. We can tie arms to the mechanical arts, and use both in the service of scientific learning. To that end, Hamilton argues that, at least where national defense is concerned, the power of the federal government to raise armies and equip fleets must exist "without limitation."[68] The "science of

[64] Hamilton, *Federalist* 7, p. 57; Hamilton, *Federalist* 16, p. 109.

[65] Hamilton, *Federalist* 11, p. 82.

[66] Hamilton, *Federalist* 25, p. 161. *Federalist* 26 also condemns this proposed amendment as originating in "a zeal for liberty more ardent than enlightened," 164.

[67] Bacon, "Of the Vicissitude of Things," 516–517.

[68] Hamilton, *Federalist* 23, p. 149.

war"[69] can be mastered and advanced, just as was the science of politics. For Hamilton, the instauration of American power can only be accomplished with all parts of the society, commercial, political, and military, working together towards a common end.

Conclusion

This portrait of Alexander Hamilton as a Baconian thinker illuminates some of the more commonly neglected aspects of his plan for the United States' political development. In order to truly grasp the scope of Hamilton's vision for the fledgling republic, it is necessary to first grasp the colossal scope of the early Enlightenment thinkers' ambitions regarding the new science of politics. And while the influence of later Enlightenment thinkers such as Locke, Smith, Hume, and Montesquieu on the American Founders is well-documented, little attention has been paid to the influence of the architect of modernity itself: Francis Bacon. This is not to argue that Bacon's influence supersedes that of the other thinkers listed. The nuances of Bacon's Instauration are, after all, meant to be worked out by succeeding generations, and the more direct influence of Locke, Smith, Hume, and Montesquieu is clear in the writings of the American Founders. That said, it is valuable to consider how all of these thinkers fit together into the plan for modernity originally laid out in Bacon's Instauration.

Moreover, Hamilton's status as a philosophically sophisticated thinker is often overshadowed by scholarly attention paid to the thought of John Adams or Thomas Jefferson. When discussing Hamilton's philosophical education, one commonly encounters the anecdote about Hamilton passed on from Jefferson, who relates that Hamilton failed to recognize the portraits of Francis Bacon, Isaac Newton, and John Locke decorating Jefferson's home. According to Jefferson's account, Hamilton asked who they were, and Jefferson responded that, "They were his [Jefferson's] 'trinity of the three greatest men the world had ever produced,' but they meant little or nothing in Hamilton's philosophy. 'The greatest man that ever lived,' said the Colonel [Hamilton] 'was Julius Caesar.'"[70] This story is oft cited as proof that Hamilton was an unapologetic

[69] Hamilton, *Federalist* 29, p. 178.

[70] Dumas Malone, *Jefferson and His Time, Vol. II: Jefferson and the Rights of Man* (Boston: Little Brown and Company, 1951) 287.

proponent of monarchism, and dangerously close to embracing the idea that power is the root of justice. Yet, as Thomas P. Govan demonstrates, Hamilton's own writings do not reveal a particular affinity for Caesar, or Caesarism.[71] Jefferson and Hamilton's mutual distrust of each other is well established, and we should not, perhaps, be eager to condemn Hamilton's philosophical outlook on the basis of his rival's account.

Hamilton writes in *Federalist* 31 that "In disquisitions of every kind there are certain primary truths, or first principles, upon which all subsequent reasonings must depend."[72] This is as true, Hamilton argues, in politics and ethics as it is in geometry. Failure to accept the truth of such principles is attributed either to faulty sense perception or prejudice. While men are capable of comprehending mathematical truths, "in the sciences of morals and politics, men are found much less tractable."[73] Hamilton acknowledges that moral and political science has not yet risen to the same level of certainty as mathematics. Yet, he implores his fellow Americans to not let that uncertainty dissuade them from the possibility of uncovering universal political truths. The modern science of politics is new, and bound to err, as he acknowledges. The Founders' plan is admittedly experimental and ambitious, but it also offers possibilities of justice and prosperity undreamed of in prior ages. That said, Hamilton also firmly grasps the precarious position of the new republic. He would not risk the complete failure of the American experiment by "expos[ing] the Union to the jeopardy of successive experiments in the chimerical pursuit of a perfect plan."[74]

We know that Hamilton was well read, despite his youthful age. His arguments are also more nuanced, and his vision for American political development more thoughtful, than is commonly credited. Hamilton spent the long winter of 1777–1778 with the Continental Army at Valley Forge, unable to continue their military campaign against the British. He was far from idle during this period, however. During this winter, he completed his education in political philosophy, reading texts from thinkers

[71] Thomas P. Govan, "Alexander Hamilton and Julius Caesar: A Note on the Use of Historical Evidence," *The William and Mary Quarterly* 32, 3 (1975): 475-480. Bacon is likewise skeptical of Caesar's greatness. In his essay "Of Friendship" Bacon discusses how Caesar was blinded to the conspiracy against him by virtue of his friendship with Brutus. Caesar is thus not a paragon of statesmanship, nor an ideal ruler.

[72] Hamilton, *Federalist* 31, p. 189.

[73] Hamilton, *Federalist* 31, p. 190.

[74] Hamilton, *Federalist* 85, p. 523.

ranging from Plutarch to Hume, and including the works of Francis Bacon.[75] Undoubtedly, his time as Washington's aide-de-camp during the war would have influenced his views on the role of executive leadership and the need for military power in the new republic. It perhaps also convinced him of the real possibility of forming a plan for the new republic that was Baconian in both its grand scope and nature. Bacon envisioned a modern society founded on scientific principles, guided by wise political thinkers, and led by statesmen versed in both natural and moral philosophy. The American republic finally offered the world a possible chance to see this vision realized.

[75] John C. Miller, *Alexander Hamilton and the Growth of the New Nation*, (Abingdon: Routledge, 2017) 46; Philip Stadter, "Alexander Hamilton's Notes on Plutarch in His Pay Book," *The Review of Politics* 73, no. 2 (2011): 199–217, 199.

PART II

LEGACY AND APPLICATIONS

6

THE AMERICAN CONSTITUTION AND STATESMANSHIP: AN ARGUMENT FROM LINCOLN

Jon D. Schaff

Toward the end of his classic *What the Anti-Federalists Were For*, Herbert Storing makes two allusions to Abraham Lincoln. The first refers to Lincoln's 1838 address to the Springfield Young Men's Lyceum, about which I will say more below. In this famous oration Lincoln raises reverence for the law to the level of a "political religion." In his second allusion to Lincoln, Storing declares:

> It is a simplification, but not a misleading simplification, to say that the crisis faced by Abraham Lincoln seventy years later required a synthesis of the Federalist solution and the Anti-Federalist reservation. And if the major element in the synthesis was still the Federal one, yet it is due the Anti-Federalists to say that it was they, more than the defenders of the Constitution, who anticipated the need. The Anti-Federalists saw, although sometimes only dimly, the insufficiency of a community of mere interest.[1]

If Storing is correct, and I believe he is, in his assessment that the debate between Federalists and Anti-Federalists has continued across American history, then it makes sense in light of his statements regarding Lincoln to explore the ways in which Abraham Lincoln represents a synthesis between Federalist and Anti-Federalist thought.

Lincoln's thought, I contend, is in dialogue with Federalist and Anti-Federalist thought in two different ways. First, Lincoln's own political vision harmonizes with various aspects of both Federalist and Anti-Federalist thought. While it is fair to say along with Storing that Lincoln's thought has more in common with the Federalists, there is a perhaps surprising congruence between certain aspects of Lincoln's political

---

[1] Herbert Storing, *What the Anti-Federalists Were For* (Chicago: University of Chicago Press, 1981) 76.

philosophy and those of Anti-Federalists. In this essay I wish to demonstrate some ways in which Lincoln's thought integrates various ideas on both sides of the Constitutional debate. To this end, while pointing to the essential harmony between Lincoln and Federalist ideals, I stress the ways in which certain Anti-Federalist values complement various principles articulated by Lincoln. Lincoln, who led the Union to the defeat of the agrarian-based Confederacy and who was a supporter of Henry Clay's nationalizing economic program called the American System, is not an obvious inheritor of Anti-Federalist ideas. But I will show that on matters such as labor and territorial expansion Lincoln's arguments echo certain values of the Anti-Federalists.

Second, Lincoln moves beyond the Federalist/Anti-Federalist divide by overcoming crucial limitations of both camps. One of the key differences between Federalists and Anti-Federalists was the extent to which good government depends on virtue. Anti-Federalists were more likely to say that republican virtue was essential to just government. Federalists, notably James Madison despite his own republican proclivities, were more likely to have an institutional view of government, insisting that it is not virtue that keeps government in check, but well-crafted institutions. I wish to argue that Lincoln added another variable, namely that of statesmanship.

Federalists and Anti-Federalists: A Lincolnian Synthesis

Let me begin by discussing how Lincoln's thought partakes of arguments from the contending sides of the framing debate. Given Lincoln's defense of the Union, it is not surprising he agrees with the Federalists in the promotion of the Union over the states. The Anti-Federalists argued that liberty is best maintained if government resides geographically close to the people and remains relatively local. Anti-Federalist pamphleteer Brutus derided the Federalist defense of the extended republic: "Now, in a large extended country, it is impossible to have a representation, possessing the sentiments, and of integrity, to declare the minds of the people, without having it so numerous and unwieldly, as to be subject in great measure to the inconveniency of a democratic government."[2] How can unity be

[2] Ralph Ketchum, ed., *The Anti-Federalist Papers and the Constitutional Convention Debates* (New York: Mentor, 1986) 276–277.

founded given such a geographical expanse? Brutus echoes the contention of classical thought that republican government can only justly operate within the "small republic" where citizens have much in common and a vigilant citizenry can easily keep tabs on elected officials.

Publius, in contrast, famously argues that it is in the extended republic, with its promotion of economic diversity, where rights are actually protected. In *Federalist* 2, 3, and 15, to name just a few examples, the importance of Union for this extended republic is emphasized. In *Federalist* 2, to cite one instance, Publius writes, "With equal pleasure I have as often taken notice that Providence has been pleased to give this one connected country to one united people...who, by their joint counsels, arms, and efforts, fighting side by side throughout a long and bloody war, have nobly established general liberty and independence."[3] By contrast, in *Federalist* 15 Publius derides as "absurd" and "impracticable" the notion that confederacy can produce a stable, orderly government that promotes peace and the protection of rights.[4]

Lincoln's dedication to the Union is well known. In Lincoln's famed letter to Horace Greeley in 1862 he wrote:

> My paramount object in this struggle is to save the Union, and is not either to save or to destroy slavery. If I could save the Union without freeing any slave I would do it, and if I could save it by freeing all the slaves I would do it; and if I could save it by freeing some and leaving others alone I would also do that. What I do about slavery, and the colored race, I do because I believe it helps to save the Union; and what I forbear, I forbear because I do not believe it would help to save the Union."[5]

Lincoln had spoken similarly in his First Inaugural Address, stating plainly that "The Union of these states is perpetual," concluding with one of his most poetic turns of phrase, "The mystic chords of memory, stretching from every battlefield, and patriot grave, to every living heart and hearthstone, all over this broad land, will yet swell the chorus of the Union, when touched again, as surely they will be, by the better angels of our nature."[6] Like the Federalists, Lincoln defended the notion of the United

---

[3] Clinton Rossiter, ed., *The Federalist Papers*, introduction by Charles Kesler (New York: Mentor, 1999) *Federalist* 2, p. 32.

[4] *Federalist* 15, p. 104.

[5] *The Collected Works of Abraham Lincoln*, ed. Roy P. Basler, vol. 2. (New Brunswick, NJ: Rutgers University Press, 1953) 5: 387–389.

[6] Abraham Lincoln, *Collected Works*, 4: 264, 271.

States as one whole rather than separate and competing state entities.

In the fundamental dispute about the nature of the Union, Lincoln is decidedly in the Federalist camp. Anti-Federalists such as Luther Martin said that at the time of the Declaration of Independence, each of the thirteen colonies was in a state of nature, thus the ensuing union is that of thirteen states, not a nation of individuals.[7] The Federalists argued, accurately, that the states declared independence as a unit, thus the rights of the Declaration are national concerns. Thus, as Publius argued in *Federalist* 15 and 23, the national government must have the power to act upon individuals, not just states. This became important during the 1850s with the debate over slavery. It hardly bears defending the idea that is ubiquitous in Lincoln's thought that the Declaration's principles applied to all individuals and thus, as with the injustice of slavery, the nation had a duty to act in its corporate capacity.[8] Lincoln, alluding to scripture, described the Declaration of Independence as an "apple of gold" framed by the silver of the Constitution.[9] The national constitution had as its purpose the securing of the principles articulated in the Declaration.

Lincoln's support of the Union is echoed in his economic views. As a young Whig, Lincoln was a strong supporter of Henry Clay's economic program, dubbed The American System. This economic vision, borrowing heavily from the nationalist economics of Alexander Hamilton, saw economic ties as one way in which a nation could be formed out of diverse states. "Lincoln's policies were rooted in Hamilton and Clay's American System," writes Stephen F. Knott, "and his Hamiltonianism was evident in his support for internal improvements such as railroad and canal expansion and land-grant colleges."[10] Clay believed that the Union would be "invigorated by an intimate, social and commercial connexion between all

---

[7] Storing, *What the Anti-Federalists Were For*, 13.

[8] To cite just a couple of examples, Lincoln, while in Philadelphia on his way to his inauguration in 1861, noted, "I have never had a feeling politically that did not spring from the sentiments embodied in the Declaration of Independence" (Abraham Lincoln, *Collected Works*, 4:240). One should also peruse the Cooper Union address of 1860, which makes a systematic argument that the founding generation wished to use national power to promote the principles of the Declaration and limit the expansion of slavery. See Lincoln, *Collected Works*, 3: 522–550.

[9] Lincoln, *Collected Works,* 4: 169. The biblical reference is to Proverbs 25:11, "A word fitly spoken is like apples of gold in pictures of silver."

[10] Stephen F. Knott, *Alexander Hamilton & The Persistence of Myth* (Lawrence, KS: University Press of Kansas) 54.

parts of the confederacy."[11] The national government should bind the nation together with a system of roads, rivers, and canals. Lincoln advocated for similar policies in Illinois as a state legislator and in his one term in Congress. As president he supported the Homestead Act, the Pacific Railroad Act, Banking Act, and a currency bill that were motivated by economic nationalism.

Like the Federalists, Lincoln also thought that just government required not simply dependence on the will of the people, but the rule of law. As Publius famously puts it in *Federalist* 51, "A dependence on the people is, no doubt, the primary control on the government; but experience has taught mankind the necessity of auxiliary precautions."[12] This is what Storing alludes to when he discusses Lincoln's elevation of rule of law, and specifically the Constitution, to the level of "political religion." In Lincoln's Lyceum address, Lincoln warns against that most democratic of phenomena, the mob. The people should not get whatever they want, falsely equating passing desires for justice. And so Lincoln said:

> As the patriots of seventy-six did to the support of the Declaration of Independence, so to the support of the Constitution and Laws, let every American pledge his life, his property, and his sacred honor;—let every man remember that to violate the law, is to trample on the blood of his father, and to tear the character [charter?] of his own, and his children's liberty. Let reverence for the laws, be breathed by every American mother, to the lisping babe, that prattles on her lap—let it be taught in schools, in seminaries, and in colleges;—let it be written in Primmers, spelling books, and in Almanacs;—let it be preached from the pulpit, proclaimed in legislative halls, and enforced in courts of justice. And, in short, let it become the political religion of the nation.[13]

The auxiliary precaution to which Publius refers largely consists in the separation of powers. The justification is similar to Lincoln's in his invocation of the rule of law. In both cases we can see that democracy is the secondary good that serves the primary good, the protection of rights. Once democracy ceases to serve this higher purpose it creeps toward despotism. Crude majoritarianism is to be discouraged; democratic tyranny is still tyranny.

---

[11] Robert Remini, *Henry Clay: Statesman for the Union* (New York: W.W. Norton and Company, 1991) 226.

[12] *Federalist* 51, p. 319.

[13] Abraham Lincoln, *Collected Works*, 1: 112.

It would seem, then, that Lincoln breathed much of the Federalist air. Yet, Anti-Federalist notions also steal into Lincoln's political thought. First, while Lincoln was what we might call an economic nationalist, he was also, like Anti-Federalists, skeptical about the concept of empire, most enthusiastically embraced among the Founders by Alexander Hamilton. Anti-Federalist John Dewitt cautioned against such notions, stating, "In short, my fellow-citizens, it can be said to be nothing less than a hasty stride to Universal Empire in this Western World, flattering, very flattering to young ambitious minds, but fatal to the liberties of the people."[14]

Here we do well to note Lincoln's opposition to that first American imperialism, Manifest Destiny. Lincoln was opposed to its most obvious expression, the Mexican-American War, which he saw as a land-grab unworthy of a decent people. He was steadfastly opposed to the Young America movement, of which his arch-rival Stephen Douglas was a prominent member, which sought a swift extension of control over the lands of the West. This achieved, Young America cast its gaze upon Cuba and Central America for potential American conquests. In his unjustly neglected Lecture on Discoveries and Invention, Lincoln condemns Young America's "fond desire…longing after territory." Young America, he notes, is interested in "liberating" nations, even those who "have not any liking" for Young America's form of liberation through conquest. As for those who have no land, such as slaves, "Young America is not interested in their liberation."[15]

Secondly, while Lincoln supported Whig economics, his view of labor expresses Anti-Federalist ideals. Anti-Federalist Melancton Smith wrote, "He who is controlled by another is a slave."[16] Anti-Federalists—with notable echoes of Jefferson's agrarian praise for the yeoman farmer—believed that those who are self-sufficient and tied to the land were best able to cultivate the republican virtue they thought essential to maintenance of democracy. This describes Lincoln's theory of labor well. In his annual message of 1861, Lincoln wrote of the supposed conflict between labor and capital, "The error is in assuming that the whole labor of community exists within that relation. A few men own capital, and that few avoid labor themselves, and, with their capital, hire or buy another few to

[14] Ketchum, *Anti-Federalist Papers*, 313.
[15] Abraham Lincoln, *Collected Works*, 3: 357.
[16] Ketchum, *Anti-Federalist Papers*, 341.

labor for them. A large majority belong to neither class—neither work for others, nor have others working for them."[17] Most people, Lincoln posits, are neither purely capitalists nor purely laborers. Because they own their own labor by working their own field or overseeing their own shop, they partake of both roles. "Men with their families—wives, sons, and daughters—work for themselves, on their farms, in their houses, and in their shops, taking the whole product to themselves, and asking no favors of capital on the one hand, nor of hired laborers or slaves on the other."[18] "Lincoln's America was the world of the small producer," argues Eric Foner.[19] This is what Lincoln means by free labor. While wage-labor is superior to slave labor, it is not truly free labor. In his 1859 agricultural address in Wisconsin, Lincoln stated that before long "the most valuable of all arts, will be the art of deriving a comfortable subsistence from the smallest area of soil." This kind of self-sufficiency is a bulwark against despotism. Lincoln proclaims, "No community whose every member possesses this art, can ever be the victim of oppression in any of its forms. Such community will be alike independent of crowned-kings, money-kings, and land-kings."[20] So Lincoln is with the Federalists in regards to his views on proper political institutions and the nature of the Union, but he shared with Anti-Federalists concern over economic consolidation and imperial expansion.

Given that Lincoln believed that America was justly conceived, the question becomes how a people maintains that justice over time. As Storing notes, even James Madison appreciated the prudence of having "the prejudices of the community" on the side of the Constitution and the need for some kind of republican virtue.[21] But the Constitution, Storing concludes, is marked by "a lack of much attention to the question of how that

[17] Abraham Lincoln, *Collected Works*, 5:52.

[18] Ibid.

[19] Eric Foner, *Free Soil, Free Labor, Free Men: The Ideology of the Republican Party Before the Civil War* (New York: Oxford University Press, 1995) xxvi.

[20] Lincoln, *Collected Works*, 3:481. Lincoln's political economy is not entirely in harmony with the Hamiltonian emphasis on manufacturing and banking, while having much in common with Jefferson's promotion of individual economic independence.

[21] Storing is referring to Madison's comment in *Federalist* 49: "But a nation of philosophers is as little to be expected as the philosophical race of kings wished for by Plato. And in every other nation, the most rational government will not find it a superfluous advantage to have the prejudices of the community on its side" (Rossiter, *Federalist Papers*, 312).

necessary republican virtue can be maintained."[22]

Anti-Federalists had an answer to that, namely a reservation of most power to small, relatively homogenous states where habits of citizenship were promoted by a government easily accessible and responsible to the people. Melancton Smith urged a government based on what he called the "Middling Class." Smith opined:

> Those in middling circumstances have less temptation; they are inclined by habit, and the company with whom they associate, to set bounds to their passions and appetites. If this is not sufficient, the want of means to gratify them will be a restraint: they are obliged to employ their time in their respective callings; hence the substantial yeomanry of the country are more temperate, of better morals, and less ambition, than the great.[23]

To highlight the contrast: for the Federalists, rights are protected through properly formed institutions that channel and form conflicting interests and opinions in such a manner as to protect minority rights. This is the institutional view. For Anti-Federalists, protection of rights comes from a virtuous people vigilant in defense of their rights. These different prescriptions for protection of rights by Federalists and Anti-Federalists respectively arise from different assessments of the threat to rights. For Anti-Federalists, generally speaking, the threat to rights stems from elites who wish to use government to enrich themselves at the expense of the common man. The solution to this problem is to keep government close to the people where the "middling sort" have a greater say and to put strict boundaries on the central government so as to limit the possibility of abuse. On the other hand, the two main authors of *The Federalist Papers*, James Madison and Alexander Hamilton, have their own diagnoses and solutions. For Madison rights are most threatened by factious majorities. His cure is to create a diversity of opinion, external to governing via the extended republic and internally in the separation of powers. Majorities will form as a result of compromise and moderation, helping secure the rights of minorities. Hamilton added to the Madisonian approach a concern for the centrifugal force of disunion. Hamilton's economic nationalism has as its goal, in part, the encouragement of unity. As he wrote in *Federalist* 11, anticipating the language of Henry Clay's economic system, "Let the thirteen States, bound together in a strict and indissoluble Union,

---

[22] Storing, *What the Anti-Federalists Were For*, 73.

[23] Ketchum, *Anti-Federalist Papers*, 344.

concur in erecting one great American system."[24] Without strong union there is a tendency for states to see each other as rivals and for a confederacy to descend into chaos, as was hinted at in the experience under the Articles of Confederation. As with Madison, Hamilton's approach is institutional rather than the more populist view espoused by Anti-Federalists.

Federalists and Anti-Federalists alike saw the good of both liberty and order. Liberty taken too far produces the ill of chaos. Order taken too far produces the ill of authoritarianism. If we can take as our guide what each side feared, the Anti-Federalists feared authoritarianism more than chaos, and concomitantly the Federalists believed the threat to democracy was more likely to come from disorder than through excessive stability.

The Necessity of Statesmanship

There are three approaches to the threat to rights within a democracy: a fervent republicanism coupled with strict limits on government, a Madisonian multiplication of interests channeled through properly formed institutions, and Hamilton's strong union that prevents infighting. These relate to the respective threats to democracy, either from consolidated government on the one hand or instability caused by faction and lack of union on the other. To these three options Abraham Lincoln adds a fourth, that of statesmanship. From a Lincolnian point of view, Anti-Federalists were insufficiently attentive to the possible corruption of the people or the dangers of public opinion run amok. This is the danger of an unrestrained populism. But the institutional solutions of the Federalists are similarly inadequate, given their reliance on the channeling of self-interest. Anti-Federalists, Storing is correct to note, saw the "insufficiency of a community of mere interest."[25] Lincoln overcomes the Federalist/Anti-Federalist divide by showing that while proper institutions and virtue are necessary, both must be taken care of by statesmen. Just democracy does not arise naturally from an ever-virtuous people; neither does it arise from a people who are entirely dependent upon institutions rather than virtue to promote justice. Surely enlightened statesmen will not always be at the helm, but a people that cannot regularly produce statesmen will not long maintain a free government.

[24] *Federalist* 11, p. 86.

[25] Storing, *What the Anti-Federalists Were For*, 76.

The virtues of the statesman are prudence and moderation. The tools of the statesman are dedication to the rule of law and political rhetoric. "Prudence" is right reasoning about legitimate ends. Assuming that we have reasoned properly about the proper ends of government, which is the work of theoretical wisdom, we then need to know how to achieve those ends. This is the work of practical wisdom, or prudence. The additional virtue of the statesman is that of moderation. Moderation means having each good thing in its proper amount. Moderate eating is not simply a middle point between starvation and obesity but a proper balance of various types of food. Such moderation will also take into account our life situation. The proper diet for a professional athlete will be different from that of the common person. The diet of a teenager will differ from that of someone middle-aged. An individual genetically predisposed to high blood pressure will have different dietary restrictions than someone who is diabetic, and so on. Moderation implies balance. In politics there are various competing goods. In the American context, we tend to value goods such as natural right, equality, liberty, and consent. The statesman tries to balance these goods.

As stated, if prudence and moderation are the virtues of the statesman, rule of law and rhetoric are among his tools. We have seen above in the reference to the Lyceum speech that Lincoln proposed to make the rule of law a "political religion" so as to curb the rising tide of mob violence. For Lincoln this was not idle talk. He lived the rule of law as a lawyer and was surprisingly scrupulous as president. It is commonplace to note Lincoln's aggressive use of executive power during the war, and one is reminded of Clinton Rossiter's so-called "dictatorship thesis." Rossiter claims that Lincoln, "faced with an overriding necessity for harsh, even dictatorial action…used the commander in chief clause, at first gingerly, in the end boldly, to justify an unprecedented series of measures that cut deeply into the accepted liberties of the people and the routine pattern of government."[26] Lincoln was, in Rossiter's estimation, a "constitutional dictator," as he alone judged what was best for the survival of the republic.[27] But this characterization doesn't hold up under scrutiny. Let us stipulate that in time of civil war the limits of the law will be tested. I do not wish to argue that Lincoln never tested nor exceeded those limits. But given the

---

[26] Clinton Rossiter, *The American Presidency* (New York: Time, Inc., 1956) 12.
[27] Rossiter, *The American Presidency*, 13.

situation, Lincoln showed admirable restraint. First, it is worth noting that Lincoln was under the oversight of Congress, including the Committee on the Conduct of the War. Also, elections still occurred during the war with Lincoln's Republican Party experiencing significant losses in the 1862 midterm election. Importantly, Lincoln was careful not to confuse his own will with the law. We see this in the many times Lincoln conceded that slavery, which he despised, did have legal rights under the Constitution. William Lee Miller directs our attention to Lincoln's commutation of almost all death sentences against Native Americans implicated in a massacre of settlers in Minnesota in 1862.[28] Lincoln commuted those sentences precisely because of denial of due process.

Perhaps the best example of Lincoln's placement of the law over will is in the Emancipation Proclamation. It is to be remembered that Lincoln had telegraphed his plan in the open letter to Horace Greeley in August, 1862, namely that he would emancipate slaves in those parts of the nation under rebellion as of January 1, 1863, but not all slaves everywhere. At the end of that famous letter Lincoln states, "I have here stated my purpose according to my view of *official* duty; and I intend no modification of my oft-expressed *personal* wish that all men every where could be free."[29] After the issuance of the proclamation, Lincoln was criticized by his abolitionist Treasury Secretary Salmon Chase for Lincoln's refusal to emancipate more fully. Lincoln responded that the proclamation had no "constitutional or legal justification, except as a military measure." What defense was there of an extension of the proclamation to areas not in rebellion "except the one that I think the measure politically expedient, and morally right? Would I not thus give up all footing upon constitution or law? Would I not thus be in the boundless field of absolutism? Could this pass unnoticed, or unresisted?"[30]

The rule of law teaches that the passions of the people don't win the day. Arbitrary government is the definition of tyranny, whether of a majority or a minority. Rule of law advances moderation by forcing the good of consent to follow a particular predetermined process. At the heart of tyranny is the notion of a government that can operate without limits. This

[28] William Lee Miller, *President Lincoln: The Duty of a Statesman* (New York: Vintage, 2008) 318, 325.

[29] Lincoln, *Collected Works*, 5:389. Emphasis in the original.

[30] Lincoln, *Collected Works*, 6: 428–429.

is true whether it is the tyranny of one or of many. Rule of law in a democracy teaches the people that its consent must be tempered by due process, helping to protect the goods of liberty and natural rights.

In his work on religion and violence, William Cavanaugh notes that pre-modern religion was not held to be simply a set of internal dispositions and beliefs. In the same vein as Aristotle, religion was considered a virtue that required the perfection of habit. "As a virtue, *religio* is a type of habitus, a disposition of the person toward moral excellence produced by highly specific disciplines of the body and soul. *Religio* is not so much a matter of learning certain correct universal propositions about the world, but of being formed in bodily habits."[31] If Lincoln preached a political religion, that religion cannot be simply a set of interior dispositions assented to in the mind. It requires practice, as do other virtues. The political religion of Lincoln needs its own habits. Among those habits is the habit of abiding by the law. The tendency of democracy is, it is said, to confuse the will of the people with the will of God. By asking the people to submit to preordained processes the good of consent is moderated and put in closer harmony with other political goods.

Regarding rhetoric, what makes Lincoln distinctive is his ability to be forceful, to stake out the moral high ground, while recognizing the valid claims of his opponents. He was able to direct the people to the right course while not stooping to demagoguery. Lincoln stated in 1856, "Our government rests in public opinion. Whoever can change public opinion, can change the government, practically just so much."[32] Lincoln deftly used rhetoric to promote moderation and prudence. He promoted moderation by consistently recognizing the legitimate claims of his opponents. "If you would win a man to your cause, *first* convince him that you are his sincere friend," Lincoln stated.[33] One does not achieve this via fiery denunciations or thunderous condemnations of one's political opponents. Success is more likely if one shows sympathy with one's opponents, recognizing the partial legitimacy of their claims while encouraging them down a more just path. The statesman effectively communicates that he is balancing the competing just claims of various sides, simultaneously

[31] William Cavanaugh, *The Myth of Religious Violence: Secular Ideology and the Roots of Modern Conflict* (New York: Oxford University Press, 2009) 66.

[32] Lincoln, *Collected Works*, 2: 385.

[33] Lincoln, *Collected Works*, 1: 273. Emphasis in the original.

practicing moderation while rhetorically encouraging it in the people. Lincoln's own synthesis of Anti-Federalist and Federalist values illustrates how a statesman might incorporate competing legitimate claims into his own political thought.

Lincoln also avoided the imprudence of much of the abolitionist movement by advocating the limitation of the expansion of slavery rather than its immediate abolition, abolition being a view with little public support and of dubious constitutional legitimacy. Lincoln's caution was vindicated as when finally given an opportunity to act decisively against slavery he did so with vigor in the Emancipation Proclamation and his advocacy of the Thirteenth Amendment.

Lincoln, in his prolonged contest with Stephen Douglas from 1854 to 1860, rejected the notion that insisted "that there is no right principle of action but self-interest."[34] Douglas had argued that his popular sovereignty approach to slavery, which would leave the legality of slavery in new territories up to a vote of territorial residents rather than the U.S. Congress, would keep slavery out of the West because slavery would be contrary to the economic self-interest of Western settlers. In rejecting this notion, Lincoln declared that self-interest is not sufficient grounds for justice. A statesman must care for the opinion of the people, and using thoughtful, well-crafted political rhetoric, reshape the architecture of the republic's soul, cultivating the soul that it may be more fertile ground for justice and liberty. This may be the statesman's greatest task. To this end he must use poetry as much as prose.

By arguing for popular sovereignty and dismissing the claims of natural right, Douglas was flattering democratic prejudices but ultimately undermining the very grounds of democracy, namely the natural equality of all. While Douglas declared popular sovereignty to be the truly democratic option, Lincoln argued that the real import of popular sovereignty was, "That if any one man, choose to enslave another, no third man shall be allowed to object."[35]

Lincoln heaped scorn on the indifference toward slavery indicated in Douglas's "don't care" attitude toward the institution. This indifference, Lincoln maintained, was logically no different than outright advocacy as it signified a common ground between Douglas and pro-slavery forces,

[34] Lincoln, *Collected Works*, 2: 225.

[35] Lincoln, *Collected Works*, 2: 462.

namely that slavery is not a wrong. Lincoln stated, "The difference between the Republican and the Democratic parties on the leading issue of this contest, as I understand it, is, that the former consider slavery a moral, social and political wrong, while the latter do not consider it either a moral, social or political wrong."[36] Lincoln opined:

> This declared indifference, but as I must think, covert real zeal for the spread of slavery, I can not but hate. I hate it because of the monstrous injustice of slavery itself. I hate it because it deprives our republican example of its just influence in the world—enables the enemies of free institutions, with plausibility, to taunt us as hypocrites—causes the real friends of freedom to doubt our sincerity, and especially because it forces so many really good men amongst ourselves into an open war with the very fundamental principles of civil liberty.[37]

This lowering of sights from the natural rights of the Declaration to the mere expedience of self-interest was contrary to just democracy. When Lincoln proclaimed that "right makes might" he was arguing against a simplistic democracy in which the majority, due merely to its superior might in numbers, was always right.[38] Even if successful in keeping slavery out of the West, Douglas's position taught a dreadful lesson: natural rights can be trumped by self-interest and power of numbers. Douglas seemed to believe that there was no need for statesmanship as the people needed no improvement. Thus any appeal to a standard beyond the aggregate interests of the people would be unjust. Douglas was teaching the people not to care about natural rights and to think only about what is convenient or in their selfish interest. A majority unconcerned with justice is a mob, the very definition of an immoderate democracy.

Conclusion

Madison claims that the "latent causes of faction are thus sown into the nature of man."[39] If this is the case, then political incivility and disorder should always be lurking just below the surface of politics, periodically manifesting themselves in various political disorders. These disorders might include rank demagoguery, partisanship, corruption, and other ills

---

[36] Lincoln, *Collected Works*, 3: 92.
[37] Lincoln, *Collected Works*, 2: 225.
[38] Lincoln, *Collected Works*, 3: 550.
[39] *Federalist* 10, p. 73.

that tend to infect the body politic. Incivility in this case is akin to illnesses caused by viruses that may linger in an individual's system but only periodically become symptomatic under specific conditions. The statesman attends to the health of the body politic, ensuring that either political disorder does not arise or if it should that the disease is quarantined. The tools for this art are those of rhetoric and the rule of law.

American politics of recent years is defined by nothing if not a dearth of statesmanship. One can safely say that wisdom is not a primary pursuit of today's politician. Most politicians have internalized, intentionally or by accident, that unhappy meeting of the Baconian notion that "knowledge is power" with the post-modern skepticism that language is connected to anything real. Communication, then, becomes not an expression of truth but is instead simply another expression of power, the desire to control and manipulate for one's benefit. Such a regime might abound in a kind of Machiavellian statecraft, but statesmanship will be rare. This is the result of thinking of power as the only political good worth pursuing. With power at the center of our politics, our political practice becomes more about creating spectacle than reasoned discourse. To be sure, one can agree with Madison regarding the unlikelihood of a race of Platonic philosopher-kings, but surely we can do better than the philosophic equivalent of the Three Stooges. One need only consider the embarrassment of the recent hearings regarding Judge Brett Kavanaugh's nomination to the Supreme Court to see how the performance art of American politics degrades our respect for rule of law, due process, and even common decency. And those hearings were merely an exaggerated example of what is all too typical of congressional debate.

One cannot help but wonder why we suffer a shortage of statesmanship. There are many reasons. Some of them are institutional. Our electoral system, now thoroughly plebiscitary, encourages candidates to act in a manner most likely to attract attention. Weak parties lack the power to discipline demagogic members. Combine weak parties with a campaign finance system that promotes interest groups—almost by definition more extreme than the general public—and we have a perfect storm of irresponsible politics.

Forgive the college professor if he also points to the failure of our educational system, particularly higher education. As literature and history are cut in favor of Science, Technology, Engineering, and Math (STEM) curriculum, there is an increased tendency to see the world as something to be manipulated for the sake of enhancing our own power. When students do take the humanities they are often exposed to a metaphysic (frequently masquerading as the absence of metaphysics) that, as alluded to above, sees language as nothing more than an expression of power. Thus do the humanities become politicized in the crudest sense. There is little here to educate the statesman. We suffer from a kind of moral obesity brought about in part by educational fast food. Patrick Deneen has recently argued that "an education for a free people [has been] displaced by an education that makes liberal individuals servants to the end of untutored appetite, restlessness, and technical mastery of the natural world. Liberal education is replaced with servile education."[40]

It is of note that Abraham Lincoln, who had far less formal education than virtually everyone in contemporary politics, possessed wisdom that most of today's politicians lack. Lincoln's education, such as it was, was poetic rather than technical. Lincoln's own religious beliefs could best be described as heterodox, yet Lincoln had a near encyclopedic knowledge of the Bible and drew on it constantly for rhetorical use. While he did not quote Shakespeare much in his public speeches, Lincoln had a similar familiarity with key Shakespearean plays. Lincoln did not read Shakespeare broadly, but he returned to certain plays on a regular basis, plays such as *Richard III*, *Hamlet*, *Macbeth*, and *King Lear*. Lincoln was able to recite long passages from these plays from memory.[41] It is not an accident that Lincoln's interests in Shakespeare tended toward the historical and the tragic, interested as he was with the nature of power and its ability to corrupt good men. The art of governing is not simply the technique of acquiring and enhancing one's power, but the ability and wisdom to use that power well. An education that is as devoted to cultivating statesmen as it is in cultivating economically efficient producers and consumers would help our polity immeasurably.

No doubt Madison was right that properly formed institutions are necessary for sound, just government. No doubt the Federalists were right to be skeptical of crude majoritarianism. Similarly, Anti-Federalists were correct that consolidation of power away from the hands of ordinary

---

[40] Patrick Deneen, *Why Liberalism Failed* (New Haven, CT: Yale University, 2018) 111.

[41] Lincoln, *Collected Works*, 6: 392–393. See also, Michael Anderegg, *Lincoln and Shakespeare* (Lawrence: University Press of Kansas, 2015).

citizens, as promoted in the Constitution, might lead to anti-republican tendencies. But history has taught mankind the necessity of auxiliary precautions. Among those precautions, Lincoln teaches us well, is that of sound statesmanship.

7

FEDERALISTS AND ANTI-FEDERALISTS THEN AND NOW: THE UNFINISHED RATIFICATION DEBATE

Roger Barrus

The debate over the ratification of the Constitution might seem to be over and done with. The story seems simple and straightforward: two political parties debated the fine points of the new Constitution; the Federalists won, the Anti-Federalists lost, and the Constitution went into effect. The reality, however, is much more complicated. The two sides were not political parties, but rather broad coalitions with more or less similar opinions. While the Constitution's supporters called themselves "Federalists," its opponents probably never called themselves "Anti-Federalists:" as far as they were concerned, they were the true "Federalists," and their opponents were usurpers.

It is not even quite correct to say that the Constitution as implemented was the one that the Federalists proposed: it was substantively changed during the first Congress in response to the Anti-Federalists' criticism that it lacked a Bill of Rights. For the Federalists, the omission was not an oversight. Alexander Hamilton argues that "bills of rights are, in their origin, stipulations between kings and their subjects, abridgements of prerogative in favour of privilege," and "have no application to constitutions professedly founded upon the power of the people." In fact they are dangerous: to "declare that things shall not be done, which there is no power to do" might "afford a colourable pretext to claim more [powers] than were granted."[1]

The adoption of the Bill of Rights illustrates two points that are critical to understanding the Federalist/Anti-Federalist debate. First, it shows

[1]Alexander Hamilton, *Federalist* 84, in Alexander Hamilton, John Jay, and James Madison, *The Federalist,* ed. George W. Carey and James McClellan (Indianapolis: Liberty Fund, Inc.) 445.

that the debate did not come to an end with the Constitution's ratification, because it was not about the Constitution alone, but about the proper ordering of American society—the American "regime"—of which its form of government was but one element, albeit a very important one. Second, it shows that the Federalists and Anti-Federalists were not ideological enemies but practically minded opponents who were open to compromise. They agreed on the fundamental principles that guided the debate, while disagreeing on how those principles should be implemented. The debate was thus a dispute over more or less specific matters of disagreement within more basic agreements. The great question concerning the debate is whether it was truly comprehensive, that is, whether the participants considered all the issues relevant to it, or whether they might have missed something important. With the debate focusing on the functions, powers, and institutions of the national government, little attention was given to the role of the states and even localities in the functioning of the new system of democratic self-government under the proposed Constitution.

Agreements in Principle

The most obvious agreement between the Federalists and Anti-Federalists concerned the stakes in the debate. Both sides were convinced that the Americans were involved in something rare if not unique in history: a people attempting to form a government by rational deliberation and choice alone. The ratification debate was thus the decisive test of human beings' real capacity for self-government. Hamilton observes that "it seems to have been reserved to the people of this country to decide, by their conduct and example, whether societies of men are really capable or not, of establishing good government from reflection and choice, or whether they are forever destined to depend, for their political constitutions, on accident and force."[2]

The Anti-Federalist "Brutus" (most likely Robert Yates) makes the same point, even more emphatically:

> The most important question that was ever proposed to your decision, or to the decision of any people under heaven, is before you, and you are to decide upon it by men of your own election, chosen specially for this purpose. If the constitution, offered to your acceptance, be a wise one, calculated to preserve the invaluable rights of mankind, and promote human happiness, then, if

[2] *Federalist* 1, p.1.

> you accept it, you will lay a lasting foundation of happiness for millions yet unborn...But if, on the other hand, this form of government contains principles that will lead to the subversion of liberty...then, if you adopt it, this only remaining asylum of liberty will be shut up, and posterity will execrate your memory.[3]

A second point of agreement was the Declaration of Independence with its self-evident truths that all human beings are equal and as such possess certain unalienable rights; that governments are instituted by the consent of the governed to secure those rights; and that if any government fails in that purpose, it is the people's right to abolish it and establish a new one. While these principles can be found in John Locke's political philosophy, Thomas Jefferson insisted that he wrote the Declaration as "an expression of the American mind."[4] These principles pointed to the establishment of something unprecedented, a true "new order of the ages": a democratic society dedicated to securing its people's liberty. Hitherto there had been democratic societies (e.g., ancient Athens) that were by no means liberal, and more or less liberal societies (e.g., Britain) that were at best only marginally democratic.

Federalism was another area of agreement. Both sides were convinced that the Americans should be united politically, but that union had to take the form of an association of the separate states, rather than a consolidation of the people into one national state. This understanding was at least in part the result of the experience of the Revolutionary War, which demonstrated on the one hand, that the Americans had very important interests in common that made union necessary, but on the other hand, that there were also important differences among them that would make their union in a national state undesirable, and even impossible.

One last agreement was the acceptance of the French philosopher Montesquieu as the ultimate authority on constitutions and laws. This might appear surprising: a more likely authority would seem to be Locke, the philosopher of the American Revolution. The reason for their choice of Montesquieu concerns the fundamental difference between the two philosophers' principle political works. Locke's *Second Treatise of Government* is an abstract theory of political right, applicable to any society,

---

[3]Brutus 1, in *The Anti-Federalist*, ed. Herbert J. Storing, with selection by Murray Dry (Chicago: The University of Chicago Press, 1981) 109.

[4]Thomas Jefferson to Henry Lee, May 8, 1825.

anywhere, and at any time. It has little to say about the concrete circumstances that must be taken into account in making laws for a particular society. Montesquieu's *Spirit of the Laws*, in contrast, presents a more practical teaching, showing how the circumstances that the *Second Treatise* abstracts from—climate, geography, economics, religion, modes of warfare, and many more—relate to states' laws, governmental institutions, and politics.

Practical Disagreements

While the Federalists and Anti-Federalists both look to Montesquieu for guidance, they turn to two different sections of the *Spirit of the Laws* to find it. The two sections deal with the two distinct but related elements of the liberal democratic regime, democracy and liberty. For the Anti-Federalists, the key text is the chapters on democracy in the *Laws'* first nine books. Montesquieu defines democracy as the regime in which "the people as a body have the sovereignty," which means that "the people are, in certain respects, the monarch," while "in other respects they are the subjects." They must be able to both rule and be ruled, meaning that they must possess what Montesquieu calls "virtue," which he defines as "love of the homeland, that is, love of equality." Such virtue is democracy's "principle," the "spring" or the "human passion" that must animate it, if it is to succeed. In the absence of such virtue, "ambition enters the hearts that can admit it, and avarice enters them all," with the result that the citizen who had been "free under the laws," now "wants to be free against them," like "a slave who has escaped from his master's house." "The republic" in this condition "is a cast off-husk, and its strength is no more than the power of a few citizens and the license of all."[5]

Since this virtue is a kind of "renunciation of oneself, which is always a very painful thing," Montesquieu argues that democracy has a special need for the education of its citizens. He points to the nature of this education when he praises the ancient Greeks and Romans, who "lived in governments that had virtue for their principle," and as long as "that virtue was in full force, things were done in those governments that we no longer see and that astonish our small souls." Their secret was that their societies

[5]Montesquieu, *The Spirit of the Laws*, trans. and ed. Anne M. Cohler, Basia C. Miller, and Harold S. Stone (Cambridge, U.K.: Cambridge University Press, 1989) Author's Preface, p. xli; Part I, Book II, Chapter 2, p. 10; I. III. 1–3, pp. 21–23.

were organized in such a way that what they were taught as youths "was never contradicted." Thus the Spartan Epaminondas, at the end of his life "said, heard, saw, and did the same things as at the time he was first instructed." Epaminondas' "education" was really a comprehensive way of life that turned ordinary human beings into beings of a special type, "Spartans," who were totally dedicated to the preservation of their city and its unique institutions.[6] The requirement of virtue and the consequent need for such an education sets a limit to the size of a democracy. Montesquieu argues that in "a large republic, there are large fortunes, and consequently little moderation in spirits." "Interests become particularized," so that "at first a man feels he can be happy, great, and glorious without his homeland; and soon, that he can be great only on the ruins of his homeland." In general, in "a large republic, the common good is sacrificed to a thousand considerations; it is subordinated to exceptions; it depends upon accidents. In a small one, the public good is better felt, better known, lies nearer to each citizen; abuses are less extensive there and consequently less protected."[7]

Montesquieu completes his analysis of democracy in Book 9, where he discusses the issue of national security. In this regard, democracies appear to be caught in a vicious dilemma: "If a republic is small, it is destroyed by a foreign force; if it is large, it is destroyed by internal vice." The problem is so serious that if it could not be resolved, it would mean that human beings would be "obliged to live forever under the government of one alone." The solution that suggests itself is for democracies to band together in a "federal republic," a "kind of constitution that has all the internal advantages of republican government and the external force of monarchy." Montesquieu recommends the ancient Lycian League, in which the votes of the member states and the taxes imposed on them were proportionate to their size, as the best "model" of a federal republic. He does not mention, however, that according to Strabo, his source, this best of all federal republics lost its independence to the Roman Empire, meaning that it ultimately failed in its specific purpose.[8] In this way, he perhaps hints that national security might well be an irresolvable problem for the traditional democratic republic.

---

[6]Ibid., I. IV. 4–5, pp. 35–36.
[7]Ibid., I. VIII. 16, p. 124.
[8]Ibid., II. 9. 1–3, pp. 131–133. See Strabo, *Geographica*, 14. 3. 3.

The Federalists have for their key text *Spirit of the Laws* Book 11: "On the Laws that Form Political Liberty in Relation to the Constitution." In this book, which not coincidentally follows two on war, Montesquieu discusses a plan for a new kind of republic, one that while not a traditional democracy—most obviously, because through the principle of representation it can be expanded well beyond democracy's narrow limits—does nevertheless have important democratic elements. This new republic, which Montesquieu says is exemplified in the English constitution, has "political liberty" as its "direct purpose." To explain this purpose, he first has to define "liberty," which is not what people typically take it to be, particularly in democracies, where "the people seem to do whatever they want," and the "power of the people has been confused with the liberty of the people." Real "political liberty" is something quite different: "In a state, that is, in a society where there are laws, liberty can consist only in having the power to do what one should want to do and in no way being constrained to do what one should not want to do." In another formulation, "Liberty is the right to do everything the laws permit; and if one citizen could do what they forbid, he would no longer have liberty, because the others would likewise have this same power."[9]

Something more than equal justice under the law is required, however, to make liberty actual: the government must be structured in such a way that the people will feel themselves safe in exercising their liberty. Political liberty is "that tranquility of spirit which comes from the opinion each one has of his security, and in order for him to have this liberty the government must be such that one citizen cannot fear another citizen." Liberty is thus not an inherent feature of any particular regime form; rather it exists "in moderate governments" of whatever form, in which no one can "abuse power" because power is made to "check power by the arrangement of things." Liberty requires not only the separation of powers among different branches of government, as Locke argues in the *Second Treatise*, but also a system of checks and balances, in which the powers are allocated in such a way that the branches can function as brakes on one another. The purpose of this system is not to prevent government from acting, but rather to create the condition in which its branches are normally in a state of "rest or inaction," but capable of acting together when "constrained to move by

[9] *Spirit of the Laws*, II. XI. 2–3, pp. 154–155.

the necessary motion of things."[10]

While Locke argues for the separation of powers based on considerations of both safety, as a defense against tyranny, and efficiency, in the exercise of the powers themselves, Montesquieu argues for checks and balances on the basis of safety alone. His procedure is puzzling, given that the context of his discussion of the constitution of liberty is the danger of war, where efficiency might appear to be the paramount consideration. The reason concerns the proper role of fear in founding a liberal democracy. For Montesquieu, the fear of conquest seems to be the necessary motivation to get democratic peoples to think about a different kind of republican regime, one that allows for expansion beyond democracy's narrow limits, and thus offers a solution to its national security dilemma. Such fear is not, however, the proper motivation for thinking about the political structure of such a republic, because it points, in the fashion of Thomas Hobbes' argument for absolute monarchy in *Leviathan*, to the extreme centralization of political power. Montesquieu criticizes Hobbes' argument as based on a mistaken conception of human nature, as inherently aggressive.[11] Human beings are not naturally aggressive but rather naturally fearful. The problem with respect to any question is to know what fear to consult. While in establishing an extended republic the operative fear is foreign conquest, in organizing its government the fear of conquest gives way to the fear of tyranny, which does not mean that the fear of conquest is no longer real, but only that it must be pushed into the background. That is in essence Montesquieu's method in his analysis of checks and balances: while he argues that if the legislative, executive, and judicial powers are not separated, and the different branches given the means to protect themselves from the others, then "all would be lost," he argues at the same time that the executive power, which "almost always needs immediate action," should be vested in one "monarch," who would have charge of the military, since it is concerned "more with action than deliberation."[12]

Federalists and Anti-Federalists in 1787

Out of their agreements and disagreements, the Federalists and Anti-Federalists elaborated more or less coherent theories of liberal democracy,

[10]Ibid., II. XI. 4, p. 155; II. XI. 6, pp. 157, 164.
[11]Ibid., I. I. 2, p. 6.
[12]Ibid., II. XI. 6, pp. 157, 161, 165.

more in the case of the Federalists, thanks in large part to the *Federalist Papers*, less in the case of the Anti-Federalists, who do not seem to have recognized the need for a comparable work on their side. The core of the Federalists' case for the large republic is presented in three numbers of the *Federalist Papers*: paper 23 by Hamilton and papers 10 and 51 by Madison. Of the three, the most important is 23, which makes the argument for "the necessity of a government at least as energetic as the one proposed" for the preservation of the Union.[13] The significance of *Federalist* 23 is in the way that it reverses the priorities of the Anti-Federalists' small republic, for which the first concern is democracy. The requirements for democratic government define the parameters within which all other matters–institutions, laws, social organization, the very size of the state–must be resolved. This applies even to the critical issue of national security: Brutus argues that "the just way of reasoning" on the subject of national security is that since "the general government is to provide for the protection and defense of the community against foreign attacks," it "therefore ought to have authority sufficient to effect this," but only "so far as is consistent with the providing of our internal protection and defense."[14]

Hamilton argues in a direction diametrically opposed to Brutus. He begins with the question of the ends the federal government is to attain, and then proceeds to the powers necessary for these purposes. Only after these questions are resolved does he bring up the issue of democracy. Hamilton derives the purposes from the Constitution's preamble, and then to clarify the issue of powers, he chooses one, the common defense, for careful analysis. His choice is not accidental: national security is the extreme case that demonstrates how the question of government powers in general must be resolved. The powers in this case are to raise armies and navies, provide for their support, and direct their activities. These powers, he argues, "ought to exist without limitation," since "it is impossible to foresee or to define the extent and variety of national exigencies, and the correspondent extent and variety of the means which may be necessary to satisfy them." He bases his argument on a self-evident truth, that "the *means* ought to be proportional to the *end*" and "the persons from whose agency the attainment of any *end* is expected, ought to possess the *means* by which it is to be attained." In this case, the means could be limited, by

[13] *Federalist* 1, 4.
[14] *The Anti-Federalist*, Brutus 7, p. 146.

constitutional prohibitions, if and only if "the circumstances which may affect public safety" were "reducible within certain determinate limits."[15]

In essence, the order of priorities for the Anti-Federalists is first democracy then national security, while for the Federalists it is first national security then democracy. The practical implications of the two approaches are reflected most clearly in one particular disagreement between the two sides, over standing armies in peace time. Brutus criticizes the Constitution for not including a prohibition on standing armies, arguing that they "have always proved the destruction of liberty" and are "abhorrent to the spirit of a free republic." He concludes that "it is impossible that the liberties of the people in any country can be preserved where a numerous standing army is kept up."[16] In *Federalist* 41, Madison responds by going even beyond Hamilton in 23, warning that "The means of security can only be regulated by the means and danger of attack. They will in fact ever be determined by these rules, and by no others. It is vain to oppose constitutional barriers to the impulse of self-preservation. It is worse than vain: because it plants in the constitution itself necessary usurpations of power, every precedent of which is a germ of unnecessary and multiplied repetitions."[17]

As national security is the fundamental problem in foreign affairs, so factionalism, at least in democracies, is the fundamental problem in domestic politics. For the Anti-Federalists, it is precisely this problem that requires the United States to be a federation of small republics, since only in such societies would the people develop the love of country that would lead them to subordinate their own interests to those of the community. "In a republic," Brutus argues, "the manners, sentiments, and interests of the people should be similar"; otherwise "there will be a constant clashing of opinions, and the representatives of one part will be continually striving against those of the other." For this reason "a free republic cannot succeed over a country of such immense extent, containing such a number of inhabitants." History provides the proof, presenting "no example of a free republic, anything like the extent of the United States," but rather showing how the Greek and Roman republics, which "extended their conquests over large territories of country" changed their "free governments to those

[15] *Federalist* 23, p. 113.

[16] *The Anti-Federalist*, Brutus 1, p. 115, and 8, p. 152.

[17] *Federalist* 41, p. 209.

of the most tyrannical that ever existed in the world."[18]

In contrast, Madison in *Federalist* 10 argues that the large republic offers the most effective solution to the problem of factionalism, which also happens to be the only solution that is really consistent with the liberty of the people. Like Hamilton in his argument on government powers, Madison begins his argument on factionalism one logical step below the Anti-Federalists, by analyzing the nature and origins of the problem. He defines a faction as "a number of citizens, whether amounting to a majority or minority of the whole, who are united and actuated by some common impulse of passion, or of interest, adverse to the rights of other citizens, or to the permanent and aggregate interests of the community." Factionalism originates in the structure of human nature itself, in which there is a "connection" between "reason and self-love," with the result that "opinions and passions will have a reciprocal influence on each other." While the "latent causes of faction" can be triggered by just about any difference of opinion or interest, the "most common and durable source" is "the various and unequal division of property."[19]

For Madison, the solution to factionalism must take into account its natural origin. In principle, it can be solved in either of two ways: by removing its causes, or by controlling its effects. The first approach amounts to the suppression of human nature itself, which might be accomplished either "by destroying the liberty which is essential to [faction's] existence," or "by giving every citizen the same opinions, the same passions, and the same interests." The first alternative, which is truly a cure "worse than the disease," is despotism; the second alternative is the small republic, or at least what the small republic aims to be. If factionalism's causes cannot be removed, then the rational approach to the problem is to control its effects, which can be accomplished through the establishment of a representative democracy—what Madison calls a "republic," as opposed to a "democracy," in which the people rule themselves directly—and the "enlargement of the orbit" of society that representation makes possible. The great advantage of such an extended republic is that with "the greater number of citizens, and extent of territory," the factions in society will be multiplied and diversified, making it less likely that a tyrannical majority will be able to organize itself, than in a smaller society with fewer factions. The way to

[18] *The Anti-Federalist*, Brutus 1, pp. 113–114.
[19] *Federalist* 10, pp. 43–44.

make "factious combinations less to be dreaded" is therefore not to attempt to extinguish factionalism, which in any event is likely to fail, but in a way to encourage it, by giving it a larger arena within which to develop.[20]

One major problem of democracy remains: the oppression of the people by the government. In the Anti-Federalists' small republic this is presumably impossible, since the government in it remains close to the people and subject to their immediate control. In the large republic, the government is far removed from the people and subject to them only intermittently, at election time. Madison thus argues, in *Federalist* 51, that while "dependence on the people is, no doubt, the primary control on the government," what he calls "auxiliary precautions," in the form of the proper organization of government, are necessary. The first requirement in this regard is the separation of government powers, since "the accumulation of all powers...in the same hands, whether one, few, or many...may justly be pronounced the very definition of tyranny." The mere separation of powers is insufficient, however, because power is "of an encroaching nature," so there must be some means for containing the branches within their respective spheres. The solution to this problem is the system of checks and balances, "so contriving the interior structure of the government as that its several constituent parts may, by their mutual relations, be the means of keeping each other in the proper place." Specifically, "Ambition must be made to counteract ambition," connecting "the interest of the man" with "the constitutional rights of the place," by "giving to those who administer each department, the necessary constitutional means, and personal motives, to resist encroachments of the others."[21]

On the deepest level, Madison's solutions to factionalism—the large republic—and government tyranny—the system of checks and balances—rest on precisely the same principle, which he explains as supplying "by opposite and rival interests, the defect of better motives."[22] Viewed abstractly, this approach seems quite elegant, but it is also perhaps a bit simplistic: it assumes that good ends—liberty and democratic self-government—can really be brought about by the use of bad means—self-interest and personal ambition, which might seem to violate the self-evident truth that like produces like. At least a few Anti-Federalists recognized that

[20]Ibid., 10, pp. 45–48.
[21]Ibid., 47, p. 249; 51, pp. 268–269.
[22]Ibid., 51, p. 269.

there was something problematic about the Federalists' fundamental principle. Thus "Centinel" (likely Samuel Bryan) questions whether a government founded on it would answer "the great purposes of civil society; if the administrators of every government are actuated by views of private interest and ambition, how is the welfare and happiness of the community to be the result of such jarring adverse interests?"[23] More pointedly, Melancton Smith criticizes "the ardent advocates for the new system" who "reprobate republican principles as chimerical and such as ought to be expelled from society. Who would have thought ten years ago, that the very men who risqued their lives and fortunes in support of republican principles, would now treat them as the fictions of fancy?"[24]

Federalists and Anti-Federalists Now

The Federalists won the ratification debate, in the sense that the Constitution was finally ratified. In a way they won it a bit too easily, however. The cause lay with the Anti-Federalists' strategy in the debate, which was to counter the Federalists' comprehensive proposal with a series of specific criticisms rather than with a comprehensive proposal of their own. Their strategy was misconceived, perhaps because they did not fully understand the condition of the country in 1787. As demonstrated by the Congress' very call for a convention, the American people generally had come to the conclusion that substantial changes needed to be made to the Articles of Confederation. The political situation was objectively more "revolutionary" than it might have appeared: for many Americans, the existing government had failed so signally that it had lost whatever legitimacy it once enjoyed. In this situation, to defend the existing government, the Anti-Federalists needed to go back to first principles and present an argument for the small republic as robust as the Federalists' argument for the large one.

The point is not that with a little extra effort, the Anti-Federalists would have won the debate. Hamilton's argument on the powers of the federal government is ultimately dispositive: in order for a society to be good, it must first simply exist. Rather, there was something crucial missing from the ratification debate, something that could have been supplied

[23]Centinel 1, in *The Anti-Federalist Papers*, ed. Ralph Ketcham (New York: Signet Classics, 1986) 236.

[24]Melancton Smith, Speech of June 23, 1788, in ibid., 371.

if the Anti-Federalists had made a more serious argument. The consequence of their failure was a defect in the Federalists' case for the Constitution. What was missing was a discussion of the good of democratic self-government as such—meaning not the mere forms of democracy, but the active life of a citizen—which would have led naturally to a consideration of how the Constitution would attain that good. The Anti-Federalists' failure in effect allows the Federalists to commit the fallacy of arguing that the Constitution conforms to the principles of democratic self-government—the subject of *Federalist* 39–84—without first showing how it is a good thing. Perhaps the closest they come to this issue is in *Federalist* 39, where Madison claims that only a "strictly republican" government "would be reconcilable with the genius of the American people; with the fundamental principles of the Revolution; or with that honorable determination which animates every votary of freedom, to rest all our political experiments on the capacity of mankind for self-government."[25] While everything Madison says might very well be true, it proves only that democratic self-government is good for the Americans, and perhaps only in their present condition. It does not prove that it is a good thing as such.

The Federalists' problem is reflected in what appears as a significant contradiction in their case. At the beginning of the *Federalist Papers*, Hamilton appeals to the American people to deliberate dispassionately on the great question before them, making their decision based on "a judicious estimate of our true interests, uninfluenced by considerations foreign to the public good," and advises them to be on their "guard against all attempts, from whatever quarter, to influence your decision in a matter of the utmost moment to your welfare, by any impressions, other than those which may result from the evidence of truth."[26] The *Federalist Papers* culminate, however, in Madison's defense of the Constitution as offering solutions to democracy's major problems that do not require the exercise of such dispassionate rationality, and even seem to cast doubt on its possibility. Madison would undoubtedly dismiss this thought, pointing out perhaps that the purpose of his devices—the most important in this case being the multiplication and diversification of factions in the extended republic—is to bring about a kind of equilibrium of the passions, in order to make it possible for the people's representatives to govern in accordance

[25] *Federalist* 39, pp. 193–194.

[26] *Federalist* 1, p. 1.

with reason. The Constitution thus secures a "space" for the few—the rulers in the democratic republic—to exercise the kind of rationality called for by Hamilton. The logical next question is how, if at all, it does the same thing for the many, the people who elected the rulers.

The Anti-Federalists, in their critique of the large republic, put forth what is at least the beginning of an argument for the good of democratic self-government, but unfortunately they do not properly develop it. The beginning is Montesquieu's assertion that what he calls "virtue" is the "principle" of democracy. The virtue he is referring to is not one of Plato's four cardinal virtues, Aristotle's eleven moral or six intellectual virtues, or Thomas Aquinas' four theological virtues. It is something more primal: the political virtue of the "love of the laws and the homeland," which he argues is "singularly connected with democracies," because they require a "continuous preference of the public interest over one's own." Because democracies vest government power in the mass of the people, and make them responsible for its exercise, they also offer the most favorable environment for such virtue's general development. Montesquieu argues that the "preference" that democracy inculcates—the common good over the private—is productive of much more than the democratic regime's political success. It is, in practice, the source of "all the individual virtues," which are in different ways expressions of that preference, since the "less we can satisfy our particular passions, the more we give ourselves up to passions for the general order." The result is a virtuous circle: "Love of the homeland leads to good mores, and good mores lead to love of the homeland."[27]

To develop the argument, the Anti-Federalists could have proceeded from Montesquieu to Aristotle, whose works were available and possibly even well known to them. In the *Nicomachean Ethics* and the *Politics*, Aristotle shows why virtue is a good thing, and how it is related to political life. A "virtue" (*areté*), Aristotle argues, is an excellence of the soul, and "happiness" (*eudaimonía*)—the supreme human good because all other good things are sought for its sake, while it is not sought for the sake of anything higher than itself—is "action in accordance with virtue, and if there are a number of virtues, then it is in accordance with the best and most complete."[28] Human beings associate together in many different "communities" to pursue the many goods that they need to live well, but

[27] *Spirit of the Laws*, I. IV. 5, p. 36; I. V. 1, pp. 42–43.
[28] Aristotle, *Nicomachean Ethics* I, 1098a16–20.

one stands above all the rest: the "city" (*pólis*) or "political community," the "most authoritative of all communities," that "includes all the others," and thus "aims at the most authoritative of the goods." Aristotle discerned in the Greek experience of the city something fundamental about human nature: the specific power of human beings, that which makes them "human," is *logos*—"speech" or "reason"—and that power makes them by nature "political animals"—literally "beings of the *polis*," a small, independent, self-governing society. The reason is that the function of *logos* is not merely to register pain or pleasure, as is the case with the "voice" of brute animals, but rather to "make clear the beneficial and the harmful, and therefore also the just and the unjust." Human beings are "political" because only in an association like the *polis*—a "community" in a conception of the "good and bad, and just and unjust"—can they exercise that power in full.[29] The highest practical expression of *logos* is the common deliberation of fellow citizens concerning the good they seek as a society, then acting together to attain that good, in a system of ruling and being ruled in turn. Aristotle, who has his reservations about democracy as a political regime, would nevertheless agree with the Declaration of Independence in its placement of government by consent of the governed as the highest of the rights of nature, and the culmination of the rights of life, liberty, and the pursuit of happiness. It is a kind of corollary to his claim that man is by nature a political animal.

If the Anti-Federalists had made this argument—or if the Federalists had brought it up on their own—then the Federalists could have responded that the Constitution they proposed actually created a space for such active self-government. It did so in the new kind of federalism that it created: instead of a league of sovereign states, it formed a state of shared sovereignty. As Hamilton explains in *Federalist* 23, the Constitution's allocation of a limited number of essentially national functions to the federal government, along with all the powers necessary to fulfill them, leaves all other governmental functions and the powers to fulfill them to the states. Under this new "dual sovereignty" system of federalism, the federal government would be sovereign in the areas of national security, foreign affairs, and interstate and foreign commerce, while the states would be sovereign in the remaining functions of domestic affairs. The states could therefore still operate largely as they more or less always had, as small,

[29]Aristotle, *Politics* I, 1252a1–7, 1253a7–18.

independent republics. When the Federalists discuss the new federalism, however, they do not explain it in these terms. Thus Madison in *Federalist* 51 portrays it as providing a "double security" for the people's liberty, but ascribes no higher moral or political purpose to it.[30]

The case is different with Alexis de Tocqueville who, when he came to America in 1831 to see the new democracy in action, discerned something much more significant about its federalism. In *Democracy in America*, he calls it "an entirely new theory that will be marked as a great discovery in the political science of our day," showing how it is possible to combine the advantages of large and small societies, while compensating for their respective disadvantages. Because of the new federal system, he argues, "The Union is free and happy like a small nation, glorious and strong like a great one."[31] Of all the remarkable features of the Constitution, it is this one that Tocqueville most highly praises. At the same time, since it is a complicated and delicate balance of powers, he warns that it will be diffi cult to maintain. The near term threat, as he and many others recognized, was the dissolution of the Union, from the power of the states as organic communities, and the weakness of the federal government as an artificial creation. In the long run, however, he perhaps alone foresaw a very different danger: a pronounced tendency in modern democracies to the centralization of political power—originating in the people's passionate love of equality, along with a number of social pathologies deriving from it—which if not curbed will culminate in a new, softer but nevertheless real kind of despotism.[32]

The debate between the Federalists and Anti-Federalists thus left the American people with a more or less clear understanding of the necessity of union—although that would be tested in the conflict over slavery that culminated in the Civil War—and a clear understanding of the necessity of governmental checks and balances. What they lacked was an understanding of the necessity of federalism, with the limited sovereignty of the states as the necessary complement to the different but also limited sovereignty of the general government. They were thus unprepared to recognize and respond appropriately to the kind of centralizing tendencies that

[30] *Federalist* 51, p. 270.

[31] Alexis de Tocqueville, *Democracy in America*, trans. Harvey C. Mansfield and Delba Winthrop (Chicago: University of Chicago Press, 2000) 147, 154.

[32] On the new despotism and its relationship to the passion for equality, see *Democracy in America*, Volume II, Part IV, Chapters 2–3, 6.

Tocqueville warned about, when they appeared in company with the powerful reform movements that began in the late nineteenth century. The problem is not that the proposed reforms—which included Theodore Roosevelt's Square Deal, Woodrow Wilson's New Freedom, Franklin D. Roosevelt's New Deal and Second Bill of Rights, Harry Truman's Fair Deal, Lyndon Johnson's Great Society, George W. Bush's Compassionate Conservatism, and Barack Obama's Fundamental Transformation, along with the Civil Rights Movement and Earl Warren's Rights Revolution—were not popular, and in some cases even necessary. Rather the problem is that there was no commonly understood and accepted argument for the necessity of federalism—equivalent to the argument for the system of checks and balances that was the root cause of the defeat of Roosevelt's so-called Court Packing scheme in 1937—to make it possible for critics of the proposed reforms to mount a principled and effective resistance, to minimize the centralization involved in the reforms that were really essential, and perhaps to defeat those that were not.

This situation has led to a long and almost continuous process of what Tocqueville calls "administrative centralization," with the federal government assuming a wide range of new, non-national political functions, along with the powers necessary to fulfill them. The functions might be welcomed, but the mass of new powers is intimidating, so the people look illogically for ways to limit them. The centralization process is in effect a drive to complete what Tocqueville calls the "incomplete nationalism" of the American federal system and create a national community.[33] What it has actually created is not that, however, but rather the modern bureaucratic, regulatory, administrative state that many Americans, on both the Left and the Right, decry as too powerful, too intrusive, and too remote from the people. Many of the dissatisfactions of modern American society, which seem to multiply even as it becomes more wealthy, secure, and powerful, can be traced to this development. The people do not understand the mighty leviathan that touches on so many aspects of their lives. They believe it to be manipulated and its power abused by some hidden, nefarious force, whether Wall Street, the Establishment, the Deep State, or something even more sinister. They blame it for the defects in their social circumstances, which they want to reflect their standards and their

[33]On administrative decentralization, see ibid., I. I. 5, p. 82. On the Constitution's "incomplete nationalism," see I. I. 8, p. 149.

interests, but instead seem to be determined by malign forces centered in Washington, D. C. Above all, they think that it is deaf to their concerns, leaving them with no effective voice in their putatively democratic government.

The complaints of the American people today are reminiscent of the Anti-Federalists' criticisms of the Constitution during the ratification debate. The United States is now in a kind of "Anti-Federal" moment, perhaps not so revolutionary as the "Federal" moment of 1787, but nevertheless quite volatile. Americans today are peculiarly inconsistent Anti-Federalists, however: while they find the source of many of their problems in the Washington behemoth, they think the solution to these problems is to take control of its great power. Some even want to expand that power, by adding gigantic new programs. Of course, what the Right would do with that power is anathema to the Left, and vice versa, so every Presidential election, every midterm Congressional election, and every selection of a new Supreme Court justice is approached as the political equivalent of Armageddon. The parlous state of American politics demonstrates the truth of the Anti-Federalists' fundamental premise, that it is impossible to create a true community of millions of people, and every attempt to do so will involve some degree of unjust coercion. A community requires a commonality of opinions, principles, and interests, along with a mutuality of concern. All this might come together in a large society in a time of national emergency—which accounts for the tendency on both the Right and Left to attempt to define present problems as such emergencies—but that unity inevitably dissipates when the emergency passes.

Perhaps the best way to explain the present situation is to say that it is the result of a deep but ill-defined desire on the part of Americans of all political stripes for real democratic self-government, that is, for the opportunity to participate actively in a system of ruling and being ruled, in which they can cooperate with fellow citizens to define and attain a common good. In effect, what they desire is to actualize their nature as "political animals." For this to occur, the "administrative" functions and powers that have been assumed by the federal government would have to be devolved to the states, to revitalize them as separate and distinct communities. The devolution of power should perhaps go even further, where possible, from the states to localities. Returning to the Constitution's dual sovereignty federalism would allow for the development of a diversity of real state communities, in place of the hollow and ultimately impossible national community presently on offer. That in turn would require the people of the various states to recognize the legitimacy of the possibly very different forms that should be adopted by other states. "Live and let live," within the limits defined by the Declaration's natural rights, would have to be recognized as a political virtue, and not just a personal one. It might be utopian to hope for the recovery of the Constitution's original federalism, given all the changes that have been made in the past hundred plus years. On the other hand, without the recovery of such federalism it is difficult to imagine how the deep and increasingly bitter disagreements over fundamental moral and political issues might ever be resolved. Which side in the battle for the soul of the promised national community is going to surrender?

8

THE SEPARATION OF POWERS OR THE NORMALIZATION OF TYRANNY? REVISITING *FEDERALIST PAPERS* 47-51

Elizabeth Kaufer Busch

Introduction

The U.S. Constitution's republican nature, separated powers, and divided sovereignty collectively aim to prevent tyrannical and incompetent government. While some Anti-Federalists critique the system's unnecessary complexity and divergence from classical republicanism, the Federalists insist not only that their Constitution is decisively republican, but also that its proposed blending of authority amongst the branches is the best way to secure a Montesquieuian separation of powers.

While *Federalist* 39 defends the republican features of the Constitution, *Federalist Papers* 47–51 outline the separation "of power among its constituent parts."[1] The proper division and balance of authority, Madison explains, is *the key* to avoiding tyrannical and incompetent governing. To punctuate the centrality of preserving "separate and distinct" branches, Madison defines "tyranny" as the polar opposite: "The accumulation of all powers, legislative, executive, and judiciary, in the same hands, whether of one, a few, or many, and whether hereditary, self-appointed, or elective, may justly be pronounced the very definition of tyranny."[2] This definition is a direct descendent of Baron de Montesquieu's *Spirit of the Laws,* but a similar notion of tyranny can also be found in Locke's *Second Treatise of Government.* Indeed, when the whole power of two or more branches is held by one set of hands, "the fundamental principles of a free constitution

---

[1] James Madison, *Federalist* 47, in *The Federalist: A Collection*, by Alexander Hamilton, John Jay, and James Madison, ed. George W. Carey and James McClellan (Indianapolis, IN: Liberty Fund, 2001) 249.

[2] *Federalist* 47, p. 249.

are subverted."[3]

But today this subversion is lauded as standard operating procedure in what has become known as the Administrative State. Frustrated by a "broken" Congress, President Barack Obama has sought "the authority to consolidate the federal bureaucracy" in order to act in a "leaner, quicker, and more responsive" way "to the needs of the American people."[4] This effort merely followed the lead of bureaucratic champion Woodrow Wilson, who lamented the stifling mechanistic structure of the government's checks and balances, which have "hampered and limited" presidential action.[5] His solution was to weaken these constitutional shackles to allow the president to act quickly through executive orders and other bureaucratic actions.

While such prerogatives may seem wise in the short term, or in the cases in which the president is of the party one prefers, constitutional scholar Jonathan Turley recognizes the growth of the Administrative State as "neither benign nor inevitable," with little on course to arrest its development.[6] Indeed, those who praise or remain ignorant to the Administrative State's predominance may need a refresher on why such a merging of delegated power is synonymous with tyranny itself. After laying out the roots of the Federalists' conception of tyranny in Locke and Montesquieu, this chapter outlines the rationale for the tripartite constitutional structure in *Federalist Papers* 47–51 as tyranny's antidote. Next, I describe the nature of the Administrative State to see if it violates Madisonian republicanism. Finally, I question whether the Federalist vision has been protected in light of the current role of the Administrative State, whether the vision was faulty, and whether it can be reinstated.

---

[3] Ibid., 251.

[4] Barack Obama, "Fourth State of the Union," (January 24, 2012).

[5] Woodrow Wilson, *Constitutional Government in the United States* (New York: Columbia University Press, 1908) 54–62, cited from https://teachingamericanhistory.org/library/document/constitutional-government-chapter-iii-the-president-of-the-united-states/.

[6] *The Administrative State: An Examination of Federal Rulemaking* (2016) (statement of Jonathan Turley). Accessed March 25, 2019. https://www.hsgac.senate.gov/imo/media/doc/Testimony-Turley-2016-04-20.pdf.

What is Tyranny?

John Locke's *Second Treatise of Government* posits the rule of law as the polar opposite of tyranny, will, and caprice. This rule of law has two components—orientation towards a proper end (the protection of property in Locke's case) and a detailed structure for the devising of law towards this end. Locke describes tyranny as "the exercise of power beyond right, which nobody can have a right to."[7] Locke contrasts the stability of settled law with the arbitrariness of an individual leader's will. Tyranny occurs, for example, "when the governor, however intitled, makes not the law, but his will, the rule; and his commands and actions are not directed to the preservation of the properties of his people, but the satisfaction of his own ambition, revenge, covetousness, or any other irregular passion."[8] In other words, an individual's will, when directed towards one's own private desires, is lawless, for this is a failure to serve society's proper end. But acting on will is also tyranny in another sense because "however intitled" the leader may be, he would still be directing society by an "irregular passion," which is by nature lawless. At minimum, the rule of law would thus entail the leaders' dispassionate outer-directedness towards a set, agreed-upon end (the protection of property).

"Wherever law ends, tyranny begins," Locke elaborates as he describes three additional ways in which tyranny might emerge after law has been set.[9] In addition to failing to serve the end the law requires (i.e. the protection of property), or acting erratically or selfishly (that is, based upon mere passion), tyranny emerges "if the breach of the law brings harm to someone else; and anyone in authority who exceeds the power given him by the law, using the force at his disposal to do to the subject things that aren't allowed by the law."[10] If the leader causes harm to another by breaking an agreed upon law, exercises power beyond right, or if the leader forces things that are not permitted by law, he acts arbitrarily, and thus, tyrannically. Consequently, the rule of law does not only refer to the existence of an agreed upon end goal, but also entails the manner and set procedures by which the law is constructed and exercised. The rule of law

---

[7] John Locke, *Second Treatise of Government*, ed. Thomas P. Peardon (New Jersey: Prentice-Hall, Inc., 1997) Sec.199, p. 112.

[8] Ibid.

[9] *Second Treatise of Government*, Sec 202, p. 114.

[10] Ibid.

includes not only permissible end goals towards which it may be oriented, but also of a set of procedures by which that end may be secured.

Laws of course are not manufactured out of thin air, but are made by men, and more specifically, the legislature. Locke stresses the importance of establishing the specific form of government and detailing the limited functions of each part by asserting that "The people alone can appoint the form of the commonwealth, which is by constituting the legislature and appointing in whose hands that shall be."[11] One of the many ways to prevent legislators' wills from replacing the rule of law is Locke's stipulation that "the legislature can have no power to transfer their authority of making laws and place it in other hands."[12] The law specifies the kind of power those in authority have and what they may and may not do with that authority.

Tyranny thus falls into two general categories—the violation of the end goals *and* violation of the process or set parameters that may be used to make and enact law. The "corruption and viciousness of degenerate men" explains why the process of making laws is as significant as the content of the laws themselves.[13] Locke is not only referring to a few bad apples, for "most men are not strict observers of fairness and justice."[14] Without very specific guidelines by which elected leaders should behave, the people would remain "constantly exposed to invasion by others" and "full of fears and continual dangers."[15] While Locke seems to grant that in extraordinary circumstances a leader might violate the letter of the law in content or procedure, in general the mere breaching of that authority can be understood as tyranny itself, and certainly if that breach causes harm to another or fails to secure property.[16]

Montesquieu, another of the Federalists' (and especially Anti-Federalists') touchstones, similarly juxtaposes despotic will and the rule of law. There are "no fundamental laws" in a "despotic government, that in which

---

[11] *Second Treatise of Government*, Sec 141, p. 81.

[12] Ibid.

[13] *Second Treatise of Government*, Sec 128, p. 72.

[14] *Second Treatise of Government*, Sec 123, p. 70.

[15] Ibid.

[16] *Second Treatise of Government*, Sec 159–168, p. 91–96.

a single person directs everything by his own will and caprice."[17] Montesquieu associates tyranny explicitly with the failure to separate powers: "All would be lost if the same man or the same body of principal men, either of nobles, or of the people, exercised these three powers: that of making the laws, that of executing the laws, and that of judging the crimes or the disputes of individuals."[18] In other words, when such extensive types of power merge in one individual or group, the self-regarding will and dangerous caprice of that entity would naturally result in "an end of everything." In sum, human beings plus power equals danger.

In *Federalist Papers* 47–51, Madison's emphasis on the elaborate web necessary to protect the people's interests follows both Locke's and Montesquieu's process notions of tyranny, as well as their dismal views of human nature. We will see that Madison similarly insists on creating a proper structure in government because this is the only way to enact the rule of law.

What is a Constitutional Republic?
End Goals

The *Federalist Papers* do not systematically lay out the proper ends towards which the constitutional republic ought to be oriented, but they provide in exquisite detail the form and processes that must be in place to secure those ends. These ends are more easily found in the Declaration of Independence and, to a lesser extent, the Preamble to the Constitution. While the preamble provides some overarching principles, such as the need to "establish Justice, insure domestic Tranquility, provide for the common defense, promote the general Welfare, and secure the Blessings of Liberty," the Declaration lists the origin and content of specific rights. The "Laws of Nature and of Nature's God entitle" all peoples to "certain unalienable Rights," among which are "Life, Liberty and the pursuit of Happiness." Further, the government is created by the people only "to secure these rights."

For having failed to recognize that leaders only derive "their just powers from the consent of the governed," King George has been guilty of

[17] Charles de Secondat Montesquieu, *The Spirit of the Laws*, ed. Harold Samuel Stone, Basia Carolyn Miller, and Anne M. Cohler (Cambridge: Cambridge University Press, 1989) Part I, Book II, Chapter 4, p. 19.

[18] Montesquieu, II. XI. 6, p. 157.

"repeated injuries and usurpations, all having in direct object the establishment of an absolute Tyranny." The grievance section of the Declaration details two types of violations perpetrated by George upon the colonies—the violations of rights (injuries) and violations of process (usurpations). The rejection of George's imposition of taxes and quartering of solders without consent mirrors Locke's end of property protection.

As in Locke and Montesquieu, the Declaration also conceives tyranny as the failure to maintain the proper structure of government. The inclusion of George's alleged violation of sensible institutional boundaries echoes Locke's and Montesquieu's insistence that law and process must replace arbitrary will. A few of the Declaration's allegations include:

> The refusal to "Assent to Laws, the most wholesome and necessary for the public good."
>
> The dissolution of the "Representative House."
>
> The forbidding of "his Governors to pass Laws of immediate and pressing importance."
>
> His obstruction of the "Administration of Justice by refusing his Assent to Laws for establishing Judiciary Powers."
>
> "He has made Judges dependent on his Will alone."

As stated in the Declaration, these and other actions that appear to be acts of arbitrary will rather than law "define a Tyrant...unfit to be the ruler of a free people." Following Locke and Montesquieu, the end goal of protecting the liberties of the governed, which is grounded in consent, necessitates a particular form of government to moderate the actions of any particular leader. That proper form at minimum requires the rule of law, a representative lawmaking branch, and an independent Judiciary.

Constitutional Form and Process

The thesis of *Federalist Papers* 47–51 is that the only way to avoid tyranny, given the vicissitudes of human nature, is to construct the institutions of government to neutralize the natural threat posed by individuals in power. Madison elaborates that "the real welfare of the great body of the people, is the supreme object to be pursued; and that no form of government whatever has any other value than as it may be fitted for the attainment of this object."[19] The end goal of protecting unalienable rights necessitates a very specific form of government, that is, republicanism. A republic alone holds the potential to secure unalienable rights, for "no other form would be reconcilable with the genius of the people of America; with the fundamental principles of the Revolution; or with that honorable determination which animates every votary of freedom, to rest all our political experiments on the capacity of mankind for self-government."[20] The proper form necessitates at least four protective layers. In addition to being republican, sovereignty must be divided between the national and state units, the powers of the national government must be enumerated and divided amongst three somewhat separate branches, and the rule of law must be the standard. While many of these aspects are Lockean, Montesquieu's theories of republicanism and separation of powers also exerted significant influence.

Republicanism and Federalism

The Federalists and Anti-Federalists agreed that the republican form ought to be maintained, yet the size and operation of the republic was a matter of serious dispute. In *Federalist* 39, Madison provides the "*essential*" criteria by which a republican government "derives all its powers directly or indirectly from the great body of the people."[21] This appears to be consistent with Montesquieu's argument that "in a free state, every man, considered to have a free soul, should be governed by himself, the people as a body should have legislative power."[22] But, Montesquieu elaborates, "as this is impossible in large states and is subject to many drawbacks in small ones, the people must have their representatives do all that they themselves cannot do."[23] In other words, it would not be practical to have the entire citizen body enact all legislation, so the selection of representatives to administer government is needed. Large states make direct governing impossible, while "many [unnamed] drawbacks" make it undesirable in general for the body of the people to legislate.[24] Montesquieu recommends local governing and inclusive suffrage, for "members of the legislative body must not be drawn from the body

---

[19] *Federalist* 45, p. 238.
[20] *Federalist* 39, p. 194.
[21] Ibid.
[22] Montesquieu, *Spirit of the Laws*, II. XI. 6, p. 159.
[23] Ibid.
[24] Ibid.

of the nation at large; it is proper for the inhabitants of each principal town to choose a representative from it."[25] And while Montesquieu acknowledges that large republics may exist, he recommends inclusive participation at the local level to ensure that the great body of the people will have spoken.

Madison seemingly diverges from Montesquieu by adding that it "is *sufficient* for such a government that the persons administering it be appointed, either directly or indirectly, by the people; and that they hold their appointments" for limited terms or good behavior.[26] While perhaps not proposing the identical formulation to Madison, Montesquieu allows certain citizens to be excluded from suffrage,[27] expresses concern with the fitness of the people for direct governing,[28] and he asserts that execution of the laws "altogether exceeds the people's capacity."[29] The people themselves must be moderated by the form of representation itself. Madison later reveals why indirect consent or even appointment of leaders is adequate—humans are not to be trusted with power—even with the power to select leaders.[30]

Republicanism alone is not adequate to protect against despotism, so the sovereignty must also be divided between state and nation. Responding to the Anti-Federalist desire to preserve state sovereignty, Madison explains that the "powers reserved to the several States will extend to all the objects which, in the ordinary course of affairs, concern the lives, liberties, and properties of the people, and the internal order, improvement, and prosperity of the State."[31] The national government "will be most extensive and important in times of war and danger; those of the State governments, in times of peace and security." Because times of peace should outnumber the times of war, presumably the states will hold more authority over the daily lives of citizens than will the national government. Madison further argues that the "more adequate" the national powers are with respect to national defense, "the less

---

[25] Ibid.

[26] *Federalist* 39, p.194.

[27] He states that "all citizens in the various districts should have the right to vote except those whose estate is so humble that they are deemed to have no will of their own." Montesquieu, II. XI. 6, p.160.

[28] "The people are not at all appropriate for such discussions; this forms one of the great drawbacks of democracy." Montesquieu, II. XI. 6, p.159.

[29] Montesquieu, II. XI. 6, p.160.

[30] *Federalist* 51, 268–269..

[31] *Federalist* 45, p.241. This reading of the separation of powers between the state and federal government is informed by Emmett McGroarty, Jane Robbins, and Erin Tuttle, *Deconstructing the Administrative State* (Liberty Hill Press, 2017) 14-17.

frequent will be those scenes of danger which might favor their ascendancy over the governments of the particular States."[32] Above all, the national government is "to guard them against those violent and oppressive factions which embitter the blessings of liberty, and against those military establishments which must gradually poison its very fountain," not to dictate the daily lives of individuals living within the many states.[33]

Separate and Blended Powers[34]

While "the more respectable" Anti-Federalist critics contend that the Constitution fails to adhere to "the political maxim, that the legislative, executive, and judiciary departments ought to be separate and distinct," Madison insists that the Anti-Federalists misunderstand Montesquieu's call for a separation of powers. Tyranny, for Madison, is the complete accumulation of all three kinds of power—legislative, judicial, and executive power—in a single set of hands.[35] While Madison acknowledges that the structure devised lacks an absolute separation or even a "symmetry and beauty of form," this would only be due to the fact that human beings are not angels and cannot be expected to behave gracefully or graciously when power is at stake.[36] A true separation of powers, as recommended by Montesquieu, requires a blending of powers amongst the branches.

For some Anti-Federalists, the Constitution did not adequately maintain the barriers between the three departments as recommended by Montesquieu. Madison responds to this charge by distinguishing between *some* authority and *complete* power. Montesquieu only required that the departments be separated; he did not insist on complete isolation of each independent type of authority (judicial, legislative, and executive). Instead, Montesquieu meant that "where the *whole* power of one department is exercised by the same hands which possess the *whole* power of another department, the fundamental principles of a free constitution are subverted."[37] Montesquieu "did not mean that these departments ought to have no *partial agency* in, or

---

[32] Ibid.

[33] Ibid., 238.

[34] This reading in the next few paragraphs of the degree of separation of powers required by Monesquieu and his influence on Madison is influenced by Jonathan Turley in "Madisonian Tectonics," 327–335.

[35] *Federalist* 47, 219.

[36] *Federalist* 51, 269.

[37] *Federalist* 47, p. 251. See also Turley, "Madisonian Tectonics," 328.

no *control* over, the acts of each other."[38]

Mere separation of powers would not provide adequate protections against the abuses of government due to the viciousness of human nature. Montesquieu had already intimated that the people themselves need to be checked or limited. [39] And if laypeople themselves need to be checked, elected officials require even more deterrents, for "it has eternally been observed that any man who has power is led to abuse it; he continues until he finds limits."[40] Madison similarly asserts:

> It may be a reflection on human nature, that such devices should be necessary to control the abuses of government. But what is government itself, but the greatest of all reflections on human nature? If men were angels, no government would be necessary. If angels were to govern men, neither external nor internal controls on government would be necessary.[41]

Thus, Madison explains, "in framing a government which is to be administered by men over men, the great difficulty lies in this: you must first enable the government to control the governed; and in the next place oblige it to control itself."[42] Humans will naturally seek to aggrandize their own power, no matter what kind or how much power he or she has been delegated, so adequate weapons of defense also need to be distributed to the members of each branch. Typically called "checks and balances," Madison refers to these tools as a blending of powers. The blending of legislative, executive, and judicial authority is the means by which government will control itself. Each branch will be allocated the necessary tools by which to exercise their own authority and to control the misdeeds of others, that is, each will be provided with a measure of the other branches' authority in order to prevent any one branch from usurping the others' power.

For example, the Executive has a share of legislative power—the veto—to limit the lawmaking authority of the legislature. However, the Legislature can override the veto. The blending allows these two branches mutually to check one another and keep each other in their respective lanes. The Judicial branch can declare a law unconstitutional, but Congress can respond by passing a new and very similar law. In practice, this is how, as Montesquieu

---

[38] Ibid. See also Turley, "Madisonian Tectonics," 328.

[39] Montesquieu, II. XI. 6, p. 160.

[40] Montesquieu, II. XI. 4, p. 155. See also Turley, "Madisonian Tectonics," 330.

[41] *Federalist* 51, 268–269.

[42] *Federalist* 51, 269.

recommended, "power must check power."[43]

This elaborate design aims to ensure that law, rather than the despotism of will and caprice, rules. Locke had similarly recognized the need for the blending of legislative and executive power. When the "executive power is placed anywhere but in a person that has also a share in the legislature, it is visibly subordinate and accountable to it [the legislature], and may be at pleasure changed and displaced."[44] Both Locke and the Federalists feared that the legislature would predominate without such a blending of powers.[45]

The Rule of Law

The American Experiment aims to establish a society ruled by laws, not men. The rule of law, i.e., the avoidance of tyranny, entails two things: the rule of the laws themselves and the procedures by which governing itself occurs. The words that comprise laws themselves are a great protection of the people. These laws ought to be stable and not "living" or changeable based upon the political preference of any individual interpreting them. Law provides stability that is not subject to the capricious whims of any individual in the legislature, executive, or judicial branch. Second, the existence of a constitution itself provides another protective mechanism. The document enumerates "few and defined" powers in order to limit what leaders with delegated authority may and may not do.[46] Montesquieu explains that settled law is preferable to individual judgments, even of judges. "If judgments were the individual opinion of a judge, one would live in this society without knowing precisely what engagements one has contracted."[47]

What Is the Administrative State

As outlined in *Federalist Papers* 47 through 51, each of the three branches has a specific function that separates it from the others; however, each of the branches is also blended with the others. This means that each department is allocated some defensive tools, such as the veto, appointee confirmation, and judicial review to prevent the other branches from gaining too

---

43 Montesquieu, II.XI.4, p. 155.

44 Locke, Sec 152, p. 86.

45 *Federalist* 48, 257-258.

46 *Federalist* 45. See also McGroatry, Robbin, and Tuttle, *Deconstructing the Administrative State*, 14.

47 Montesquieu, II. XI. 6, p.158.

much authority. Congress is the deliberative body whose primary responsibility is to debate, interpret, and pass laws. The Executive Branch is tasked with enforcing them through its bureaucratic agencies. The purpose of the Federal Courts is to protect the civil rights of individuals against violations by state and federal governments and to ensure that federal regulations are consistent with the Constitution and with the public meaning of the laws they intend to enforce.

Administrative agencies in the Federal Executive Branch, however, do not only explain what the laws mean in practice; they also enforce the law by investigating whether individuals or agencies are violating those laws. These agencies also possess judicial authority to determine if violations occurred and what the punishment for infractions should be. Typically, when a complaint is made, the bureaucratic agency conducts an investigation, and, if found to be in violation, the agency determines the punishment or recommends the steps to be taken by the violating institution.

Bureaucratic enforcement, which entails interpretation of the law, often means creating new rules and regulations under the laws they enforce. The authority for issuing new rules under a law is limited by the 1946 Administrative Procedure Act (APA).[48] The APA was passed to prevent the encroachment of a "fourth branch" of government as well as the "unconstitutional usurpation of power" by the executive department. [49] The APA provides guidance on the means by which laws are to be enforced when the U.S. Constitution is silent. Any interpretation of the law must be consistent with the public meaning of the law's text. The APA does not grant these interpretations the power and force of law, though most act as if they are law, and the Supreme Court generally defers to bureaucratic interpretations of the laws they enforce.[50]

To illustrate the prerogative that administrative agencies have in defining, enforcing, and judging infractions against the laws, consider just one law—Title IX of the Educational Amendments of 1972.[51] The mere thirty-seven words that comprise the law state:

---

[48] 5 U.S.C.A. §§ 501 et seq.

[49] Peters, Gerhard and John T. Woolley, "Summary of the Report of the Committee on Administrative Management," *The American Presidency Project* (January 12, 1937).

[50] *Auer v. Robbins,* 519 U.S. 452 (1997).

[51] These amendments are also known as the Higher Education Amendments of 1972.

> No person in the United States shall, on the basis of sex, be excluded from participation in, be denied the benefits of, or be subjected to discrimination under any education program or activity receiving federal financial assistance.[52]

Since its passage, the Federal Executive Branch and the U.S. Supreme Court have expanded and transformed Title IX's enforcement, scope, meaning, and goals to include hundreds of new regulations. Students today can invoke Title IX not only to receive equal opportunities in admissions, activities, and programs, but also to attain equal numerical outcomes in athletics, receive protections against sexual harassment and assault by teachers or students, and recover monetary damages when a school fails to ensure any of these things. These changes have been enacted not by Congress, the legislative body whose primary purpose is to create law, but by appointed officials in the agency responsible for enforcing Title IX—the U.S. Department of Education's Office of Civil Rights (OCR).[53] Although the Supreme Court facilitated the statute's transformation, the OCR's informal guidance documents and Dear Colleague letters created substantive changes to Title IX. This means that the agency's *rulemaking*, which substantially altered Title IX, is analogous to *lawmaking*. The minimal role of Congress in the transformation of Title IX provides a window into the process by which laws can be extended in the United States.

As a number of scholars have argued, non-legislative measures ultimately transformed Title IX over more than four decades.[54] Title IX's transformation depicts the Office of Civil Rights as a lawmaker, enforcer, and interpreter of Title IX law. The OCR's interpretations have added new requirements; they judge compliance according to whether schools adopt the OCR's interpretations, and the OCR doles out punishments for failure to comply. The agency is the combination of legislative, executive

---

[52] Public Law No. 92-318, 86 Stat. 235 (June 23, 1972) codified at 20 U.S.C. §§ 1681–1688.

[53] Before the creation of the Department of Education, the Department of Health, Education, and Welfare was responsible for enforcing Title IX.

[54] Elizabeth Kaufer Busch and William E. Thro, "*Title IX: The Transformation of Sex Discrimination in Educaiton* (Routledge, 2018); R. Shep Melnick, *The Transformation of Title IX* (Brookings Institution Press, 2018); Task Force on Federal Regulation of Higher Education, "Recalibrating Regulation for Colleges and Universities," February 12, 2015; American Association of University Professors, "The History, Uses, and Abuses of Title IX," *2016 Bulletin*.

and judicial authority. According to Supreme Court Justice Anthony M. Kennedy:

> Although modern administrative agencies fit most comfortably within the Executive Branch, as a practical matter they exercise legislative power, by promulgating regulations with the force of law; executive power, by policing compliance with those regulations; and judicial power, by adjudicating enforcement actions and imposing sanctions on those found to have violated their rules. The accumulation of these powers in the same hands is not an occasional or isolated exception to the constitutional plan; it is a central feature of modern American government.[55]

If the OCR interprets Title IX beyond its statutory language, it is also exercising legislative authority in potential violation of the separation of powers, regardless of whether one views a particular rule as good or bad.

This type of administrative lawmaking appears to circumvent the institutional limitations that Madison vociferously defends. Not only are bureaucrats largely unchecked by the other branches of government, they are also unelected and hidden from the public. Individual citizens rarely understand the work of the bureaucracy, so they have very few means of checking them short of voting against the President who appointed them. Though it is unclear whether the OCR or other bureaucratic agencies are able to attain the "*whole*" power of two or three of the departments,[56] it seems that administrative lawmaking would be precisely the kind of blending that the Anti-Federalists and Federalists feared. Perhaps they would call it by the name of "tyranny."

Ultimately, it is the role of the governed to judge whether the bureaucracy is failing to adhere to legitimate procedural boundaries; however, how many of "the people" can be trusted to watch over these obscure bureaucrats and how many even know that those procedural boundaries exist? Could this tyranny become the new normal?

The rule of law—both end-goal and procedural—is the alternative to the normalization of tyranny. As Locke, Montesquieu, and Madison teach, the law in a republic should have the end of protecting the rights of the governed. The procedures in place to make such laws are dictated by this end goal and by the flaws of human nature. While the Declaration of

---

[55] *Arlington v. FCC* 569 U.S. ___ (2013). Also cited in Joseph Postell, *Bureaucracy in America* (University of Missouri Press, 2017) 3, 323.

[56] *Federalist* 47, 251.

Independence clarifies the goals towards which the United States ought to be oriented, the foundation of the United States' constitutional republic are the Constitution's procedural limits to the power of the government.

Potentially the most powerful protective mechanism in the United States is the rule of law, or the language of the law itself. The language of the Constitution and of any particular statute can serve as an interpretive guide, providing a stable foundation for future interpretation, precedent, and enforcement. The clear meaning of the words comprising a law at the time it was adopted tells the public what rules the lawmakers were creating. This is why the *Federalist Papers* are such a helpful guide in explaining the meaning of the Constitution's provisions. Laws have no meaning without the carefully selected language chosen to comprise their scope. Without the stability of the words that comprise the procedural limits within the Constitution, Madison teaches that the only thing left would be tyranny.

9

OLD AND NEW TESTAMENTS IN AMERICAN GRAND STRATEGY, AN OVERVIEW

Karl Walling

Sometimes American popular culture can offer keen insight into American political culture. The various versions of the television series *Star Trek* and the film series *Star Wars* are good examples. In *Star Trek*, Captain Kirk and his crew serve the United Federation of Planets on the Starship *Enterprise.* Life forms from many galaxies unite to preserve peace within the Federation and provide security from external threats, like the Klingons. As the ship's crew goes boldly into space, the final frontier, where none have gone before, it is governed by the "prime directive" of non-intervention in the affairs of the planets and the new life forms it discovers. It is governed by respect for freedom and self-determination. In *Star Wars*, an extended republic, consisting of many different planets, faces the danger of universal tyranny from an empire led by Emperor Palpatine and his evil henchman, Darth Vader. Somehow the republic had become corrupt and lost its way. Only a few are left, the Jedi knights, who still understand "the force," but we never learn exactly what the force happens to be. It has a mystical character suggesting perhaps great confusion over the purposes of political life. It has a dark side and a light side, however. Those who serve the dark side use power for tyrannical ends; their opponents, drawing their energy from the other side of the force, use it to serve some form of freedom. These icons of pop culture reveal something deep in the American character, however inchoate, which exemplifies how Americans think not only they but also others should be governed if they have the chance, something with global, perhaps even universal significance. But what is it?

That question requires some reflection on the meanings of the terms "republic" and "federation." Volumes have been written on the meaning of republicanism;[1] for the purposes of this essay, three features are especially salient. Republics, especially as understood by the American Founders, must derive their authority, originally and through some continuing form of representation, from the consent of the governed.[2] As the Latin origins of the term suggest, their purpose is to serve the *res publica*, the public good, usually understood not merely in terms of security and prosperity, but also, in the American case especially, of civil, religious, and political liberty. And republics must follow the rule of law rather than the rule of any individual or group. To paraphrase Thomas Paine, in England during the American War for Independence, the King was law; in America, the law was, or ought to be, King.[3] All of this distinguishes republics from empires, which tend to rule by force, not consent; to serve the advantage of the rulers, not the governed; and to be unrestrained by law.

Traditionally, republics have been small, so they have often been conquered by large empires. No less traditionally, republics have sought to solve this strategic problem by uniting their strength in federations. The traditional purpose of republican federations is to provide for the common defense while securing the freedom of each of the members. But as Thucydides revealed long ago, these alliances of free communities often tend to be too strong to be safe for liberty or too weak to defend themselves and preserve peace among their members. Commonly, one member, like Athens in the Delian League or Rome in the Latin Federation, comes to dominate the others, thus transforming a consensual union into an empire, or the members quarrel so much over how to govern themselves that the union falls apart, either violently, through civil war, or quietly, through neglect as different members lose faith in and cease to contribute to preserve the federation.[4]

The original purpose of republican federations was strategic: the

[1] Most useful for the purposes of this essay have been Thomas L. Pangle's *The Spirit of Modern Republicanism: The Moral Vision of the American Founders and the Philosophy of Locke* (Chicago: University of Chicago Press, 1988) and Michael Zuckert's *Natural Rights and the New Republicanism* (Princeton: Princeton University Press, 1994).

[2] See James Madison, *Federalist* 39, in *The Federalist,* by Alexander Hamilton, James Madison, and John Jay, ed. George W. Carey and James McClellan (Indianapolis: Liberty Fund, 2001) 194.

[3] Thomas Paine, *Common Sense and Other Political Writings*, ed. Nelson F. Adkins (New York: Liberal Arts Press, 1953) 32.

[4] *The Landmark Thucydides*, ed. Robert B. Strassler, trans. Richard Crawley (New York: Free Press, 1996) 1.97–99.

common defense, peace among the members, and the freedom of each member. Thus, it is necessary to offer a provisional definition of strategy, which comes from a Greek word, *strategos*, for general. Strategy is the art of the general. Obviously, that includes what generals do in war, but properly understood, strategy applies in both peace and war. As Sun Tzu observed, "to win one hundred battles is not the acme of skill. To subdue the enemy without fighting is the acme of skill."[5] From that point of view, the ideal strategist would never fight a war—and that form of strategy might often, indeed usually, require cooperative, "win-win" strategies rather than competitive strategies to succeed. Strategy is a form of instrumental reasoning. Strategists identify objectives and reason backwards, step by step, through the means required to accomplish them, while recognizing that others, whether opponents, neutrals, or allies, often have different objectives and strategies, which sets up an interaction. As one player moves, the others must adapt; original strategies must be reassessed, sometimes abandoned to achieve their original objectives. And sometimes the objectives must be abandoned or scaled back to suit the means available to achieve them. In all these ways, strategy is much like sailing. Sailors rarely move in a straight line directly to their destination. They tack back and forth to take account of winds and currents; not to do so would be self-defeating.

In the twentieth century it became increasingly common to speak of grand strategy, a term invented after the First World War. Grand strategy required the coordination of efforts in multiple theaters and of multiple instruments of power on land, at sea, and in the air. And in protracted struggles, like the Cold War, it required large-scale thinking, both spatially and temporally, about the world and its future for generations to come. A common way of thinking about grand strategy today employs the DIME paradigm, which is short for the coordination of diplomacy, information and intelligence, and military and economic power. Grand strategy is thus a total package synthesizing all means at a country's disposal to achieve its objectives. Above all, it is a matter of managing risk. No strategy is ever without risk and costs; good grand strategists manage them more

[5] Sun Tzu, *The Art of War*, trans. Samuel B. Griffith (Oxford: University Press, 1971) 77.

effectively than others.[6]

How did the United States rise from the condition of what we today might call a Third World country, struggling for its independence in 1776, to become both a great and, so far, a durably free federal republic? One answer might be that, over time, piece by piece, sometimes intentionally, but not always, it developed an extremely effective grand strategy. And in time a deep national consensus came to support that strategy—which explains the quasi-religious language of Old and New Testaments in this essay.

That strategy is a species of a larger genus, sometimes termed "republican security theory."[7] Its great themes are *e pluribus unum* and *ex uno plura*, uniting the strength of many for the common defense and peace among the members while dividing power to prevent its abuse. Americans did not invent this theory. Greeks and Romans experimented with it. In modern times, theorists like Machiavelli and Montesquieu explored its characteristic strengths and weaknesses. And the American Founders, the Federalists and Anti-Federalists especially, but also, later, the Federalist and Republican Parties and their descendants up to the present, quarreled deeply about its meaning and application. One might even say that how each understood the theory led it to see the other as a threat to American liberty, with Anti-Federalists clinging to an older species of the theory (in which republics must be small and federations weak for liberty to be secure) and the Federalists advancing a new version in which republics needed to be large and diverse and federations strong for liberty to endure. In that sense, the Anti-Federalists were defending the Old Testament in American grand strategy; the Federalists were advancing a New Testament, and American quarrels ever since have often been based on which testament citizens and their leaders have chosen to give priority.[8]

Note: the end was liberty—civil, political, and religious especially; the disagreement between Federalists and Anti-Federalists was emphatically not over ends, but how to accomplish them. Thus, it was fundamentally

---

[6] See B. H. Liddell Hart, *Strategy* (London: Penguin, 1967) 319–330, 353–360; and Hal Brands, *What Good is Grand Strategy? Power and Purpose in American Statecraft from Harry S. Truman to George W. Bush* (Ithaca, N.Y.: Cornell University Press, 2014) 1–16.

[7] See Daniel H. Deudney, *Bounding Power: Republican Security Theory from the Polis to the Global Village* (Princeton: University Press, 2008).

[8] See Herbert J. Storing, *What the Anti-Federalists Were For* (Chicago: University of Chicago Press, 1981) 7–23.

about strategy. The struggle was never over liberty versus order, but rather, over the kind of order best suited to serve liberty. From a strategic point of view, the agreement on ends is a very good thing. You cannot have a coherent strategy without clarity about objectives. Although the different kinds of liberty are often in tension with each other, and that tension helped produce the collapse of the American republican security community in 1860, the common objective of liberty first is crucial. All countries have an interest in security and prosperity, but each country has a particular interest in preserving its regime. Liberty first has been the enduring definition of the American national interest from 1776 to the present. What changed was the strategy to serve that national interest.

In America since the passage of the National Security Act of 1947, the organ most responsible for coordinating American grand strategy is the National Security Council, whose members, to employ the DIME paradigm effectively, consist of representatives from the State Department, the Department of Defense, the intelligence agencies, and, as needed, those who oversee American economic policies. These people sit on committees that issue reports. Each report commonly has a number, like NSC 68, which expressed much of American grand strategy for the Cold War.[9] In keeping with that tradition of numbering grand strategic documents, one might say that the grand strategy of the American Founders is expressed in six national security documents, each of which deserves a number. The first is the Declaration of Independence in 1776.

National Security Document No. 1: The Declaration of Independence—Liberty First, Independence, and Union

Americans usually do not understand the Declaration of Independence as a national security document, but that just means they have forgotten their own history, as they are often wont to do. What was the point of declaring independence from England? Establishing and preserving a free society came first; that was the fundamental objective. This is most evident from the truths the authors of the document took to be self-evident, at least to Americans. All human beings are created equal. They possess certain inalienable rights, including life, liberty, and the pursuit of happiness.

[9] *NSC 68: United States Objectives and Programs for National Security, a Report to the President* (Washington: National Security Council, 14 April 1950).

Governments are instituted to secure these rights, deriving their just powers from the consent of the governed. And when any government becomes destructive to these rights, it is the right of the people to alter or abolish it and to institute new ones as seem to them most conducive to their safety and happiness.[10] This is a liberal statement of republican security theory. It roots legitimate government in popular consent. It defines the public good in terms of freedom. And it suggests our weakness as individuals requires us to unite our strength in institutions governed by law. Because the American "republic of republics" (republican security federation) has endured for almost two and one-half centuries, we tend to look at these principles from a merely domestic point of view, but that was not the original purpose of the Declaration of Independence. The purpose was to declare independence because the English government had, in the minds of the authors, become a threat to liberty. Strategically speaking, independence was a means necessary to secure liberty.

Strategists often distinguish between enduring interests and particular objectives. By July 4, 1776, Congress (originally a diplomatic term) had reached the conclusion that liberty, the national interest, could not be secured while Americans remained part of the British Empire, which made independence their political objective in the struggle with England. The Declaration of Independence is a syllogism. Its major premise is that a people have a right to revolt if their government becomes dangerous to their rights. Its minor premise, in the part of the Declaration that few read any more, is that the British government, under the King and with the aid of Parliament, had become a danger to American rights. But the evils of war and revolution are so dangerous that they ought not to be risked for light and transient causes. So facts were submitted to a candid world to demonstrate, first, that it was legitimate to declare independence, and second, that it was prudent too. The king and his supporters in Parliament had taxed Americans without their consent. They had suspended the Massachusetts legislature. They had imposed martial law. Despite numerous peaceful appeals from the American people, they continued with these offenses. Prudence dictated not resorting to force until all peaceful appeals had been exhausted, but prudence also required acting before it was too late to act, before the colonies were divided and conquered into abject

[10] *The Constitution of the United States and the Declaration of Independenc*e (Washington, D.C.: Commission on the Bicentennial of the United States Constitution, 1987) 35.

slaves of the empire. The overwhelming weight of the evidence was that there was "a design of tyranny" against Americans, so it was legitimate for the Americans to declare their independence and establish new governments safer to their liberties. But was doing so wise?

In declaring independence, Congress was also declaring war (and the Declaration of Independence became a model for future American declarations of war, like President Madison's War Message in 1812).[11] Since Americans have not declared war since 1943 (against Bulgaria, which became an Axis ally), one might ask what is the point of declaring war? We seem to be able to fight many wars without them. One answer is rooted in the DIME paradigm and strategic reasoning. The Declaration of Independence is a model of what some call strategic communications. It constructs a narrative to justify a potentially costly war and build confidence that victory was possible. The narrative was designed to convince Americans that it was more prudent to risk the evils of war than to submit to the evils of tyranny. It puts the I in the American DIME. But it also puts the D in the DIME by establishing the foundations of a winning wartime coalition, first, among the thirteen newly minted states, and second, with European powers.

While independence was a necessary means to liberty, union of the thirteen states was necessary for independence. The Declaration styles itself the unanimous declaration of the thirteen United States of America—that is how the country got its name, as a coalition of states fighting to achieve their independence. The truth, however, is that not every delegate in Congress supported independence in July, 1776. Some wanted to give peaceful appeals and economic sanctions more time to work.[12] That is often the question: not merely whether to go to war, but when, with *whether* often very much dependent on *when*. In the American case, this would mean shifting from armed rebellion within the empire, which might have allowed for a peaceful compromise with Americans still subject to British authority, to complete revolt, with England more than able and willing to bring its full military might to bear to crush resistance. So it is no wonder that some wanted to try any means short of all-out war to secure their

---

[11] James Madison, *War Message to Congress*, June 1, 1812, in *James Madison: Writings* (New York: Library of America, 1999) 685–692.

[12] Robert Middlekauff, *The Glorious Cause: The American Revolution, 1763-1789* (Oxford: University Press, 2005) 312–332.

liberty. The Declaration styles itself "unanimous," however, for the sake of coalition unity, so each state could enjoy the protection and support of all. Each state was represented by a delegation of what we today would have to call diplomats, since members of each delegation were selected by their legislatures, not the people of their states. Congress was a place where ambassadors from different states met to deliberate on common policies and strategies for attaining them, with Philadelphia more like Brussels (where ambassadors from the North Atlantic Treaty Organization, NATO, meet) than Washington, D.C., today. As is true in NATO today as well, each state had one vote, so if a majority of each state delegation voted for independence, then the decision for independence could aptly be described as the unanimous decision of the United States in Congress assembled.

If the syllogism of the Declaration explains why the American cause was legitimate, the unanimity of Congress was no less valuable for bolstering public confidence in the wisdom of Congress. The "Fallujah" of American resistance, Boston alone had no chance against England, arguably the greatest military power of the age, especially at sea; nor did Massachusetts or New England (the "Sunni Triangle" of North America), full of Minutemen armed to the teeth against the tyrant from overseas, have good odds of winning independence without the aid of others. But if all the states united their strength, this war would be not merely a contest between an empire and individual states, but also one between a tiny island and a continent, a sea power against a land power, with Americans having plenty of room to retreat if necessary and British forces getting overextended the further they moved into the interior, as occurred most famously at Saratoga, the pivotal battle of the war. Union, in other words, was the precondition of General George Washington's Fabian strategy throughout the war.[13]

Treat the American union in 1776 as what we today call a start-up company, or as the Founders might say, a new "enterprise" based on daring and ingenuity (hence the continuity with the Starship *Enterprise* in the television series). Start-up companies are usually short of financial capital, so they develop business models to attract investors. Who might invest in the new American enterprise?

---

[13] For Washington's Fabian strategy, see Russell F. Weigley, *The American Way of War: A History of United States Military Strategy and Policy* (Bloomington and Indianapolis: Indiana University Press, 1977) 3–17.

Note that the three Americans who had the most influence on the form and content of the Declaration of Independence, Benjamin Franklin, John Adams, and Thomas Jefferson, were all diplomats, that is, understand the Declaration of Independence as a diplomatic document. Almost immediately after helping Thomas Jefferson draft the Declaration of Independence, and signing it themselves, Franklin, and later Adams, were dispatched as American diplomatic envoys to Europe (and Jefferson would later join them at the peace talks in Paris after the decisive Franco-American victory at Yorktown). Adams appealed to Dutch bankers to invest in the war; Franklin appealed to France for a military and commercial alliance. Both the Dutch and the French had suffered at the hands of the British. The Dutch lost New Amsterdam (later New York City) in 1674; the French lost Canada and Louisiana in 1763. Both wanted payback, and so too did Spain, for the loss of Gibraltar in 1704 especially. The task of America's diplomats was to convince these powers to intervene, covertly or overtly, on the American side, because the E and the M in the American DIME were weak. Americans lacked specie and they had to import almost all the weapons and tools of war from Europe. Supporting the American cause might be in these powers' interest if England were distracted from other regions of its Empire, the West Indies especially, or so weakened by war with the Americans that it could not confront a coalition of France, Spain, and the Netherlands. Paradoxically, however, to convince these powers to invest in the American enterprise required military victories, with none more important than crushing the British at Saratoga in 1777, which persuaded the French to shift from covert aid to the Americans to an overt alliance. Franklin's success in Paris with the D in the DIME depended on Washington's success with the M, and vice versa.

So it ought to come as no surprise that the National Security Document No. 1 ended by stating that the United States had a right to contract alliances with foreign powers. The message to Europe: The United States was open for business, not merely commercially, now that its trade was no longer controlled by England, but also strategically, as a coalition partner in what would develop into a global maritime war (in which North America was just one theater).[14]

---

[14] On the American War for Independence as just one theater in a global maritime conflict, see Alfred Thayer Mahan's classic, *The Influence of Sea Power on History, 1660-1783* (New York: Dover, 1987).

The American people were one audience for the Declaration. So too were foreign powers, but a third audience for this masterful work of strategic communication is sometimes easily forgotten: the opposition in the British Parliament. Members of Congress understood that not every member of Parliament supported the King's efforts to end the revolt in America by force. They knew that some, sometimes called the Old Whigs, with Edmund Burke their most illustrious champion, thought the King might have done better to conciliate the Americans, to win without fighting as Sun Tzu said, through some form of political compromise. They knew that some in the opposition saw the war in America as a threat to England itself, either because habits of tyranny practiced in America might come back to haunt Englishmen at home or because France, Spain, and the Netherlands might take advantage of England while it was stuck in a quagmire, England's Vietnam, so to speak, in North America. The Declaration supplied talking points, as we might say today, to the opposition in Parliament, who could question both the legitimacy and the wisdom of a war with fellow Englishmen.[15]

And that, in a nutshell, is the strategy by which Americans won their independence. They never had a chance of winning the war militarily, but they did not need to. If they were united, they could exhaust the British with a Fabian strategy. If foreign powers intervened, they could supply aid to compensate for American economic and military weakness, especially their lack of a trained navy capable of operating in fleets. Eventually France, Spain, and the Netherlands became belligerents too (though only France allied with the United States), and the British were overwhelmed fighting in too many theaters, fearful of a cross-channel invasion, and worried about losing their (at the time) most lucrative colonies in the West Indies. The shock of the combined Franco-American victory at Yorktown proved too much for Lord North and the governing party, which called for negotiating peace, with the opposition waiting in the wings to take power and cut British losses before it was too late for England to recover. Americans won the war not on the battlefield, but in Parliament, with the Declaration of Independence providing the strategic outline for victory.[16]

---

[15] Edmund Burke, *Speech of Edmund Burke on Moving Conciliation with the Colonies, in Select Works of Edmund Burke* (Indianapolis: Liberty Fund, 1999) 221–243.

[16] Samuel Eliot Morison, *The Oxford History of the American People, Volume One: Prehistory to 1789* (New York: Meridian, 1972) 331–353; and Middlekauff, *Glorious Cause,* 579–602.

National Security Document No. 2: The Articles of Confederation—an Imperfect Union

While liberty depended on independence, independence depended on union, so it should come as no surprise that almost before the ink was dry on the Declaration of Independence, Congress called for establishing the terms of union among the states. The Articles of Confederation were completed in April, 1777; they were submitted to the states in June, 1778; and they were finally ratified by all the states in March, 1781, just six months before the great Franco-American victory at Yorktown and two years before the Treaty of Paris ending the War for Independence in 1783. Congress under the Articles accomplished much that was good and worthy of admiration, not least the enactment of the Northwest Ordinance in July, 1787. Most importantly, under the Articles Americans were united long enough to win the war for fear, to paraphrase Benjamin Franklin, that if they did not hang together, they might hang separately.[17] Alas, despite Congress's best efforts, the Articles left much to be desired both for waging the war effectively against England and for preserving the peace after the war among the states and between the United States and foreign powers.

A fundamental problem was money. Not surprisingly, given that the American Revolution originated in large part from a struggle against the authority of Parliament to tax Americans without the consent of their colonial legislatures, Congress was dead set against granting the union the authority to tax citizens directly. No state legislature would have supported such a drastic measure at the time. Congress did have the authority to make requisitions, that is, to ask each state to supply funds for the war effort, but few states complied completely or on time. So Congress was always short of funds and was obliged to print money, thus leading to inflation and the virtual collapse of the American economy during the war. There is a reason for the phrase, "not worth a Continental." A continental dollar printed in 1776 was worth a penny by 1778 and almost worthless by the end of the war. Without a trustworthy medium of exchange to pay for its expenses, Washington's Continental Army was compelled to "impress" supplies more and more. Supply officers were issued printed I.O.U.s.

[17] For this famous (possibly apocryphal) quip, see Paul M. Zall, *Ben Franklin Laughing: Anecdotes from Original Sources by and about Benjamin Franklin* (Berkeley: University of California Press, 1980).

When the army needed supplies, they would give the I.O.U.s to merchants and farmers with the promise that they would be paid back once independence had been won. Increasingly, however, farmers and merchants began to doubt Americans would win the war or that they would be compensated for their lost property. In 1781, in Virginia, which had been reduced to a barter economy because the currency was worthless, farmers began to hide the grain and livestock for fear that either the British or the American forces, or both, would rob them of their livelihoods. But how could Americans win the war if the people were hoarding supplies? And how could Congress justify the war if the only way to support it was by robbing the people? The necessities of supplying the army were fundamentally at odds with the principles of the Declaration of Independence.

Wealth is often called the "sinews of war."[18] Congress and General Washington did have a viable strategy to win the war, but there was precious little E in the American DIME. Recognizing this problem, Congress passed an impost, a tax on imports, to be paid in specie, but ratification required unanimous consent of the states. Eleven states ratified the impost; Georgia never acted, and tiny Rhode Island, the smallest state in the union, fearing it would have to pay more than its fair share, refused to ratify, thus forcing the Americans to fight the war against the wealthiest military power of the age with one hand tied behind their backs.[19]

This was no way to run a war. Indeed, said Alexander Hamilton, a twenty-three-year-old colonel serving on George Washington's staff, in 1780, while the army was starving for lack of supplies, the Articles of Confederation were "fit neither for war nor peace."[20] They were unfit for war because, without sufficient E in the American DIME, the M in the DIME was bound to get weaker and weaker. Indeed, Washington's Continental Army was wracked by the desertions of often unpaid soldiers with families to support. True, Washington was able to win his greatest victory at Yorktown, and peace talks with England ensued, but this depended on

[18] James A. Huston, *The Sinews of War: Army Logistics, 1775-1953* (New York: Center for Military History, 1997); and John Brewer, *The Sinews of Power: War, Money, and the English State* (Cambridge: Harvard University Press, 1988).

[19] E. James Ferguson, *The Power of the Purse: a History of American Public Finance, 1776-1790* (Durham, North Carolina: University of North Carolina Press, 1961).

[20] Alexander Hamilton to James Duane, September 3, 1780 in the *Political Writings of Alexander Hamilton*, eds. Carson Holloway and Bradford P. Wilson (Cambridge: University Press, 2017) Volume I, 130–142.

foreign aid, with France supplying over 90% of the muskets, gunpowder, artillery, and above all, money for Washington's fledgling army.[21] And without French aid, decisive victory would have been impossible. A French fleet defeated a British squadron off the Chesapeake Bay and enabled a blockade of British General Cornwallis's forces. And the French actually brought a larger army to Yorktown than Washington himself. Abject dependence on a foreign power was humiliating—and such aid could not be counted on in the future.

The Articles were unfit for peace for many reasons. First, although they aspired to a "perpetual" union of the states, the reality was that Americans had fought the war as members of a coalition—and coalitions tend to collapse at their moment of victory, just as the coalition of Athens and Sparta against Persia collapsed at the end of the Persian Wars and just as the Grand Alliance of the United States, Great Britain, and the Soviet Union collapsed at the end of the Second World War. At such moments, wartime allies tend to become post-war rivals and sometimes adversaries. Second, the Treaty of Paris ending the War for Independence depended on the states to enforce its terms, but in the aftermath of a bitter war the state governments were in no mood to practice malice toward none and charity toward all defeated Loyalists. Far from it, fearing Patriot retribution, Loyalist refugees often took shelter within British lines in New York City, Charleston, Savannah, and elsewhere. And then they took ship to Nova Scotia, Jamaica, and the Bahamas rather than suffer Patriot vengeance. And the states were often reluctant to uphold the terms of the treaty, including reenfranchising defeated Loyalists and returning property confiscated from them during the war. This failure to enforce the treaty gave the British a legal right to renew the war at a time and place of their choosing. Third, the Articles were a compact among the states, not the American people. So Congress represented the states, not the people themselves. Its legitimacy was questionable—and so too was the loyalty of the people to the union it established. A sense of history might well have suggested to anyone who thought about the future that it was not a question whether the union would collapse, but when.

---

[21] See Robert J. Allison, *The American Revolution: a Concise History* (Oxford: University Press, 2011) 44.

National Security Document No. 3: The Constitution of 1787—a Less Imperfect Union

The story of the origins of the Constitution of 1787 has been told so often that it is hard to think of anything new to add, but here is an attempt. True, the Annapolis Convention of 1786 emerged from calls for giving Congress authority to promote commerce more effectively. True too, Shays' famous rebellion in 1786–1787 added great urgency to the thoughts of those who presided over framing the document, especially to their fears of factions and demagogues. But the first recorded call for a new Constitution this author has seen occurred during the War for Independence, in 1780, at General Washington's headquarters—with Washington's most trusted aide, Colonel Alexander Hamilton, writing Major James Duane, who had also served at Washington's headquarters but left the Army to serve in the New York legislature and later in Congress. To this author, these communications look like the nucleus of a strategic reform movement with Colonel Hamilton saying bluntly to Major Duane (and thus to Congress) what perhaps General Washington, whose authority depended on the complete trust of Congress, could never have said directly to Congress himself. As Hamilton understood the matter, three reforms were necessary to win the War for Independence (and secure the peace thereafter). First, Congress had to be granted complete authority to raise revenue and troops for the war. This included establishing a draft with three-year terms of service. Second, Congress needed to establish a national bank to help fund the war. And third, a new constitution had to replace the committees that had managed the Confederation's war efforts with executive departments to supply system and method to the administration of the war. This was also the nucleus of the Federalist agenda in the Washington administration and especially of Hamilton's agenda as Secretary of the Treasury seeking to establish the powers of the purse (the E in the DIME) and the sword (the M).[22]

It would be hard to think of two men more dissimilar than Hamilton and James Madison in their experiences and style of presenting themselves, but Madison actually shared many of Hamilton's strategic objectives. He too feared the union might collapse. He too feared this might lead to civil war. He too feared that civil war might offer foreign powers a pretext to

[22] See, again, Hamilton to James Duane, *Political Writings*, Volume I, 130–142.

meddle in North America. So he too advocated a much stronger national government and came to the Federal Convention of 1787 with a bold vision for reconciling the necessary powers of government with liberty in a more perfect union.[23]

So what is the grand strategy of the Constitution of 1787? It too places liberty first with independence a means to secure it. But it moves toward a less imperfect union than under the Articles. First, consistent with Hamilton's wartime proposals, the Constitution establishes the power of the purse and the sword. It vests Congress with unlimited authority to raise revenue and troops for war. It makes it possible for the United States to put the M in the DIME by giving it the authority to fund as much military power as the United States might need.[24] Second, it *republicanizes American federalism.* It makes federal authority legitimate by resting it on popular consent, both originally through the ratification of the Constitution and continually through the elected branches.[25] Third, it makes federal authority effective by applying it directly to individuals rather than through the medium of the states. Whereas a single state or coalition of states might resist such authority or merely pay it no heed, which risked civil war, individuals are just too weak to do so.[26]

In that sense, the Constitution is an example of a famous formula from Jean Jacques Rousseau who summarized social contract theory by saying that in a republic the citizen is to the sovereign as the sovereign is to the subject.[27] The first half of this formula is about legitimacy; the second, about effectiveness. The first is about the origins of authority; the second, about giving it sanctions. Through such means, *e pluribus unum* could become a reality. When it was necessary to be one for all and all for one, especially in time of war and other crises, Americans could unite their strength for the task at hand. Fourth, to ensure this Leviathan did not become tyrannical, the Constitution divides power. *Ex uno plura*, the complicated system of separated institutions with shared powers, requires the

---

[23] See Madison, "Vices of the Political System of the United States," April, 1787; and Letter to George Washington 16 April 1787, *Writings*, 69–85.

[24] *Federalist* 23, p. 113.

[25] *Federalist* 22, p. 112.

[26] *Federalist* 16, pp. 75–80.

[27] Jean Jacques Rousseau, *On the Social Contract with Geneva Manuscript and Political Economy*, ed. Roger D. Masters, trans. Judith R. Masters (New York: St. Martin's Press, 1978) 11:46; 2:63; 1:79.

cooperation of the different branches for any sustained national purpose, thus making it less likely that any one of them will dominate the whole.[28]

A classic example of *ex uno plura* as a strategy to preserve the union, and to keep it free, is the Great Compromise of the Philadelphia Convention. The great danger in all federations is that one member will dominate the whole or that fearing such domination the different members will resist, thus leading to civil war. The solution was to represent the states equally in the Senate, so none need fear domination by larger, more populous and wealthier states, but represent the people proportionally in the House, so that citizens of more populous states feel they have an influence commensurate to their numbers—then extend the compromise to the Electoral College, so both states and people feel protected by the system. In that way, the Constitution *federalizes American republicanism* not merely by applying federal law directly to individuals, but also by including so many diverse passions, interests, and opinions as to make majority faction, James Madison's dreaded bane of republican government, exceedingly difficult, if not impossible for a sustained period.[29]

Perhaps none of the "inventions of prudence" in the Constitution was new or never seen before, but the synthesis was indeed novel.[30] The synthesis made it possible for the American states to be *united states*. It gave Americans full command of the DIME, when and if it was necessary to employ it. And it gave them tools to ensure the powers necessary to govern effectively could be controlled in such a manner as to remain safe to liberty. The Constitution of 1787 is the quintessential expression of republican security theory in the modern age.

National Security Document No. 4: *The Federalist Papers* as Strategic Commentary

Since the eighty-five essays by Alexander Hamilton, James Madison, and John Jay in *The Federalist* are often considered the most insightful American reflections on free government, it was perhaps inevitable that they have already been referenced in this essay. But there is a special reason for students of strategy to think about them carefully and for students of American political thought to consider them from a strategic perspective.

---

[28] *Federalist* 51, pp. 267–272.

[29] *Federalist* 10, p. 42–49.

[30] *Federalist* 9, p. 38; *Federalist* 14, p. 60–67; *Federalist* 51, p. 269.

The strongest arguments in favor of ratifying the Constitution in *The Federalist* are strategic arguments; indeed, it is not too much to say that American grand strategy ever since has been the gradual working out of strategies either explicit or implicit in these essays.[31]

Consider, for example, essays 3–8 and 11 in the first section of *The Federalist* on the utility of a well-constructed union. It bears mentioning that one of the authors, John Jay, had served as President of Congress during the War for Independence and understood the problems of holding the coalition together. He was also the most experienced diplomat of his time, with the possible exception of Benjamin Franklin, having served as American ambassador to Spain during the war, as a peace negotiator for the Treaty of Paris to end the war, and as secretary of foreign affairs after the war. Another of the authors, Alexander Hamilton, who wrote two-thirds of the essays, was a soldier and Washington's right-hand man throughout the war. James Madison lacked similar military and foreign policy experience, but all three were lawyers who understood that the law could be a powerful instrument of statecraft, for nation-building especially.

John Jay's contributions are often overlooked, but he was the most well-known of the authors at the time. To the extent the identity of the authors writing under the pseudonym of Publius was public knowledge, his prestige in matters of foreign policy was vital to any warm reception of *The Federalist.* So he began the argument for a well-constructed union in *Federalist* 3 by considering the role such a union might play in providing for safety from wars with foreign powers, which led him to discuss just and unjust causes of war. Most striking in his account is his complete lack of self-righteousness, which is uncommon in Americans but necessary in diplomats. Unjust wars might arise from foreign attacks on Americans, but also if Americans provoked them by violating treaties or committed acts of violence against foreign powers or their citizens or property. Jay understood all too well that Americans could be their own worst enemies. He

[31] Alas, Alexander Hamilton is the only one of the Founders treated as a strategist in the classic *Makers of Modern Strategy from Machiavelli to the Nuclear Age*, ed. Peter Paret (Princeton: University Press, 1986). A mid-twentieth century editor of the *Federalist*, Edward Mead Earle, wrote the chapter, "Adam Smith, Alexander Hamilton, Friedrich List: The Economic Foundations of Military Power," 217–261. But why stop with just the economic foundations of military power? Why not see the *Federalist* as the most sustained and comprehensive discussion of grand strategy among the Founders for the sake of a DIME designed to ensure liberty, independence, and union for generations to come?

noted that Americans already had treaties with six foreign nations, most of them maritime powers able to threaten American trade, or worse, able to project power by sea to North America itself. And such powers were likely to look for continental allies, the Native Americans in the West, for example, to annoy Americans and hinder their expansion. Motive for such alliances was not lacking, since Americans on the frontier had already engaged in direct violence against the various tribes.

Jay worried that an errant state or two or more might drag the United States into war by violating treaties, like the Treaty of Paris ending the War for Independence, or through acts of violence committed by their governments, or through vigilantes and filibusterers. Since the Confederation lacked the authority to prevent states from violating treaties, and the state governments were vulnerable to majority factions who might provoke war, it was too weak to prevent the foreign wars Jay feared.[32] But the future first Chief Justice of the Supreme Court understood that if federal authority applied directly against individuals, then the American judiciary, which few today count for much as an instrument of national security, might play an important, though often invisible role in protecting the American people from foreign wars. By making the Constitution and all laws and treaties passed pursuant to it the Supreme Law of the Land, the courts could punish state officers and private citizens for violating treaties as well as for acts of violence against Native Americans and the citizens or property or territory of foreign powers. They could prevent war by deterring Americans from provoking it.[33]

Jay of course understood that it was not enough to deter American citizens or states from provoking a war for which all Americans might be held responsible. Indeed, he understood well that complaints about injustice are often mere pretexts for going to war in the service of power and interests. So he told a story about the republic of Genoa in the age of Louis XIV. Genoa had offended the Sun King, who demanded that it send their *doge*, or chief magistrate, to Versailles to beg Louis's forgiveness. He asked whether Louis would have demanded any similar humiliation from Spain, or England, or any other powerful country. The moral of this worldly story

[32] *Federalist* 3, p. 9–12. See also Frederick W. Marks III, *Independence on Trial: Foreign Affairs and the Making of the Constitution* (Wilmington, Delaware: Scholarly Resources, Inc., 1984) 3–51.

[33] *Federalist* 80, p. 411–416.

thus seems to be that if you want to avoid war with foreign powers, establish a government strong enough to prevent your citizens or states from provoking war, but all governments are led by fallible human beings; thus all governments err and commit injustices from time to time. Since "acknowledgements, explanations, and compensations are often accepted from a strong united nation, which would be rejected as unsatisfactory if offered by a state or confederation of little consideration or power," a well-constructed union might prevent war by deterring foreign powers from going to war, even when they were in the right. A well-constructed union able to employ all tools of the DIME might render Americans so strong that they could get away with their injustices, so to speak, though Jay did stress making apologies and compensations when, as was bound to be the case from time to time, Americans were in the wrong.[34]

Republican security theory seeks to protect small republics not only from great empires like England, France, and Spain in the 1780s, but also from civil war. In that sense, the Constitution of 1787 was a "peace pact" among the states.[35] So after Jay's contribution on preventing war with foreign powers, Hamilton turned to preventing war among the states and between some states and the federal government. Ironically, while some of his opponents among the Anti-Federalists were very old fashioned, others had seized on a new fad in international relations theory, sometimes called commercial republican peace theory in his age and democratic peace theory in our own.[36] Then and now, supporters of this theory claimed that republics do not fight wars, at least not with each other (though they frequently fight wars against non-republican governments and quite ferociously too). Wars, the argument went, are the sport of monarchs and dictators who sacrifice their people to serve their ambition. Since all the American states were republics, there was no danger of war among them—

[34] *Federalist* 3, p. 12.

[35] See David C. Hendrickson's *Peace Pact: The Lost World of the American Founding* (Lawrence, Kansas: University Press of Kansas, 2003).

[36] For the tip of this enormous iceberg of academic debate, see Immanuel Kant, "Perpetual Peace," *Perpetual Peace and Other Essays on Politics, History, and Morals*, ed. Ted Humphrey (Indianapolis: Hackett, 1983) 107–46; Michael Doyle, "Kant, Liberal Legacies and Foreign Affairs," *Philosophy and Public Affairs* 12 (1983): 205–235 and 323–353; and Christopher Layne, "Kant or Cant: The Myth of Democratic Peace," *International Security* 19, no. 2 (1994): 5–49. For the specific Anti-Federalists Hamilton sought to refute, see Murray Dry, "Anti-Federalism in the *Federalist,*" in *Saving the Revolution*, Charles Kesler et al (New York: Free Press, 1987) 40–60.

and thus no need for a stronger federal government to prevent such wars. And each of the American states was also a commercial republic. It makes no sense for trading states to war against other trading states. That would be killing the goose that lays the golden egg of prosperity. So economic interdependence would serve as a check on the states going to war with each other.

Hamilton was much more than skeptical of this theory. Sounding like a classic realist, perhaps Thucydides especially, he observed that the causes of war lie in human nature, the love of power and the fear of power. And in certain ages the structure of the international system plays an enormous role, with the mercantilist empires of eighteenth century Europe perhaps more often at war with each other than not. And the vices and virtues of leaders makes a difference. Following Plutarch (not Thucydides) he suggested that Pericles instigated the Peloponnesian War to serve his mistress. Neither commerce nor republican government would remove any of these causes of war. Indeed, the history of popular governments, both democracies and republics, and commercial states, both ancient and modern, proved his point. Sparta was little more than an armed camp; Rome was never sated of carnage. Athens and Carthage were both commercial republics, yet each destroyed itself in war with another republic. And in the modern age, Venice and Genoa, both trading republics, were almost constantly at war, as too were England and France. And come to think of it, sometimes the people have dragged their countries into war with their monarchs kicking and screaming against them. Indeed, there have been "almost as many popular as royal wars!"[37] In sum, commercial republican peace theory was reductionist because it left out important causes of war, and it was empirically false (at least so far). No one who wanted to preserve peace within the union could afford to gamble on such a flight of fancy.

Yet this apparently realist critique of commercial republican peace theory is not the whole story. At the Philadelphia Convention and elsewhere, especially in Washington's Farewell Address (most of which Hamilton drafted on Washington's behalf), Hamilton made clear that he hoped that commerce would make the states so interdependent that they would never contemplate going to war against each other. In particular, in his plans for funding the national debt and assuming the debts of the states, he hoped to make what he called "monied men" so dependent on the

[37] *Federalist* 6, p. 20–26.

survival of the union that they would do all they could in their disproportionate power to save it.[38] In truth, for Hamilton, commerce was necessary to preserve the peace of the union, but not sufficient. Each of the states could erect trade barriers against the others, which would lead to trade wars. And sometimes trade wars lead to armed conflict.[39] If Americans wanted to avoid shooting wars with each other, they had to ensure that trade among the states was free. They had to turn the United States into the world's largest free trade zone. They had to grant Congress the authority to regulate commerce so that trade among the states would be free. He knew full well that even the commerce clause would not be enough to prevent civil war, but there was no hope of peace among the states without it.

Hamilton was a military man, but he was not a militarist. It is possible to think strategically without being a warmonger. Indeed, if the best strategy is to win without fighting, the best strategists must often be opposed to militarism, if only because peace allows building up strength while war requires expending it, perhaps to the point of crippling exhaustion. So he called attention to the likely consequences of war among the states to drive home why anyone who insisted that liberty must come first had to support a stronger, well-constructed union. Bearing in mind that liberty depended on independence and independence on union, division among the states would likely lead to foreign intervention in an American civil war as weaker states called in foreign aid and then their opponents did the same. In time, the different states might then become satellites of such powers, who were no friends of republican liberty. The constant danger of war among the states would lead each to put itself in a state of constant preparation for war. It would lead to an arms race, indeed a race toward military despotism, as citizens in each state, more concerned for their safety than their liberty, concentrated ever more power in the executives of their evolving national security establishments. In time, Americans would find themselves erecting the same "engines of despotism" that had been the scourge of the Old World. And the hope that the New World might offer an alternative to government based on accident, force, and fraud (the hope that

[38] See Hamilton's Speech of June 18, 1787 in James Madison's *Notes of the Debates of the Federal Convention of 1787* (Athens: Ohio, 1966) 129–139; and President George Washington, Farewell Address, in *Annals of America* (Chicago: Encyclopedia Britannica, 1968) Volume 3, 606–615.

[39] *Federalist* 7, p. 28–31.

the New World might show that government founded on and operating by "reflection and choice" could succeed) would die of the militarism Americans had inflicted, however unintentionally, even tragically, on themselves.[40]

For Hamilton no less than other Founders, liberty came first. So if one feared military despotism, the great question was what kind of government and what kind of military establishment was most likely to avoid it. About this he was clear. Continental or land powers are far more vulnerable to military despotism than insular (and united) naval powers. The former must maintain large standing armies ever ready for war; the latter have much less need of such armies, except perhaps temporarily in extraordinary emergencies. The model for the United States in this case was the United Kingdom, but not its monarchy or House of Lords. Instead, it was the union of England, Scotland, and Wales which made a standing army almost always unnecessary for England, so long as its navy was strong enough to guard the English Channel and to protect its sea lines of communication with its empire and other trading partners.[41]

Hence, in *Federalist* 11, Hamilton, an army veteran (but also originally from the West Indies), revealed his true colors as an advocate of a strong ocean-going, blue water navy, the sort that could fight ship-to-ship with any of the navies of the age. He was not talking about a navy capable of taking on England's Royal Navy all by itself. Instead, he was thinking about the local balance of power in the Caribbean, where France, England, Spain, and the Dutch competed for trade. A few ships of the line sent from the United States might tip the naval balance of power among these trading states. And supplies from the United States would be highly useful to any of them. That being the case, Americans might enhance their security, avoid a standing army and militarism, and compel the Europeans to open their markets to American trade with the mere threat of tilting toward one great maritime power against another in the Gulf of Mexico.[42] Such a navy would be necessary for defense against these other sea powers, but properly used as an instrument of diplomacy, it might not need to fight a war. It might deter war and thus preserve peace. It might enable Americans to maintain their independence and defend their rights without fighting a

---

[40] *Federalist* 1, p.1; *Federalist* 8, p. 32–36.

[41] *Federalist* 8, p. 35–36.

[42] *Federalist* 11, p. 51.

war. It might often enable Americans to reach what Sun Tzu had called the acme of strategic skill, the ability to win without fighting.

While Hamilton was willing to discuss *realpolitik* against the Europeans locally in the Caribbean, Hamilton always thought about the big picture. The Europeans had aroused his anti-imperial, even egalitarian ire. The globe could be divided into four main regions: Europe, Africa, the Western Hemisphere, and Asia. Unhappily for the other three regions, the Europeans, by force and by fraud, by arms and by diplomacy, had made themselves masters of the other continents. Thus writers treated as profound philosophers had claimed a universal supremacy for Europe. One had even gone so far as to say that everything degenerated in the New World, that even dogs ceased to bark in the American atmosphere! Hamilton had had enough of this arrogance. It belonged to Americans, he argued, to teach their assuming brother some moderation.[43]

Union was the solution, but a union of what? About that Hamilton attempted to be discreet. Initially, he seemed to be thinking exclusively of the union of the thirteen states; indeed he was reticent about discussing matters "too far into regions of futurity," which would not be "proper for newspaper discussion," but the subject was so "striking and animating" that he could not help letting the cat out of the bag. He was talking about a "great American system, superior to the control of all transatlantic force of influence, and able to dictate the terms of the connection between the old and the new world!"[44] Herein lie the seeds of the Monroe Doctrine. Americans might vindicate their liberal republican principles, the honor of the human race, if other European colonies rebelled against their masters and the United States led them in defiance of the imperialists. If the United States led an anti-imperial coalition of Western Hemispheric republics, it could lead the New Free World against the Old Less Free World. The dangers in this vision are obvious. Americans too might succumb to the temptations of empire because, as the world goes, the strong usually do what they can and the weak suffer what they must.[45] But the strong do not always have to do what they can. With the proper self-restraint, the United States could become a regional hegemon, understood as leader of a hemispheric republican security system.

---

[43] *Federalist* 11, p. 54.

[44] *Federalist* 11, p. 55.

[45] This is the Athenian thesis in the Melian Dialogue; see *Landmark Thucydides*, 5.89.

National Security Documents 5 and 6: Washington's Farewell Address and the Monroe Doctrine—Neutrality, Non-intervention, and Counter-intervention

Their historical contexts are different, but in principle President Washington's Farewell Address in 1796 and President Monroe's Doctrine of 1823 are different sides of the same strategic coin. One counsels neutrality and non-intervention in the affairs of the Old World; the other proclaims a right of counter-intervention if the Old World empires sought to extend their rule, beyond their existing possessions, in the Western Hemisphere. What the documents have in common is dedication to a people's right to choose their own form of government; what is different is their strategy for serving this fundamental principle of freedom.

In Washington's case, the challenge was a world war, beginning in 1791 and lasting to 1815, with England and France alternately preying upon American shipping or seeking to enlist the United States as an ally. True, the United States was a Hercules in its cradle, but it was still in the cradle. Partly because the world war aggravated growing partisan differences between the emerging Federalist and Republican parties, which were growing increasingly sectional, it was not impossible that the United States might become a theater of the world war, perhaps with England playing one section and France another section against the other. National weakness counseled restraint, and thus neutrality, with the Farewell Address of 1796 partly a defense of Washington's Neutrality Proclamation of 1793.[46]

Yet it was also much more than that. As the Father of His Country, Washington stood to the Americans as Moses did to the Israelites, so he sought to lay down the unwritten law, the sort that must be written in a people's hearts to establish norms and taboos of both free government and American foreign policy. Americans could not tolerate foreign meddling in their political system, like the efforts of the French envoy, Citizen Genet, to establish Democratic Republican societies to inflame American passions in favor of France and against England. With profound implications for thinking about the breakdown of political norms in America today, George Washington's First Commandment could be expressed as: Thou shalt not tolerate nor invite foreign intervention in American

[46] See Felix Gilbert, *To the Farewell Address: The Beginnings of American Foreign* Policy (New York: Harper, 1961); and Stanley Elkins and Eric McKitrick, *The Age of Federalism* (Oxford: University Press, 1993) 489–497.

politics! "Against the insidious wiles of foreign influence," Washington proclaimed, "the jealousy of a free people ought to be *constantly* awake, since history and experience prove that foreign influence is one of the most baneful foes of republican government."[47]

His Second Commandment, so to speak, was against harboring a permanent love or permanent hatred for any country. France had been a vital ally in the War for Independence, but French interests (and France's revolutionary principles) were not the same as America's. England had been a mortal enemy once before, but it did not need to be one forever. A permanent love for France and a permanent hatred of England had nothing to do with republican freedom. Self-government, properly understood, was about controlling these passions, not succumbing to them. Indeed, the "nation that indulges toward another an habitual hatred or an habitual fondness is in some degree a slave. It is a slave to its animosity or its affection, either of which is sufficient to lead it astray from its duty and its interest." America's true policy was neutrality and non-intervention, so that the infant Hercules could grow so strong that it could "choose peace or war, as our interest, guided by our justice, shall counsel."[48]

Washington's Third Commandment was to avoid "permanent" alliances, like the alliance with France left over from the War for Independence, which risked that the United States might become a vassal of France. Significantly, however, Washington did not say "no entangling alliances." That was President Jefferson's more dogmatic expression in his First Annual Message. Washington understood that wars would happen from time to time. When they did, "temporary" alliances might become expedient, but to ensure they were expedient, they could not be permanent, though some might last longer than others, depending on the circumstances.[49]

In James Monroe's case, the challenge was that with the end of the wars of the French Revolution and Napoleon in 1815 the victorious empires of the Old World—some determined to crush republicans everywhere—might turn their attention to reclaiming rebellious colonies in the New World. And then they might focus on the United States and its growing republican security system. So Monroe proclaimed his doctrine

---

[47]George Washington, *Annals*, Volume III.

[48] Ibid.

[49] George Washington, *Annals*, Volume III, 613–615; President Thomas Jefferson, First Inaugural Address, *Writings*, ed. Merrill D. Peterson (New York: Library of America, 1984) 494.

of counter-intervention, "that the American continents, by the free and independent condition which they have assumed and maintain, are henceforth not to be considered as subjects for future colonization by any European powers." Just as respect for freedom required French non-intervention in American politics and American non-intervention in European politics, so too did it require Europeans to refrain from intervening in Western Hemispheric politics. This supplied a principle to justify counter-intervention on the part of the United States, meaning that the Monroe Doctrine, which has sometimes been abused to justify American imperial adventures, is best understood as an anti-imperial doctrine.[50] Properly understood, it is liberal to the core in its defense of the right of each people in Europe, South America, indeed everywhere, to pick their own form of government and establish their own policies for their security and freedom.

No strategy is risk-free. While defensible from the standpoint of American principles, this doctrine of counter-intervention has a slippery slope. If it were legitimate for the United States to go to war against a European power if it sought to reconquer one of its lost colonies, would it be legitimate to preempt such an attack? And if preemption were legitimate, why not prevention, that is, intervening even before the Europeans had decided to intervene themselves? Could a doctrine of counter-intervention be transformed into one of unlimited intervention anytime, anywhere, for any reason possibly relevant to American national security? And the religious language that permeates this essay to explain an evolving strategic consensus among the American Founders, much of which lasted through the Second World War, is another complication. As Tocqueville revealed, the United States was founded on both the spirit of liberty and the spirit of religion. The spirit of religion may have been essential for stabilizing enduring norms, for writing the Old Testament in the hearts of a people, but it comes with the risk of crusades for freedom, or what some might call democratic *jihad*.[51]

---

[50] President James Monroe, Message to Congress, December 2, 1823 (aka the Monroe Doctrine) in *Annals*, 73–75; Nathan Tarcov, "Principle and Prudence in American Foreign Policy," *The Public Interest* (Summer, 1984): 45–60; and Joseph M. Siracusa and Aiden Warren, *Presidential Doctrines: U.S. National Security from George Washington to Barack Obama* (New York: Rowman & Littlefield, 2016).

[51] Alexis de Tocqueville, *Democracy in America*, trans. George Lawrence (New York: Harper, 1969) Volume I, Part I, Chapter 2, pp. 46–47. See also Walter McDougall, *Promised Land or Crusader State* (New York: Houghton Mifflin Harcourt, 1997).

With a profound understanding of that risk even before President Monroe proclaimed his doctrine, John Quincy Adams, serving as Monroe's secretary of state, gave perhaps the quintessential summation of the Old Testament view of American Grand Strategy. Speaking on July 4, 1821, to Congress, in a long speech seemingly telling the history of freedom from the dawn of time, he summed up American foreign policy by stating that Americans wished well to all peoples, whether in South America or Greece or elsewhere, seeking to recover their liberties. "Wherever the standard of freedom and independence has been or shall be unfurled, there will [America's] benedictions and her prayers be.... She is the well-wisher to the freedom and independence of all.... But she goes not abroad in search of monsters to destroy." Were the United States to succumb to the crusading spirit and seek to overturn governments elsewhere it deemed insufficiently free, it would be violating its own principle that each people has a right to pick its own government. In seeking tyrannical monsters to destroy, the "maxims of her policy would insensibly change from liberty to force," and the United States would become a tyrannical monster itself. This is powerful language, but it takes great self-command to practice in the face of domestic sentiment demanding intervention against tyrants abroad. Whether the kind of restraint Adams counseled when America was weak is still possible now that America is strong is an open question.[52]

From the Old to the New Testament of American Grand Strategy

Such were the six main components of the Old Testament of American Grand Strategy: maintaining a free society comes first; independence; union; energetic and balanced republican political institutions; neutrality and non-intervention abroad (in Europe especially); and counter-intervention in the Western Hemisphere to protect a developing zone of freedom, a republican security community, so to speak, in the New World from the force and fraud by which the Old World had subjugated the rest. Alas, there is just one big problem. The strategy failed.

It did not fail completely, of course. The union expanded across the

---

[52] John Quincy Adams, *An Address Delivered... on the Occasion of Reading the Declaration of Independence* (Washington, DC, 1821) 29; and Charles N. Edel, *Nation Builder: John Quincy Adams and the Grand Strategy of the Republic* (Cambridge: Harvard University Press, 2014) 107–184.

continent incorporating ever more states into the republican security system. The United States grew so strong and prosperous that the European powers were ever less inclined to challenge it in the Western Hemisphere. Americans remained free, but the original strategy could not keep the peace among the members of the union. Slavery, America's original sin, was also its strategic Achilles' heel. Perhaps the original union might have survived if it had become all one thing or all another, but it was unable to survive with some states allowing slavery and others not. So the system collapsed in 1860; restoring peace laid the foundations of a New Testament with both domestic and international components.

Abraham Lincoln's Gettysburg Address calls for a new birth of freedom, a "born again America," based on dedication to his reading of the mother truth of the Declaration of Independence, that all human beings are created equal. And his sublime Second Inaugural Address deliberately moves from the angry God of the Old Testament who punished both North and South alike for the sin of slavery to the merciful God of the New Testament, with malice toward none and charity toward all, as the nation recovered from its self-inflicted moral and strategic disaster. Rather, Lincoln and his successors reconceptualized the union as one of hearts and convictions. To endure it could not be a mere federation of states. It had to become a nation whose dedication to its mother truth would be enshrined in the Thirteenth, Fourteenth, and Fifteenth Amendments, which deserve to be considered as the terms of peace ending the American Civil War. If these laws were written in the hearts of the people, if they did become a political religion, then (and perhaps only then) the union would be secure.[53]

Skipping over the Imperialist Era when Americans were lost in the wilderness and began to worship the Golden Calf of empire, whose temptations never cease, the international component of the New Testament might be called extending the Monroe Doctrine of counter-intervention in the Western Hemisphere to the world. Woodrow Wilson served as John the Baptist heralding a new age of collective security, while Franklin Delano Roosevelt, Harry Truman, and their successors through the Cold

---

[53] Abraham Lincoln, *Gettysburg Address* and *Second Inaugural Address*, in *The Collected Works of Abraham Lincoln*, ed. Roy P. Basler (New Brunswick, NJ: Rutgers University Press, 1953) Volume VII, 22–23 and Volume VIII, 332–333. See Also David C. Hendrickson, *Union, Nation, or Empire: The American Debate over International Relations, 1789-1941* (Lawrence, Kansas: University Press of Kansas, 2009).

War until almost today instantiated the new strategic gospel in the United Nations in general and the North Atlantic Treaty Organization especially. One for all and all for one in the original union of thirteen states became the spirit of a new world order based on counter-intervention authorized by the United Nations Security Council against aggressor states and pledged to by every member of NATO, each bound to regard an attack on any one member as an attack on all.[54]

For Old Testament fundamentalists, this was going way too far. The United States would find itself bound to intervene wherever and whenever aggression occurred. That would put it on an almost constant war footing, but war, as Hamilton revealed in *Federalist* 8, is the great destroyer of free institutions and norms, not the least of which is the right of Congress to declare war (which, again, Congress has not done since 1943 against Bulgaria). Hence for the fundamentalists, the New Testament is no testament at all, except to our capacity for folly and *hubris*. The effort to universalize the American understanding of republican security has led to the imperialization of the republic as the executive has grasped for ever more war powers, to strategic overextension in Vietnam, to monster-destroying crusades of the sort John Quincy Adams warned against in Iraq, and to a national security and surveillance state that undermines republican liberty at home. If we are serious about putting American liberty first, the Old Testament prophets today say we need to renounce not merely the Bush Doctrine of preventive war and democracy promotion by force, but also the growing habit of thinking the United States has a right to intervene abroad anywhere, anytime, for almost any reason. We have to learn to practice self-restraint again and come home to Washington's Farewell Address and the doctrine of neutrality and non-intervention.[55]

Disciples of the New Testament are not without grounds to argue that they are more faithful to the spirit of the Old Testament than the fundamentalists, however. The first three words of the Preamble of the Charter of the United Nations are "We, the peoples." The "San Francisco experiment" of 1945 and the "Brussels experiment" of 1949 sought to establish a new republican security system modeled in part on the

[54] See George C. Herring, *From Colony to Superpower: U.S. Foreign Relations since 1776* (Oxford: University Press, 2008) 595–650.

[55] See David Hendrickson, *Republic in Peril: American Empire and the Liberal Tradition* (Oxford: University Press, 2018).

"Philadelphia experiment" of 1787. True, especially when the United Nations was founded, many of its members failed a crucial test of republicanism because most member states were not founded on the consent of the governed or operated through some form of continuing representation of the people. Some of them in fact were empires. At the beginning especially, the United States, which had hoped to share the responsibilities of collective security with others, found the other members of the United Nations Security Council either hostile, like the Soviet Union, or so devastated by war, like England, France, and China, that they could not live up to their responsibilities for quite some time. So one might say that Franklin Roosevelt's vision of great power cooperation among the Four (later five) Policemen who are permanent members of the Security Council failed completely because three of the policemen were not equal to the task, the fourth appeared to be an international gangster, and the United States inherited the responsibility of policing the world—often with at best mere token support from its allies. That looks more hegemonic and imperial than republican, so it is right to question whether the New Testament is gospel or heresy that has led Americans to worship false idols.

Yet one can take this critique too far with great risk of throwing the baby out with the bath water. The United Nations, and its American-led cousin, NATO, are simply different species of the larger genus, republican security theory. They began with and continue to manifest genuine republican characteristics. They did arise from the consent of their member "peoples;" they do try to serve a common good of collective security; and they do try to abide by international law, most of the time, meaning that the system is far more republican than any previous durable international order. Despite its faults, this security system has done one thing exceptionally well: it has helped prevent great power wars, like the Second World War, from 1945 to the present. Precisely because war is the great engine of despotism, the success of the system in preventing great power war has to be considered crucial for establishing and preserving the liberal democracies of Europe and Asia and elsewhere. If so, it has to be counted as far more a blessing than a curse by all who put liberty first.

In 1782, five years before the Philadelphia Convention, Alexander Hamilton wrote a series of essays entitled *The Continentalist.* His primary objective was to get his fellow New Yorkers to think continentally, not merely locally. "Unless we can overcome this narrow disposition and learn to estimate measures by their general tendency," he observed, "we shall never be a great or happy people, if we remain a people at all."[56] Americans could not have won their independence had New Yorkers said New York First or had Virginians said Virginia First. They were too interdependent not merely economically, but also for security purposes, to survive alone, much less preserve their free governments if they became adversaries. Those who preached the strategic gospel of the New Testament in the twentieth century expanded Hamilton's continental view to a global perspective. War had become too destructive to think safety lay in shouting "America First."

Chanting "America First" in 1940 and later in 2016 is the true blasphemy, the ultimate betrayal of the spirit that links the Old and the New Testaments of American grand strategy, the idea of uniting the strength of all for security while dividing powers to secure liberty. And none of this required the United States to become an empire. It simply had to accept that the survival of the system it took the lead in founding from 1945 to 1949 depended on the consent of the members, serving their common purposes, and accepting the restraints of international law. Above all, it had to accept that the system would not survive or prosper unless it took the lead, but its leadership was not altruistic. What it paid in treasure, and sometimes blood, was more than compensated for in influence around the world. It thus had to be *primes inter pares*, first among equals, with the juridical equality and consent of the members of the system lending legitimacy to American leadership and American leadership making collective action possible. The task of republican statecraft today, it would seem, is to preserve the successes of this republican security system and to extend it to confronting new challenges, like global climate change and nuclear proliferation. Even superpowers are not supermen; the United States needs allies today as much as ever, perhaps even more. None will follow the United States willingly, and it will not deserve to be followed unless it acts like a citizen of this extended republic, seeks win-win solutions to common problems, and follows the rules of the game. If these are the preconditions of American Global Leadership, then the demagogues who chant "America First" today are the greatest American-bred danger to republican freedom and security since the Second World War.

[56] Hamilton, *Continentalist* No. V, 18 April 1782, *Political Writings*, 174.

INDEX